Muskets and Altars

Muskets and Altars

JEREMY TAYLOR

AND THE

LAST OF THE ANGLICANS

·

REGINALD ASKEW

MOWBRAY

Mowbray
A Cassell imprint

Wellington House, 125 Strand, London WC2R 0BB
PO Box 605, Herndon, VA 20172

First published 1997

British Library Cataloguing-in-Publication Data
A catalogue record for this book is available from the British Library.

ISBN 0-264-67430-8 (hardback)
ISBN 0-264-67462-6 (paperback)

The translation of the Chinese poem on p. 121 is taken from Helen Waddell,
Lyrics from the Chinese (London: Constable & Co., 1949) by permission
of Stanbrook Abbey and Molly Martin.

Typeset by Keystroke, Jacaranda Lodge, Wolverhampton
Printed and bound in Great Britain by Redwood Books, Trowbridge, Wiltshire

Contents

Christmas Day 1657   vii
Preface   viii
Some dates   xi

1   To begin Holy Living   1
2   The tears of Achilles   30
3   Political Holy Living   46
4   Merely spiritual power   68
5   Devout Holy Living   78
6   The great employment   93
7   A terrible imagining   113
8   Arresting the sun   126
9   O the death of Phoebe!   144
10 The search for Jeremy Taylor   165

    Postscript: Orinda's love letter   182
    Notes and references   191
    Index   208

for Kate

Christmas Day 1657

I WENT to London with my wife, to celebrate Christmas-day, Mr. Gunning preaching in Exeter chapell, on 7 Michah 2. Sermon ended, as he was giving us the Holy Sacrament, the chapell was surrounded with souldiers, and all the communicants and assembly surpriz'd and kept prisoners by them, some in the house, others carried away. It fell to my share to be confin'd to a roome in the house, where yet I was permitted to dine with the master of it, the Countesse of Dorset, Lady Hatton, and some others of quality who invited me. In the afternoone came Col. Whaly, Goffe and others, from White-hall, to examine us one by one; some they committed to the Marshall, some to prison. When I came before them they tooke my name and abode, examin'd me why, contrarie to an ordinance made that none should any longer observe the superstitious time of the Nativity (so esteem'd by them), I durst offend, and particularly be at Common Prayers, which they told me was but the masse in English, and particularly pray for Charles Steuart, for which we had no Scripture. I told them we did not pray for Cha. Stewart, but for all Christian Kings, Princes, and Governors. They replied, in so doing we praid for the K. of Spaine too, who was their enemie and a papist, with other frivolous and insnaring questions and much threatning; and finding no colour to detaine me, they dismiss'd me with much pitty of my ignorance. These were men of high flight and above ordinances, and spake spiteful things of our Lord's Nativity. As we went up to receive the Sacrament the miscreants held their muskets against us as if they would have shot us at the altar, but yet suffering us to finish the office of Communion, as perhaps not having instructions what to do in case they found us in that action. So I got home late the next day, blessed be God.

John Evelyn, *Diary*, 25 December 1657

Preface

THE Church of England today is being dislodged from any claim that there could be such a thing as a national Church, or an officially English religion which expresses the life of prayer in English and practises English Christianity. Had it always been a mistake, the idea of an English love of God, so reliable in faith and in moral discrimination, and so hospitable, that it could unite a bewildered realm? The Tudor and Elizabethan solution had provided an English Bible and Prayer Book for English Christians; but cohesion also depended on a measure of Euro-scepticism. Neither Spanish Catholic, nor German Protestant would suit. Something more magnanimous and mixed was needed. To make an English Church work, it needed a practical race of High Church puritans. Jeremy Taylor fits that description exactly. He is a saint. His opportunity came in the middle of the seventeenth century when the Anglican Church was knocked off its perch by Parliament.

What is attempted in this book is to judge the eloquence of the remedies proposed by someone who lived through the dislocations of the English Civil War, and found himself outside looking in. There was immediate interest in his *Holy Living* and *Holy Dying*; they remained runaway classics until quite recently. To be a spiritual classic can, however, become a disguise, or even a disqualification. The disarray of the Church of England is much closer today to Taylor's unexpectedly violent world. Parliament was legislating against episcopalians then, and putting the monarch to death; now it has merely replaced Sunday with an opportunity for car-boot sales, and is all too hungry for media coverage to defend the privacy of the Royal Family. Then they thought to ban the Feast of the Nativity as a superstitious custom. Now Christmas is the nervous anticlimax of two months of High Street spending. Jeremy Taylor was facing the prospect of the Church he understood being persecuted into extinction, and of finding himself *ultimus anglicanum*, last of the Anglicans. What was needed to survive?

He was not a kill-joy, but he and his friends understood that they would need a rule. It would make him conservative and lyrical about family life, adventurous in insecurity, unsympathetic to the drug culture but generous in what he called mercy and charity (and what we should call health) in caring for addicts, ardent for political stability, jealous for probity in public life. If Church was out, if the Prayer Book liturgy was repudiated and clergymen like him thrown in jail, he would take it as a holiday. He was not pious but practical. He loved prayer; but he fastened upon its importance for the problems of illiteracy, and hunger, and social inequality. He was not reactionary, but he would have nothing to do with the secular illusion that Heaven and hell are nowhere to be found. It is a pity we know so little about him. But his habit of spelling Heaven with a capital H, and hell with a small one, because it cannot be compared with a proper noun like Heaven, is followed in this book.

This is not a book about religious antagonism, though the explosive, mutual hatred of seventeenth-century Christian opponents was part of the power supply of the Civil War. There are two reasons for side-stepping quarrelsome Christianity. Taylor promoted peace. His *Liberty of Prophesying* burst upon the scene with the free truth that the sharpest differences of theological opinion have no business in splitting Christians from one another. One Church was all that was needed. Argument, as for example whether a set prayer out of a book was better than one made up on the spot, was inevitable, but could never become a sufficient reason for Christian disunity. Taylor's cry for peace in the Church was learned off by heart in the astonishing bloodshed of English battlefields. As with some of my theological students promoted chaplains in the armed forces, the grievous shock, willingly suffered, of ministering to the wounded and dying on both sides (these were Jeremy Taylor's bold Cavaliers and Roundhead troopers) remained long after to assail the imagination. So in this book there is no discussion of the cantankerous views of John Bunyan on extempore prayer, *I will Pray with the Spirit*, contrasted against Jeremy Taylor's *Apology for Authorised and Set Forms of Liturgie*; but there is a chapter on having a terrible imagination.

Taylor's side lost. He did not expect the Church of England to recover from this, nor did it; the Restoration of 1660 did not bring a national Church, but a measure of toleration towards Dissent. In 1650 he thought he was addressing the last of the Anglicans, without a Church to go to. In 1651 he composed the funeral of the Church of England, *Holy Dying*, and got serious about Heaven. He can speak for all those who do not go to church to this day, and are sure that it is on its way out, but think that a holy life and a holy death are too important to ignore.

I first met Jeremy Taylor as the unseen passage for a school reading prize. To A. R. D. Watkins and the late P. H. Boas my grateful acknowledgement for that introduction; to them, to E. V. C. Plumptre and R. W. Moore, I owe my first steps in Taylor's classical world. His theology I encountered at Scholae Cancelarii, Lincoln, in the teaching of Dick Milford, John Yates, Tom Baker and Oliver Tomkins. To my own students at Wells, Salisbury & Wells, and King's College London through 30 years I owe a debt for shared discoveries in Taylor's teaching. For memorable Presbyterian hospitality towards an Episcopalian lecturer in 1992 I am specially grateful to Bill Rolland and Lafayette Orinda Presbyterian Church, California. The British Institute of Human Rights invited me to lecture on Jeremy Taylor's plea for religious freedom; Westminster Abbey asked for a sermon on good writing changing lives, which became 'The tears of Achilles'. I am also grateful to the Ecclesiastical Law Society for kindly allowing me to use the lecture I gave on *Ductor Dubitantium*, published in the *Ecclesiastical Law Journal*, Vol. 3, no. 14 (1994), for my chapter 'Merely spiritual power'. Material for 'The measure of a perfect clergyman' came from my contribution to a Festschrift for Tom Baker, Dean of Worcester, *The Reality of God*, edited by James Butterworth (Severn House, 1986), entitled 'Taylor's *Abbreviature Projected*'. A retreat conference of the Servants of Christ the King put up with a draft of my essay on Jeremy Taylor's prayer of intercession 'Arresting the sun'. Remarks on George Herbert are from a sermon invited by St Luke's Chelsea in January 1996. 'The search for Jeremy Taylor' was a paper delivered to Bedford Theological Society in 1995. Lovers of Jeremy Taylor, like Harry Edwards, Vicar of Highgate, and Walter Todds, both of whom read *Holy Dying* and went on, have helped me. I am extremely grateful to those who have made friendly corrections, especially Roger Pemberton and Etain Todds. To Gonville and Caius College, Cambridge, I am obliged for the opportunity to get behind the famous nineteenth-century stable edition of the whole works of Jeremy Taylor in order to compare the informality of some seventeenth-century orthography. I have always been conscious that anything written *about* Jeremy Taylor could never compare with the liveliness of his own way of putting it. His own way of spelling it adds a tune to that.

Some dates

1606	Rembrandt born.
1608	John Milton born.
1611	Authorised Version of the Bible published.
1613	30 June, Shakespeare's Globe theatre burnt down.
	15 August, Jeremy Taylor, son of Nathanael and Mary Taylor, baptized at Trinity Church, Cambridge.
1616	Charles Stuart (15) created Prince of Wales.
	Jeremy Taylor at the Perse School, Cambridge.
1625	27 January, Accession of Charles I.
1626	Jeremy Taylor at Caius College, Cambridge; BA 1631.
1631	John Donne, Dean of St Paul's, died.
1633	William Laud becomes Archbishop of Canterbury;
	Jeremy Taylor, Junior Fellow of Caius, ordained;
	George Herbert died at Bemerton, Salisbury;
	Herbert's poems, *The Temple*, published posthumously.
1634	Milton's *Comus*, with music by Henry Lawes, performed.
1635	Rembrandt's painting of *Abraham's Sacrifice*.
1636	Taylor at All Souls Oxford and Archbishop Laud's chaplain.
1638	Jeremy Taylor appointed Rector of Uppingham.
1639	27 May, Taylor married Phoebe Landisdale; his parish sermons become material for *Great Exemplar*.
1641	Archbishop William Laud sent to the Tower.
1642	Jeremy Taylor ejected from Uppingham.
	Chaplain to Charles I, awarded DD at Oxford for *Episcopacy Asserted*; served as army chaplain.
1645	William Laud executed; 14 June, Battle of Naseby;
	Taylor a prisoner, Cardigan Castle; sanctuary at Golden Grove, home of Lord Carbery, South Wales.
1647	*Liberty of Prophesying* published.

1649   Trial and execution of Charles I. *Apology for Set Forms of Liturgy* and *Great Exemplar* published.
1650   *Holy Living* published. Death of Frances Carbery.
1651   Death of Phoebe Taylor; *Holy Dying* and *Sermons* published. Hobbes' *Leviathan* published.
1653?   Taylor married Joanna Bridges.
1654   *Real Presence* published.
1655   Taylor befriended by John Evelyn; imprisoned in Chepstow Castle for publishing *Golden Grove*.
1658   Taylor invited to Portmore, Co. Antrim; *Ductor Dubitantium* completed.
1660   Restoration of Charles II; Taylor appointed Bishop of Down and Connor and Vice Chancellor of Dublin University.
1661   *Rules and Advices to the Clergy* published.
1662   Book of Common Prayer published.
1667   13 August, Taylor died at Lisburn; buried at Dromore. Milton's *Paradise Lost* published.
1670   *Paradise Regained* published.
1725   John Wesley (23) read *Holy Living*.
1822   Reginald Heber's edition of Taylor's Works; revised and corrected by Charles Page Eden, 1847.
1838   Samuel Taylor Coleridge, *Notes on English Divines.*
1903   Edmund Gosse, *Jeremy Taylor.*
1980   Alternative Service Book includes the name of Jeremy Taylor in its Lesser Festivals and Commemorations 13 August.

I

To begin Holy Living

ONE of the bravest insights of the book which made Jeremy Taylor famous is its answer to the question: What shall we do when the Church of England has been demolished? It supplies the private English citizen with some rules for what is called *living in the presence of God* when there is no longer the old Anglican church to go to on Sunday, and no Anglican clergy available in the vicarage, 'it being now a rare thing to find a priest of the Church of England in a parish pulpit, most of which were fill'd with Independents and Phanatics', wrote John Evelyn in his *Diary*, 14 March 1652. 'Our poore Church', he had written the year before, 'now trampled on by the Rebells.' It is not impossible to imagine Jeremy Taylor addressing himself to a practical problem for Anglicans in a time of persecution, by supplying a devotional guidebook, and hoping that it would be needed only for a short time until ordinary parish life in England returned to its senses. But in the months following the execution of Charles I there was no reason for Taylor to expect either a restoration of the Stuart monarchy in England, or even a permission for the Church of England with its bishops and with the Book of Common Prayer to exist as one denomination among others. The Church he knew was being dismantled by act of Parliament; it was being replaced.

There had never been a time in our history when Parliament had not included the Lords Spiritual. In 1643 Parliament got rid of its bishops, and a bill for the abolition of the episcopacy was passed in both Houses. That was not only a reforming of the House of Lords, as it were in answer to the question: should the Church be represented, and have a place and a voice in the government of our country, or should it be excluded? It was a destruction of the way the Church understood itself and its ministry, and its ancient territorial organization into dioceses. In the face of that, could Jeremy Taylor devise an English

Christianity without obvious ecclesiastical structures at all? The native expression of Christian doctrine, the Church of England's Prayer Book, had been 'cut in pieces with a pen-knife, and thrown into the fire'. What could take its place?

The Rule and Exercises of Holy Living was his answer. It will be read quite differently when it is recognized not as a supplement to a church-goer's devotional literature, but as the whole of Christian life for the unchurched English parishioner in the middle of the seventeenth century. But it has much more than a historical interest, because its remedies challenge our secular society at the end of the twentieth century. The Church of England is not prohibited today; it has been dwindling, without any prospect of a glorious restoration. Parliament does not persecute; it merely disposes of the English Sunday.

Though there may be neither bishop, nor vicar, nor Church, nor Prayer Book to turn to, a holy life is not denied to anyone. The text of *Holy Living* shows Jeremy Taylor continually working out how to survive without them. In his first chapter, for example, there is a framework for private prayer, from getting dressed in the morning until bed-time. For those who had been used to a corporate, formal, Church liturgy, but now had 'no Opportunity to say the publick prayers', here was a very useful alternative. But his domestic version of Matins and Evensong was not just a substitute for church-going. Jeremy Taylor wanted his reader to grasp that the denial of customary church worship was an opportunity. To begin practising the presence of God in every moment does not need parish architecture. So his Introduction about the care of time, and of our motives, and of finding God in creation, and in the hearts of people, and in liberty of conscience, proposed a form of Christianity which made a virtue of being altogether church free. It is not that he had no love for the corporate and the sacramental. John Evelyn testified to the risks his friend Dr Taylor would take to preside at the Eucharist, which Parliament had expressly forbidden, and to administer baptism. But Taylor had come to see that holy life was still possible in the enforced absence of such ministry. His prayer: 'We confess, dear God, that we have deserved to be totally extinct' does not despair of Heaven for members of the C of E without their familiar and beloved parish church and set forms of liturgy.

About finding God in church, this is what is said in the introduction to *Holy Living*: God is specially present

> in the solemn assemblies of his servants. If holy People meet in grotts and dens of the earth, when Persecution or a publick Necessity disturbs the publick order, circumstance and convenience, God fails not to come thither to them; but God is also, by the same or a greater reason,

present there where they meet ordinarily by order, and publick Authority: there God is present ordinarily, *i.e.* at every such meeting. God will go out of His way to meet His Saints, when themselves are forced out of their way of order by a sad necessity: But else God's usual way is to be present in those places where his servants are appointed ordinarily to meet. But his presence there signifies nothing but a readiness to hear their prayers, to bless their persons, to accept their offices, and to like even the circumstance of orderly and publick meeting. For thither the prayers of Consecration, the publick Authority separating it, and God's love of order, and the reasonable customs of religion, have, in ordinary, and in certain degree, fixed this manner of his Presence; and he loves to have it so.[1]

Without using the term 'church' at all, the passage shows Taylor referring directly to clandestine meetings of the Church of England during this time. That it was out of the ordinary for a Church of England congregation to have to meet in secret did not mean that it was God-forsaken. Taylor shared what he took to be God's preference for an orderly establishment. He was also indicating the wisdom of his Anglican readers attending local Sunday services if required by state legislation. (The parish of Myddle, for example, evidently *preferred* the labours of the minister by whom Parliament had replaced their rector.[2] It might be said that this is but an example of 'the infidelity of the willingly-seduced multitude' complained of in *Holy Living*.[3]) But Jeremy Taylor proceeded to seek the presence of God outside the consecrated building, or authorized holy place, and its solemn assemblies.

He turned at once to spelling out what was required in order that 'we should live (1) soberly, (2) righteously and (3) godly in this present world'. The threefold formula is from the New Testament Letter to Titus;[4] but the order in which these three terms *familiarly* occur is the order in the General Confession. (Since 1552, Anglicans learned to pray 'that we may hereafter live a (3) godly, (2) righteous, and (1) sobre life' and this is echoed in Taylor's own version of Evensong, 'in all godlinesse and honesty, and sobriety'.[5]) In *Holy Living* the order of the biblical text is deliberately chosen. Jeremy Taylor expressed himself content with 'the Apostle's Arithmetick'.[6] In setting out to live *in the presence of God*, personal habits, which include practical matters of health, sex, and status, must come first; and that is what he labels as 'sober'. Then come the political and economic questions, and the issues of peace and justice; these he puts under the heading 'righteous'. Finally comes advice about prayer and Bible-reading. What is holy is not confined to the last category 'godly'.

When he began with the practice of personal virtue, he picked out temperance, chastity, humility, modesty and contentedness. It is arguable that these are qualities specially needed to survive persecution. (Uncomplaining contentment, and the skill of escaping notice by not drawing attention to oneself, are included among the reasons given by those who avoided selection in the death camps of the Holocaust.)

Next he described social and civic behaviour. God's presence was to be looked for in the decisions made in business and banking, as much as in the conduct of domestic and public relationships, in the key duties of the head of state, of judges, of parents and teachers.

Only then did he turn to the religious duties of a Christian; and put first the faith, hope, and charitable deeds which do not need church attendance to be embraced, but which thrive in evil times as well as in good. Bible reading and illiteracy, fasting and hunger, almsgiving and the gap between rich and poor, were singled out, always with a keen eye for what was practical. In a short section on how to keep Sundays and the Christian festivals, hardly a word was said about going to the parish church. It is difficult to imagine a less ecclesiastical or church-centred set of rules and exercises.

The advice is thoughtful. It was not an invitation to private piety or to scrupulosity; it took for granted an England still shaped by the habits of Christian religion. The book was being written because the services and ministry of the Church of England were being replaced by the preferences of English Presbyterians. John Evelyn would find himself without the Book of Common Prayer and without Christmas. But the English Sunday was not disturbed by the Commonwealth. Henry Vaughan, whose *Silex Scintillans* was published in the same year as Taylor's *The Rule and Exercises of Holy Living*, could still rejoice in 'Son-dayes' as Heaven once a week, as sacred time, time's bower, as time's prerogative and interest, as the holy time which gives meaning to all time:

> Bright shadows of true Rest! some shoots of blisse,
> Heaven once a week;
> The next worlds gladnes prepossest in this;
> A day to seek;
> Eternity in time; the steps by which
> We Climb above all ages; Lamps that light
> Man through his heap of dark days; and the rich,
> And full redemption of the whole weeks flight.
>
> The Pulleys unto headlong man; times bower;
> The narrow way;
> Transplanted Paradise; Gods walking houre;
> The Cool o'th'day;
> The Creatures *Jubile*; Gods parle with dust;
> Heaven here; Man on those hills of Myrrh, and flowres;

Angels descending; the Returns of Trust
A Gleam of glory, after six-days-showres.

The Churches love-feasts; Times Prerogative
And Interest
Deducted from the whole; the Combs, and hive,
And home of rest.
The milky way Chalkt out with Suns; a Clue
That guides through erring hours; and in full story
A taste of Heavn on earth; the pledge, and Cue
Of a full feast; And the Out Courts of glory.[7]

Here is an expression of the English tradition of Sunday which survived until the secular legislation of the 1990s. In its recognition of care for the holiness of time, and of the presence of God in creation, Vaughan's poetry matches Taylor's *Holy Living*. But his description of Sunday does not omit the love-feasts of the Church. The final section of *Holy Living* is about preparing for the Eucharist and its worthy reception. It is not about a service in church. Taylor invited the communicant to share the wonder of the angels 'when the holy Man stands at the *table of blessing* and ministers the rite of consecration'. But where the table was placed, whether in some nobleman's library, or in a grotto or den under the earth, was left unsaid. At the end of this section Taylor calls a return from communion into the secular world as a return *from church*. But if the blessed company of faithful people had all met under a hill, they would know on their way home that they had been to church that day. The fact is that even in his advice about the use of Sundays and the Christian festivals and the sacraments, neither church-going nor a settled ministry was relied on in *Holy Living*.

Less than 20 years earlier, George Herbert had published a collection of poems: *The Temple, Sacred Poems and Private Ejaculations*. One of the most subtle and valuable expressions of the spiritual life of the Church of England, its structure is the life of the Church, its architecture and calendar. So the floor of the church, its windows, monuments, porch, and altar, its services, feasts and fasts, all inspire the way into a poem; not descriptive, but theological and ascetical, and not ashamed of melancholy. Herbert knew how to cope with afflicted prayer; but no one had taken the Church away from him, nor the ministry of the country parson at Bemerton, which he so vividly described. How different all this is from Jeremy Taylor's England and Wales in 1650!

These general indications in the text of *Holy Living* that Jeremy Taylor was compiling un-ecclesiastical Christianity throw light upon the extraordinarily eloquent Dedication of the book made to Lord Carbery of Golden Grove, where Taylor found refuge:

> I have lived to see Religion painted upon Banners
> and thrust out of Churches
> and the Temple turned into a Tabernacle
> and that Tabernacle made ambulatory
> and covered with skins of Beasts and torn Curtains
> when Religion puts on Armour.[8]

The words reflect the turmoil of a Royalist chaplain conducting drumhead services during the Civil War. But his improvised Eucharists may also have stood upon the leather top of a gentleman's desk, and probably did, when the Church of England was out in the wilderness after the fighting,

> now that Religion pretends
> to stranger actions upon new principles
> and Men are apt to prefer
> a prosperous errour before an afflicted truth
> and some will think they are religious enough
> if their worshippings have in them
> the prevailing ingredient

Here is not just the explosive use of an alliterative p, but the admission of the shifting allegiance of nominal Anglicans which threatened the existence of the Church of England, were it not for:

> those few good People
> who have no other Plot in their Religion
> but to serve God and save their Souls

for whom *Holy Living* was being written; and

> because we now want
> the blessings of external Communion in many degrees
> and the circumstances of a prosperous
> and unafflicted People
> we are to take estimate of ourselves
> by the essential parts of Religion
> rather than by the uncertain significations
> of any exterior adherencies.

Now follow three unforgettable paragraphs, born of distress, but springing forward to describe good religion, the eucharistic community which is denied its president, and the Church which is revealed in its humiliation:

> That Man does certainly belong to God who
> 1. Believes and is Baptized
> into all the Articles of the Christian Faith

and studies to improve his knowledge in the matters of God
so as may best make him to live a holy life.
2. He that in obedience to Christ
worships God diligently, frequently, and constantly,
with natural Religion, that is, of Prayer, Praises, and Thanksgiving;
3. He that takes all opportunities
to remember Christ's Death by a frequent Sacrament,
(as it can be had;)
or else by inward acts of understanding, will, and memory
(which is the spiritual Communion)
supplies the want of the external Rite.
4. He that lives chastly, 5. And is merciful,
6. And despises the World, using it as a Man,
but never suffering it to rifle a duty;
7. And is just in his dealing, and diligent in his calling.
8. He that is humble in his spirit,
9. And obedient to Government,
10. And content in his fortune and employment.
11. He that does his duty, because he loves God.
12. And especially, if after all this he be afflicted, and patient,
or prepared to suffer afflictions for the Cause of God.
The Man that hath these twelve signs
of grace and predestination,
does as certainly belong to God and is his Son,
as surely as he is his Creature.

And if my brethren in persecution,
and *in the bonds of the Lord Jesus*,
can truly shew these Marks,
they shall not need be troubled
that others can shew a prosperous Outside,
great Revenues, publick Assemblies,
uninterrupted Successions of Bishops,
prevailing Armies, or any Arm of flesh,
or less certain Circumstance.
Theses are the Marks of the Lord *Jesus*,
and the characters of a Christian:
this is a good Religion;
and these things God's grace hath put into our powers;
and God's laws have made to be our duty,
and the nature of Men, and the needs of Commonwealths
have made to be necessary.
The other accidents and pomps of a Church
are things without our Power,
and are not in our choice:
they are good to be used when they may be had,

and they do illustrate or advantage it:
but if any of them constitute a Church
in the being of a Society and Government,
yet they are not of its constitution as it is Christian,
and hopes to be saved.

And now the case is so with us
that we are reduced to that Religion
which no Man can forbid;
which we can keep in the midst of a persecution;
by which the Martyrs in the days of our Fathers
went to Heaven;
that by which we can be servants of God,
and receive the Spirit of Christ,
and make use of his comforts
and live in his love
and in charity with all Men:
and they that do so cannot perish.

The sections of *Holy Living* deserve individual attention. Before turning to that, it will be useful to note three questions:

(1) When the Anglican Church with its bishops was re-established, and the Prayer Book (1662) re-issued, why did *Holy Living* and *Holy Dying* remain best-sellers? The huge work of Jeremy Taylor on Conscience is called *Ductor Dubitantium*. It was published in 1660 at the Restoration, and presented to Charles II. It is a serious examination of what is simply glimpsed at in *Holy Living*, that is to say, that 'God is especially present in the Consciences of all Persons, good and bad'. But *Ductor Dubitantium* is one of the unread treasures of the Church of England. And why did Jeremy Taylor not think to revise *Holy Living* after 1660?

(2) We need not suppose Taylor in any way critical of or alienated from the life of the Church to notice that the challenge of *Holy Living* is for a spiritual discipline altogether more ardent than nominal Christianity and Sunday attendance. Does this strange opportunity to devise what piety requires when Anglican worship seemed to have become inaccessible, bring Jeremy Taylor much closer to the ideals of Independents, and the fugitive essays of the new Society of Friends? Would he have been content to remain unchurched, and to practise the presence of God in a sober, just and godly life? Are there advantages for the parson and the people to be set free from ecclesiastical duties and all church concern? Was the Commonwealth not so much a threat to the Church of England as a holiday for it?

(3) *Holy Living* would appeal in the eighteenth century to that tireless priest of the Church of England, John Wesley, for being thorough, orderly and methodical. The ruled way of Christian life in England is a Benedictine inheritance. It has always been commended for its simplicity. It is not onerous. Athletes make rules about diet; musicians practise exercises. But the portrayal of holiness as a set of rules to be made routine and habitual is unsatisfactory. Discipline is virtuous. The disciple needs also to be told to 'throw away the ladder, after he has climbed up on it'.[9] If holiness, and all that is of God, is a gift, if the love of God is astonishing in its generosity but also in its spontaneity, so that a glorious liberty is spoken of as the most felicitous treasure of the children of God, is the attempt by Jeremy Taylor to elucidate rules and exercises going about it the wrong way?

OF CHRISTIAN SOBRIETY 1: TEMPERATE

Imagine being conveyed out of an anxiously hedonistic society into one in which it would not be disgraceful sometimes to express dissatisfaction with the pleasures of this life, and where the pursuit of pleasure commonly carried a health warning. Imagine bringing up children to be noble, wise, and sensible about their own appetites. Imagine not only disapproving of promiscuity, but deliberately following a training programme ('it consists in prayer, in fasting, in cheap diet, and hard lodging') in order to master temptation, and then aiming at generosity, conscientiousness and contentment instead. This is where Jeremy Taylor began with his rules for suppressing greed.

It works out how to follow Christ's 'sad and melancholy way to Felicity, rather than the broad, pleasant and easy path' simply by reducing over-indulgence, by catching desire before it grows too strong, by diverting the attention from what is tempting, by lowering anticipation in imagining what the hangover would be like after the banquet, by dwelling instead on the happiness of Heaven, and not being ashamed to be thought discriminating and censorious; to know how to look down on earthly pleasures, and upon consumers running after satisfaction

> as foolish as fishes
> thousands of them
> running after a rotten worm
> that covers a deadly hook
> or at the best but like children
> with great noise pursuing a bubble
> rising from a walnut-shell.[10]

To make a start in holy life not with Bible study but with problems of diet and drug abuse, and to fasten upon temperance primarily as a plain issue of health, shows what sort of curriculum Jeremy Taylor would have offered for RE in schools, and in what order. The seventeenth-century cases of addiction which he considered included alcoholism and nicotine addiction, as well as food-craving. But what he said about drunkenness applies to all drug abuse: 'to be perpetually longing, and impatiently desirous of any thing, so that a Man cannot abstain from it, is to lose a Man's liberty, and to become a servant of meat and drink, or smoke.'[11] He thought we should judge it as a sickness, as violence done to health. Bingeing he considered more uncharitable to the body; and drug abuse to the soul, 'the understanding part'. But these were the evil and criminal habits which needed prompt and very patient care right at the beginning of *Holy Living*.

The advice of his chapter was chiefly aimed, not at those whose obesity or addiction was out of control, but at everyone who enjoyed dinner, and could hear a warning about greediness or fastidiousness, and about too much to drink. The drunk was quite deliberately ridiculed for his red eyes and loose tongue, for becoming wanton and impotent at the same time, for immoderate laughing and stupid sleep. A reeling caricature was paraded. When Jeremy Taylor preached on the same subject, and described felicity as 'a dish of lettice and a clear fountain',[12] he was equally picturesque about intemperance. He dwelled so learnedly and in such detail about the discomfort of the overfed, that even the most restrained of congregations must have burst out laughing in Matins.

> Strange therefore it is that for the stomach which is scarce a span long, there should be provided so many furnaces and ovens, huge fires and an army of cooks, cellars swimming with wine, and granaries sweating with corn; and that into one belly should enter the vintage of many Nations, the spoils of distant Provinces, and the shell-fishes of severall seas.[13]

He was certainly as much a champion of the poor man's simple feast of 'cheese and garlick, *unctious brewages*, and the low-tasted *spinage*' as he was, like Clement of Alexandria's *Paedagogus*, a gleeful examiner of the larder of the corpulent.

He shared classical and Augustinian dismay in the face of what is irrational. 'Reason is the limit beyond which temperance never wanders.'[14] He also had an eye upon the special failings of his own Royalist acquaintance, 'valiant and brave personages' who knew how to keep their servants and children in order, but who showed which side they were on with their wild drinking parties and their inability to refuse another toast. Not until *Ductor Dubitantium* did Jeremy Taylor consider the question whether inebriation excused or aggravated criminal behaviour, and, coming closer to the case of addiction, how we are to judge the action of a will habitually depraved by drug abuse.[15] *Golden Grove*, which is the title of Taylor's book of prayers, included two prayers for deliverance from gluttony and drunkenness. To pray that sort of prayer is very hard work; and Taylor knew it. In Chapter 8 his estimation of the vocation to pray for other people is examined. He reckoned that it was not impossible, but about as difficult as trying to make the sun stand still.

Is there nothing practical that can be done to help someone who cannot stop smoking and is continually overweight, and seems to be warned off, as usual, right at the start of a holiness campaign? Jeremy Taylor's remedy comes in Chapter 5 of this book, '*The heart has to be endeared*'. It has to be so hooked, by getting directly involved in a really good cause, that it becomes more and more obvious where the money to support it has to come from.

OF CHRISTIAN SOBRIETY 2: CHASTE

Taylor's uninhibited description of boozing and gormandizing gives way to circumspection when it comes to sex. He thought it necessary to introduce this seventeenth-century topic by warning off salacious curiosity. But who, up to that time, had ever seen a book about living in the presence of God which was going to be frank about the sexual lives of virtuous married couples? François de Sales in *Introduction to the Devout Life* wanted prayer to be taken out of the cloister. He set out to instruct 'the man in the street, the family man and the VIP, those who to all appearance are completely secular'. He recognized that the devout life was not restricted to the nunnery: 'What a mistake, it's almost heretical, to want to exclude the devout life from the barrack-room or the supermarket, from high society, or from the family kitchen!'[16] But his reference to married chastity is slight, and his chapter for married people is chiefly a sermon about fidelity and the avoidance of jealousy and quarrelling. Jeremy Taylor read and appreciated François de Sales. (He would have read the French original. There is a margin reference to it in French right at the end of *Holy Living*.) But Taylor was writing in England for exactly the same sort of people, soldiers, manual workers, aristocrats and married people at home, who were (under the new Commonwealth regulations) denied their parson and the possibility of a private conversation with him. Unlike de Sales he was married. That did not guarantee wisdom; but the candour and realism of a happily married priest of the Church of England rescued Christian teaching from its very long history of theological distress over concupiscence, and its exaltation of virginity. Would *Holy Living* be the first sensible Christian handbook about married love in English?

Ever since Tertullian wrote coldly to his wife explaining that the naughty things they did in bed would not be continued in Heaven,

No restoration of marriage is promised on the day of Resurrection; nor will there be any resumption at that time of what was a disgraceful sort of pleasure between us. God promises his own no such filthy clutter.[17]

there has been within the Christian tradition unhappy use made of the teaching of the New Testament (where it has no time for anything but the end of the world) to bolster uneasiness about sex, or, as Taylor put it, to 'overact their love of single life'. Taylor's task was to show that 'chastity' was not just a word which stood in the monastic tradition between the vows of poverty and obedience. It would be a great mistake to reduce this virtue to abstinence from sex. Hardly any better would it be to present chastity as if it were a police-raid on extravagant love-making; as if good men and women held sex at bay in the interests of purity by forbidding or restraining it. Wasn't chastity the tenderest expression of mutual love and understanding between partners, and the antithesis of sexual exploitation by either side? It was clear to Jeremy Taylor that the focus of the subject must be genuine respect for married life:

> The Remedy which God hath provided,
> that is, honourable Marriage,
> hath a natural efficacy,
> besides a vertue by divine blessing,
> to cure the inconveniences
> which otherwise might afflict
> persons temperate and sober.[18]

In other places, notably in his sermon *The Marriage Ring*, Taylor would extol matrimony lovingly and generously:

> The first blessing God gave to man was society,
> and that society was a Marriage,
>
> it contains in it all sweetnesse,
> and all society, and all felicity,
> and all prudence, and all wisdome.
>
> when a man dwels in love,
> then the brests of his wife are pleasant
> as the droppings upon the hill of Hermon,

> her eyes are fair as the light of heaven,
> she is a fountain sealed,
> and he can quench his thirst, and ease his cares,
> and lay his sorrowes down upon her lap,
> and can retire home as to his sanctuary and refectory,
> and his gardens of sweetnesse and chast refreshments.
> No man can tell but he who loves his children,
> how many delicious accents make a mans heart dance
> in the pretty conversations of those dear pledges;
> their childishnesse, their stammering,
> their little angers, their innocence,
> their imperfections, their necessities
> are so many little emanations of joy and comfort
> to him that delights in their persons and society;

> this is *the marriage Ring*,
> it tyes two hearts by an eternall band;
> it is like the Cherubims flaming sword
> set for the guard of Paradise;

> Chastity is the security of love,
> and preserves all the mysteriousnesse
> like the secrets of a Temple.
> Under this lock is deposited security of families,
> the union of affections,
> This is a grace that is shut up and secur'd
> by all arts of heaven[19]

He commended chastity also for the widowed and the unmarried; and now he did mean abstinence. Virginity he highly esteemed, showing in what ways it could be considered better than marriage, even though marriage was no less holy. This enthusiastic evaluation of virginity, especially in calling it angelical, is thoroughly traditional. It would be unfair to say that Taylor was being romantic or idealistic about it. Natural virginity was allowed to stand as the treasure that it is, empty of care. It was not pitied by Taylor as unfulfilling.

Chastity was contrasted with uncleanness. Taylor described the adulterer:

> *The way of the adulterer is hedged with thorns*
> full of fears and jealousies
> burning desires and impatient waitings
> tediousness of delay and sufferance of affronts
> and amazements of discovery.[20]

He enquired '*Whether is worse, the adultery of the Man or the Woman?*' and decided both were 'equal, intolerable and damnable' for though she deserves less blame for being the weaker sex, the woman was responsible for 'bringing bastardy into a family, and disinherisons, or great injuries to the lawful Children, and infinite violations of peace, and murthers, and divorces, and all the effects of rage and madness'. The conclusion that they were equally to blame is supportable, but the argument is unconvincing. If the woman was at fault for bringing bastardy into a family, the man was equally to blame for planting bastardy into someone else's family. The description of the bitterness of marriage breakdown and its effect upon children remains accurate.

The chaste were those who guarded the eye, and the tongue, and the imagination. A special modesty was fitting for virgins, and shyness of society, as well as a loving nature. Rage and impatience were unsuitable. Widows were to give themselves time to mourn, and not to be in a hurry to marry again. The mutual love of husband and wife was not to be greater than their love of God. It ought to be simple, not violent, moderate and healthy, not time-consuming. It should not encroach upon the time set for devotion.

About what he called the troublesomeness of lust, a problem, as he saw it, for men but not women, Jeremy Taylor was a straightforward follower of the Augustinian escape route:

> When a temptation of lust assaults thee
> do not resist it by heaping up arguments against it
> and disputing with it
> considering its offers and its danger
> but flie from it

> Fly from all occasions, looseness of company,
> balls and revellings
> undecent mixtures of wanton dancings
> idle talk, private society with strange women
> starings upon a beauteous face
> the company of women that are singers
> amorous gestures, garish and wanton dressings
> feasts and liberty, banquets and perfumes
> wine and strong drinks
> which are made to persecute Chastity[21]

Here is a formidable list, even for a polite party-going Cavalier. Of course these occasions could all be 'as harmless as pickled mushromes', explained Jeremy Taylor; but where lustful excitement made it difficult for a man to control himself, the seventeenth-century night out did nothing to help. No more would it today. The rest of Jeremy Taylor's advice on dealing with lust, on the avoidance of idleness and loneliness, and on prayer and mortification, is pertinent and familiar.

This blessing, which Jeremy Taylor must have written for his wife Phoebe, is included at the end of the chapter:

the blessings of the eternal God,
blessings of the right hand and of the left,
be upon the body and soul of thy servant my wife,
and abide upon her till the end of a holy and happy life;
and grant that both of us may live together for ever
in the embraces of the holy and eternal *Jesus*,
our Lord and Saviour.
Amen.[22]

Cases of conscience which illustrate matrimonial causes were later to appear in *Ductor Dubitantium*. Of particular interest is his extended discussion of celibacy and the marriages of bishops and priests.[23] He argued that it was unreasonable and uncharitable to enjoin celibacy on the clergy, that there was no authority to make any such law, and that it was an offence to conscience. The description of chastity in *Holy Living* was now applied at some length.

He began with scandal, listing the long and impressive testimony of Catholic scholars only, including Pius II, Bernard, Cyprian, but also 'heaps of such sad complaints' which deplored 'the intolerable scandals, the infinite diminution of spiritual good, the great loss and hazard of souls, when fornicators and adulterers, paederasts and the impurest persons shall by their sermons and common talk dishonour marriage, and at the same time put their polluted hands to the dreadful mysteries'. All the complainants wished for 'the annulling of the law of single life to the Clergy'.

The Nicene fathers did not object to marriage as an honourable remedy; their banning the clergy's use of women as 'housekeepers' was showing a law of celibacy to be an intolerable burden. 'Now whether this be a burden or no will need no enquiry, when there is not in all the laws of God so much difficulty as in this very thing; insomuch that without a special gift of God, it is impossible.' It was ludicrous that holy people should have to endure such a struggle with themselves.

> *Evagrius* the Priest us'd to go into a Well in a winters night, *S. Bernard* into a Lake, to cool their burnings: *S. Francis* us'd to roll his naked body in Snows, *S. Omar* in Nettles, *S. Benedict* upon Thorns, *S. Martinian* upon burning Coals, to overthrow the strongest passion by the most violent pains. And were not that law intolerable that should command all Ecclesiasticks to do such things?

Mortification was not certainly effective; and it could be debilitating. Nor was praying for the gift of celibacy sure of success, for God requires it of none of us directly. It is sufficient that God hath given a remedy that is easie and infallible to all that love God; and it is best to use that remedy which is best, and was by the best Physician provided for all that need.

He called it an unreasonable law because, besides doing such mischief, it did no good at all. Voluntary celibacy could be imagined purer than a chaste marriage; a constrained and unwilling celibate was not pleasing to God, and was condemned to hypocrisy. But 'Virginity is not more holy than chaste marriage, and the one does not more advance religion than the other directly'. To use St Paul's advice in order to denigrate marriage was judged heretical by the early Church. Married and unmarried have different responsibilities:

> The hardest province which the married man hath is how to please his wife; but his affairs are so well order'd, that he hath not such difficulties to please God as the other hath: which thing was long since observed by *S. Gregory Nazianzen*, that indeed single life is higher and better (if it be pure and undefiled) but it is more difficult and more dangerous, and Marriage, which looks not so splendidly, is yet much more safe.

Taylor's analogy was: 'if there be any burning, if there be a fire within, it is ill dwelling in the house where there is no chimney; for that the smoke will fill every corner of the dwelling.'

Marriage might be an impediment to a ministry on the move, but to a settled pastoral ministry it was an advantage. A married man might be said to be preoccupied with worldly care; but celibates were not all innocent of worldliness. To bind the clergy to celibacy 'here was no Catholick practice' he wrote. Traditionally 'Christ and his Apostles left it free' and there is 'a plain supposition of liberty, and intimation of the thing done in the Epistles to *Timothy* and *Titus*'; thus the Council of Ancyra;

> And the practice is to this day, that the Greek and all the Eastern Priests, are, if they please, married men, and most of them actually are so: though in the Eastern Churches they always did exhort their Clergy to continence, yet they left it to their liberty, and they always took it.

He traced the story in the Latin Church, in the Second Council of Arles, in the testimony of Jerome and Ambrose, in Gregory VII's tussle with Germany, and in Anselm's single-mindedness:

> in England till the year 1100 it was not prohibited to the Clergy to marry, saith *Henry of Huntingdon*: but then *Anselm* endeavour'd to put the Popes letters in execution; And 25. years after the Cardinal of *Crema* was sent over to the same purpose: but because he was taken in bed with an

harlot, he got nothing but shame and mony, and so went away. But at last after the attempts and pressures and tyranny and arts of an hundred and thirty years continuance (for it began in 970, and was not finished till *An. Dom.* 1100, as *Polydor Virgil* computes it) the Clergy was driven from their chaste marriages, and they took themselves to Concubines, whom they could change or multiply, and they found themselves undisturbed in that; and so they rested, till God being long provok'd by their impurest services, awakened Christian Princes and Priests into liberty and holiness and reformation.

He examined the prohibition (derived from the *Apostolic Constitutions* which assume a married clergy) of marriage after ordination, and the effect of that seeming to disparage marriage, and leading to the bogus claims that orders dissolve marriage, and that orders include a vow of celibacy in their nature. But this prohibition did not prevent the clergy marrying.

> For what should hinder? The law of the Church was an evil law, made by an authority violent and usurped, insufficient as to that charge, it was not a law of God, it was against the rights and against the necessities of nature, it was unnatural and unreasonable, it was not for edification of the Church, it was no advantage to spiritual life: it is a law that is therefore against publick honesty because it did openly and secretly introduce dishonesty; it had nothing of the requisites of a good law, it had no consideration of humane frailty, it was neither necessary nor profitable nor innocent, neither fitted to time nor place nor person; it was not accepted by them that could not bear it, it was complain'd of by them that could; it was never admitted in the *East*, it was fought against and declaim'd and rail'd at in the *West*, and at last is laid aside in the Churches (especially) of the *North*, as the most intolerable and the most unreasonable tyranny in the world; for it was not to be endur'd, that upon the pretence of an unseasonable perfection, so much impurity should be brought into the Church, and so many souls thrust down to hell.

This argument about chastity and celibacy shows Taylor expanding learnedly upon what had been pithily put down in *Holy Living*. Why that book rather than *Ductor Dubitantium* became popular is not difficult to decide.

OF CHRISTIAN SOBRIETY 3: HUMBLE

Perhaps even more than passion, pride had to be taken into account by Taylor's Royalist survivors. The losing side ('if the number of thy servants be fewer') had the opportunity to learn something about humility, modesty, and contentedness.

'Humility is not a peculiar habit of self-effacement, rather like having an inaudible voice, it is selfless respect for reality.'[24] The realism which Iris Murdoch argues is needed for moral endeavour to overcome selfishness and illusion, a realism which she claims as Platonic, is also Jeremy Taylor's starting point. How unrealistic it was, he began, to be deluded by one's birth, or learning, or wealth, or excellence of character:

use the method of the Platonists
who reduce all the causes and arguments for Humility
to these seven heads.
1. The sprit of a man is light and troublesome.
2. His body is brutish and sickly.
3. He is constant in his folly and errour,
and inconstant in his manners and good purposes.
4. His labours are vain, intricate and endless.
5. His fortune is changeable, and seldom pleasing, never perfect.
6. His wisdom comes not till he be ready to die,
that is, till he be past using it.
7. His death is certain, always ready at the door, but never far off.
Upon these or the like meditations
if we dwell or frequently retire to them,
we shall see nothing more resonable than to be humble.[25]

The Sovereignty of Good is deservedly one of the most celebrated essays by an English moral philosopher in this century. What distinguishes the work of Iris Murdoch is its psychological accuracy. She pays not uncritical attention to Freud and Sartre in order to untangle the notion of original sin, and to show why humility is 'one of the most difficult and central of all virtues'. Jeremy Taylor's interest in humility was not metaphysical, but entirely practical. But he shares Iris Murdoch's flair for psychological wisdom in a cheerful way. How to be humble included, for example, neither day-dreaming,[26] nor dissembling:

Some phantastick spirits will walk alone
and dream waking of greatnesses, of palaces,
of excellent orations, full theatres, loud applauses,
sudden advancement, great fortunes;
and so will spend an hour with imaginative pleasure.[27]

Never change thy employment
for the sudden coming in of another to thee:
snatch not up a book to appear studious,
nor fall on thy knees to seem devout
nor alter any thing to make him believe thee
better employed than thou wert.[28]

Fair-mindedness was part of humility:

>we usually disparage others
>upon slight grounds and little instances;
>and towards them one fly is enough
>to spoil a whole box of ointment:
>And if a Man be highly commended,
>we think him sufficiently lessened,
>if we clap one sin or folly or infirmity into his account.
>Let us therefore be just to ourselves,
>since we are so severe to others,
>and consider, that whatsoever good
>any one can think or say of us,
>we can tell him of hundreds
>of base, and unworthy, and foolish actions,
>any one of which were enough (we hope)
>to destroy another's Reputation.[29]

Since the exemplary nature of Christ in the gospels had been the subject of his recently completed *Great Exemplar* (full title: *The Great Exemplar of Sanctity and Holy Life according to the Christian Institution; described in the History of the Life and Death of the Ever-blessed Jesus Christ, The Saviour of the World*), the imitation of Christ's humility is an essential part of Taylor's argument. Some of his paragraphs are a catena of scriptural texts:

>Pride is a great hindrance to the perceiving the things of God[30]
>
>*Humility peirceth the Clouds*[31]
>
>*God resisteth the proud, but giveth Grace to the humble*[32]
>
>the humble man will not *judge his Brother*
>*for the Mote in his Eye*[33]
>
>himself hath cast the first Stone at himself[34]
>
>the blessed Saviour of the world
>his whole Life being a great continued example of Humility[35]

Humility is also linked to candour. In his preface to *Unum Necessarium* (1655) Taylor will defend the use of private confession and spiritual direction. Even though confession to a priest is strictly unnecessary, its benefit was obvious.

>It was neither fit that all should be tied to it, nor yet that all should throw it off. There are some sins, and some cases, and some persons to whom an actual Ministry and personal provision and conduct by the Priests Office were better than food or physick . . . it were a pity that men upon the account of little and trifling objections, should be discouraged

from doing themselves benefit, and from enabling us with greater advantages to do our duty to them . . . and it is not well, if we shall be earnest to tell them that such a thing is *not necessary*, if we know it to be *good*. For in this present dissolution of manners, to tell the people concerning any good thing that it is not necessary, is to tempt them to let it alone.[36]

The benefit of spiritual direction is that it serves humility. Openness, the overcoming of pride and shame, the reliance upon 'the judgment of his friends, counsellors, or spiritual guides', are the qualities required to make a good confession. For anyone to be able to uncover and 'discover his very thoughts and fancies' marks a growth in humility:

> when the man shall tell his spiritual Guide
> the same shameful story of himself
> it is very likely he will be humbled[37]

How encouraging for Taylor's Royalists to learn that humility is not a cowardly, weak and servile virtue! Not 'going softly' but seeing things as they really are; not taking refuge in a tissue of consoling fantasy, but with fair-mindedness and candour able to see in Christ's example the way forward for themselves – are these the discoveries which will make *Holy Living* accessible in any age?

OF CHRISTIAN SOBRIETY 4: MODEST

In a footnote to what had gone before, Jeremy Taylor put together a cluster of threats to *modesty*. Some of them, like the invasion of privacy, or the sexual abuse of children, remain grave issues. They are lumped together with instances of nosiness, impertinence, bad manners, and immodesty of dress, in which mischief is not sharply distinguished from mere vulgarity. He set out shortly to get at what is offensive in being inquisitive, cheeky, indecent, and irreverent, and indicated the cause as a fundamental lack of awe. One day he will preach three long sermons about the fear of God, from the text: 'God is a consuming fire.'[38] Here, in *Holy Living*, his brevity is enigmatic. He warned against those who profaned God's secrets, and those who scoffed at natural wonders like the weather:

> He that is merry and airy at shore
> when he sees a sad and a loud tempest at sea
> or dances briskly when God thunders from Heaven[39]

was being recklessly immodest in Taylor's estimation. This is a surprise. It is ludicrous, as if we had strayed into a verse of mock solemnity by Edward Lear. Taylor's nervousness about the weather, and his corresponding beliefs about Providence, can only be accommodated now with subtlety. Perhaps if he had referred to holes appearing in the ozone layer, or to global warming, we should have agreed that it would not do to be frivolous and frisky. Modesty is indeed a proper response to the ominous and to the sublime. Cataracts and water-spouts, mighty doings in the deep, dark clouds and smoking volcanoes abashed the Psalmist dreadfully. Enlightened meteorology only began with Torricelli in 1643. The Royal Society, founded by Jeremy Taylor's friends in 1660, had to wait until 1735 for George Hadley's theory of the trade-winds and the first attempts at explaining weather.

Yet, reflected in Jeremy Taylor's forbidding to open other people's letters, or to 'listen at the doors or windows', to pry into the private lives of our neighbours, or to watch intimate scenes at the theatre, an urban, secular age can see its own concern about the boundaries of journalistic intrusion, and censorship, and the state's interference into privacy.

Taylor was satisfied with genuine scientific curiosity, and gave examples; but curiosity could become idle:

> What is it to me if my neighbour's Grandfather were a *Syrian*
> or his Grandmother illegitimate
> or that another is indebted five thousand pounds
> or whether his Wife be expensive?[40]

The vulgar curiosity which sells and buys newspapers ('they must feed upon tragedies, and stories of misfortunes, and crimes') is unsatisfied 'unless you tell them something sad and new'. So modesty was seen to be not only an expression of love and reverence, but an active defence against attacks upon innocence and integrity. This is why Taylor heaped together the nosey-parkers, the gossips, and those who laugh at funerals, with the adulterers and the incestuous. Underlying the pathetic coarseness of manners was a callous disregard of true respect and of sensibility. Immodesty was essentially destructive.

The world of learning also deserved awe in Taylor's judgement. To advance a bold opinion on slight evidence was an affront to scholarship. Pretending to knowledge which you do not have was shameless. A becoming modesty is the usual partner of very great learning. Although Jeremy Taylor did not reach back to his introductory remarks about the instruments of holy living, now it is relevant to recall his *practice of the presence of God*. For those who take on this exercise, and can use their imagination, and can see themselves 'wrapt up in the lap of his infinite Nature':

> it is the cause of great Modesty and Decency in our actions
> producing in us Reverence and Awfulness

to the Divine Majesty of God
everywhere present by his Power
he guides all the Creatures with his Eye
He it is that assists at the numerous productions of fishes
and in the Wilderness, the Bittern and the Stork
the Dragon and the Satyre, the Unicorn and the Elk
live upon his Provisions and revere his Power
and feel the force of his Almightiness.[41]

So this shy virtue, modesty, he brought to the attention of a circle of courtly friends, where exaggerated manners and daring attire, 'dissolute laughter, petulant and uncomely jests, loud talkings, jearing' had once been fashionable, but seemed pretty silly now for impoverished gentle-folk. He intended them to see that modesty was a key to a much greater, wiser seriousness. Jeremy Taylor was not peevish about merrie England. He was good-humoured. That is why more than half of his chapter on the sober virtues was devoted to contentedness.

OF CHRISTIAN SOBRIETY 5: CONTENTED

If he began to describe a happy and a holy life by considering health and diet and drug abuse, and then married love, and then selfless respect for reality and reverence for others, now he turned to what was specially important to him. He could have called it detachment, which has an honourable religious history; or *apatheia*, from the technical vocabulary of the ascetical life in the works of the Eastern Fathers whom he continually quoted. For although Cassian, Clement of Alexandria, and John Climacus appear but once or twice in the pages of *Holy Living*, their understanding of dispassion as a virtuous stage on the way to a charitable and contemplative life was not ignored by Taylor.

He could have traced *apatheia* further back, to the classical tradition of Stoicism, in which he had been educated: 'this Grace of Contentment was the sum of all the old moral Philosophy.' But, for all the influence of Stoic teachers (and by far the most frequented was Seneca, with 250 references in Taylor's works; Epictetus next, with no less than fourteen quotations in *Holy Living*, and with Zeno, Cleanthes, Chrysippus, Posidonius and even Ariston of Chios also receiving mention somewhere in Taylor's margins) he gave Stoicism an English name, and a distinct appeal. It is not at all the same as the suppression of desire; but nor does contentment merely mean cosiness, even if it does have a countrified air:

When the North-wind blows hard
and it rains sadly,

> none but fools sit down in it and cry,
> wise people defend themselves against it
> with a warm garment
> or a good fire and a dry roof.[42]

(Taylor has been called 'the Shakespeare of English prose'.[43] It is difficult to recognize that there is no echo of *King Lear* in this passage, and, ironically, no knowledge of the Fool's: 'O nuncle, court holy water in a dry house is better than this rain-water out o' door. Good nuncle, in, ask thy daughters blessing. Here's a night pities neither wise men nor fools.'[44])

Contentedness is not the appearance on the English scene of a stiff upper lip; but a certain stout-hearted, uncomplaining loyalty might be part of it. It is not just calm indifference. The Zen story of the master Hakuin[45] provides a comparison.

> A beautiful Japanese girl became pregnant. Eventually she confessed to her angry parents that Hakuin the Zen monk was to blame. All he would say was: Is that so? When the baby was born and dumped on the disgraced Hakuin, he provided exemplary care. The girl held out for a year, before admitting that the real father was the fishmonger's boy. The parents crawled back to Hakuin to retrieve the infant, and to apologize. Is that so? was all he said, yielding his charge.

Exemplary care was also provided by Silas the poor weaver in George Eliot's novel *Silas Marner*. When a shamefaced Godfrey Cass comes at last to reclaim his abandoned child, it takes a whole novel for us to enter into Silas Marner's conscientious struggle to yield the infant whom he has looked after for years as his own, because so much love is present:

> For many moments he was mute, struggling for the self-conquest necessary to the uttering of the difficult words. They came out tremulously. 'I'll say no more. Let it be as you will. Speak to the child. I'll hinder nothing.'[46]

The exquisite calm of the enlightened Zen master is admirable, even though it is humourless. Taylor worked out what is meant by contentment in a warmer emotional world. This is the world in which the English novel is also going to flourish. The fact that Taylor was referring to a large Christian tradition of unheard-of teaching about detachment (Maximus Confessor, Evagrius, Cassian, Clement and Climacus) does not mean that the subject was dry as dust.

If there was any doubt that *Holy Living* was being written for the losing side in the Civil War, the first sentence, that a contented spirit is God's remedy for every sad accident, certifies it. Taylor offered no description or commentary on the history of his times. Here and there, a reference to 'public disorder', or the choice of a moral case, like 'how to be reconciled to poverty and a low fortune', or how to behave 'when God lets loose a Tyrant upon us', provide fragmentary, oblique evidence of what it must have been like for him and his readers. Even his metaphors contribute:

> Here therefore is the wisdom of the contented Man
> to let God chuse for him:
> for when we have given up our wills to him
> and stand in the station of the battel
> where our great General hath placed us
> our spirits must needs rest.[47]

Beside metaphor, there is also his application both of Scripture and of classical allusion to what is happening round him. In the same sentence, the Psalmist and Plutarch provide Taylor with just the reassuring note of inevitable retribution he needs:

> God fails not to sow blessings in the long furrows
> which the plowers plow upon the back of the Church:
> and this success which troubles us,
> will be a great glory to God.
> and a great benefit to his Saints and Servants,
> and a great ruin to the Persecutors,
> who shall have but the fortune of *Theramenes*,
> one of the thirty Tyrants of *Athens*,
> who escaped when his house fell upon him,
> and was shortly after put to death with torments
> by his Collegues in the tyranny.[48]

It will remain to be seen if his combining both sources, classical and Christian, helps or hinders the analysis of contentedness. But if his jibe to Parliament was veiled in citing the tyrants of Athens, there followed his most outspoken piece of advice, probably representing the very limits of what could be published with impunity in 1650:

> And when thy little misfortune troubles thee,
> remember that thou hast known
> the best of Kings and the best of Men
> put to death publickly by his own subjects.[49]

There are also the rare, remarkable (because possibly autobiographical) references. It is difficult to resist guessing that he was talking about himself and his wife Phoebe in the following paragraphs, and that his own privations had been his teacher, as George Rust's eulogy testified,[50] and had given him the simple eloquence of authenticity:

The old Stoicks when you told them of a sad story
would still answer, *What is that to me?*
Yes, for the Tyrant hath sentenced you also unto prison.
Well, what is that?
He will put a chain on my leg, but he cannot bind my soul.
No: But he will kill you.
Then I will die. If presently, let me go,
that I may presently be freer than himself:
but if not till anon or to morrow
I will dine first, or sleep,
or do what reason and nature calls for, as at other times.[51]

To revisit the scenes of Jeremy Taylor's imprisonment, as, for example, at Chepstow Castle (granted to Oliver Cromwell after the Civil War, repaired by Parliament in 1650 and used as a prison), could bring to mind words about his contentedness in leg-irons. A small, ruined chapel in Marten's Tower of the castle remains. It has no floor. Its altar window and roof are open to the blue sky. Only the stone seat where the priest sits shows where a Royalist preacher serving an uncertain sentence might have been permitted to sit and pray all day long.

Or I am fallen into the hands
of the publicans and sequestrators.
and they have taken all from me:
What now? let me look about me.
They have left me the Sun and Moon,
Fire and Water,
a loving Wife,
and many Friends to pity me.
and some to relieve me,
and I can still discourse;
and, unless I list, they have not taken away
my merry countenance, and my chearful spirit,
and a good conscience:
They still have left me the Providence of God.
and all the Promises of the Gospel, and my Religion,
and my hopes of Heaven, and my charity to them too;
and still I sleep and digest, I eat and drink,
I read and meditate,
I can walk in my neighbour's pleasant fields,
and see the variety of natural beauties,
and delight in all that in which God delights,
that is, in vertue and wisdom, in the whole creation,
and in God himself.[52]

I have known an affectionate wife,
when she had been in fear
of parting with her beloved husband,
heartily desire of God his life or society
upon any conditions that were not sinful;
and chuse to beg with him
rather than to feast without him;
and the same person
hath upon that consideration
born poverty nobly,
when God had heard her prayer
in the other matter.[53]

The lot of the admirable Phoebe, to go through life aware of the embarrassing shortage of money, is a condition well known in clerical households. It was not mentioned by Taylor in his arguments against a law of celibacy (pp. 15–17). When Taylor was removed by Parliament as an 'obnoxious minister' from his living and his vicarage at Uppingham, Phoebe went with him. But the passage above implies that she had the opportunity to 'feast without him'. The Hattons of Kirby Hall must have offered to entertain Phoebe when Jeremy went off to serve as a chaplain in the king's war.

There is some jumble in Taylor's grasp of contentment. His classical writers weighed Chance and Fate. His Christian teachers spoke of 'fearless confidence' in Providence. But an English sense of humour also bobs up. These three elements cannot be easily pushed into the same essay. Taylor attempted it. After the example of Clement of Alexandria he would assimilate Stoicism to Christianity. If Stoics taught their pupils not to depend on Chance,

This in Gentile Philosophy
is the same with the discourse of *S Paul*,
I have learned in whatever state I am
therewith to be content.[54]

Holy living is about doing, not about explaining. It is the *behaviour* of one who is calm in a calamity which is impressive, whether of Seneca, or of St Paul, or of an imperturbable Royalist or of a Roundhead musketeer. The theory behind the action is not as important as to do well. To sort out what Taylor has lumped together, includes:

(i) *Fate*, which never takes a wise man by surprise, nor is ever worth bemoaning; chance which favours the prepared mind; fortune which falls out as we ourselves make it, good or bad (Epictetus), so long as it is not wholly unreasonable. The remedy was an attitude which Horace made famous as: Grasp the hour! Live for the day! Be revenged on fortune![55] Taylor reflected that philosophical tradition:

> We are in the world like Men playing at Tables
> the chance is not in our power, but to play it is;[56]

(ii) God's action in the world, working in everything for good with those who love him;[57] contentedness as a reasonable duty, because, as Taylor put it: 'God is the Master of the Scenes'; the teaching of the New Testament about the end of all things, and the promise of final judgement and heavenly beatitude for the faithful, especially for the persecuted; and, above all, the teaching of Jesus in the Sermon on the Mount:

> The Son of God told us, His Father takes care of us.
> The excellent words and most comfortable sentences
> which are our bills of exchange,
> upon the credit of which we lay our cares down,
> are these: '*Take no thought for your life* . . .'[58]

In *Holy Living* the quotation runs on, astonishingly enough, for the whole nine verses of Matthew 6.25–end (the Book of Common Prayer Gospel for the fifteenth Sunday after Trinity). This passage against anxiety, the subject of innumerable commentators, from Origen and Chrysostom to Kierkegaard and Tillich,[59] drew from Taylor:

> he is scarce a Christian
> whose faith is so little as to be jealous of God,
> and suspicious concerning meat and cloaths;
> that Man hath nothing in him
> of the nobleness or confidence of charity.
> Does not God provide for all the birds and beasts and fishes?
> do not the sparrows fly from their bush,
> and every morning find meat where they laid it not:
> Do not the young ravens call to God, and he feeds them?
> And were it reasonable that the sons of the family
> should fear the Father would give meat to the chickens
> and the servants, his sheep and his dogs,
> but give none to them?[60]

In his three Advent sermons called *Dooms-day Book*, Taylor would reach the down side of the doctrine of Providence, hell-fire. The possibility of hell was of practical, if crude, service to contentedness in *Holy Living*; especially if one's wicked enemies were seen to be prospering at one's expense:

> if we consider what unspeakable tortures
> are provided for the wicked for all eternity,
> we should not be troubled to see them prosperous here,
> but rather wonder that their portion in this life is not bigger[61]

If luck could not upset a Stoic, nor eternal punishment a seventeenth-century divine, what else was needed?

(iii) Stock proverbs of the 'sticks-and-stones' and the 'cloud-with-a-silver-lining' variety, from any English nursery;

> I have received ill language;
> but my head akes not for it,
> neither hath it broke my thigh[62]

> It may be thou art entred into the cloud
> which will bring a gentle shower to refresh thy sorrows[63]

and other common-sense sayings which judge that things 'could be worse', that taking one's medicine 'though it taste bitter, it is intended for health',[64] or that 'cutting one's coat according to one's cloth', and 'counting one's blessings', and 'being grateful for small mercies', all help a fellow to be content; and that fine fashions 'cannot cure the toothach'.[65] With these maxims, goes the characteristic attitude of being 'a good loser'.

(iv) The countryside setting is pervasive in Taylor's description of contentment, the *landscape* of such rustic wit, where 'dogs and sheep need no shooes' but we are 'full of care to get some',[66] where 'it is an unreasonable discontent that I have not so good cocks, or dogs, or horses as my neighbour',[67] 'where impatience does but entangle like the fluttering of a bird in a net' or 'like a fox catched in a trap'.[68] It is a common agricultural scene, not just the idyllic lost lands of the great Royalist families, but where a poor man may lose a cow, or an urchin throw a stone at a dog and hit his cruel step-mother. The rural scenery of England and Wales is an important ingredient in Jeremy Taylor's understanding of this sober virtue. The dialect informs with love what would otherwise be mere detachment. It is good-natured. It provides a voice for a mainly rural Church to go on adapting a cool classical opinion to its gospel, because this Church is beleaguered.

Stress, and not serenity, is a feature of our affluent lives. Taylor's virtue of temperance might sound not altogether different from club exercises in fitness and relaxation; but he was newly defining holiness in English terms. Holiness began with attention to health, and the avoidance of substance abuse. It began at home; an honest marriage is holy, but not the immodesty of the press. Respect for reality is part of holiness, but not status. Candour was required, not day-dreaming. Two questions arise:

(1) How much does Taylor's idea of holiness depend on his classical education? Already, with the idea of contentedness, he has been appealing to the ancient world. When Christopher Wren began rebuilding 51 City churches and St Paul's Cathedral after the Great Fire of London (1666) the style which replaced the mediaeval look of the English Church is confidently called Classical. Is it a name which describes not only the new external face of English Christianity but also its internal religion? The way in which Jeremy Taylor was brought up as a child in Cambridge and its influence upon his writing is the subject of the next chapter.

(2) How does Taylor's recipe for personal holiness apply in the nation's life? Chapter 3 shows how he translated 'righteousness' into political holy living.

2

The tears of Achilles

SINCE the year 362, when the Emperor Julian tried to put a stop to Christian teachers meddling with his pagan classics, and until very recently, learned Christianity freely mixed itself with the classical literary tradition. In his fifth-century block-buster *City of God* Augustine paraded his knowledge of Cicero with more than 120 quotations. But a classical education was precisely the same groundwork of Jeremy Taylor's English theology of the seventeenth century. To the consternation of his colleagues, Taylor was able to take apart Augustine's account of sex and Original Sin. But he cheerfully shared (with 215 quotations) Augustine's love of Cicero.

So full of classical references are Taylor's best-known books, that an attempt has been made to prune *Holy Living* of every Greek and Latin tag, in order to provide an edition which is accessible to those without classical studies. His preaching also was thick with classical instances. He provided such fluent asides from *Iliad* and *Odyssey* that he plainly expected his listeners to know something about the Trojan War and about Ithaca. A third of all his quotations from Homer are to be found in his sermons. Are these illustrations essential, or do they count as a dusting of scholarship (rather in the way that the Wizard of Oz keeps using the tag *e pluribus unum* to impress Dorothy and her companions)? Could the stories of Achilles and Odysseus actually have made a difference to Taylor's understanding of Christianity?

When he was writing about contentedness, for example, Jeremy Taylor thought he was able to bridge the fundamental differences between the teaching of the Stoics and the Sermon on the Mount; but is his use of ancient authors critical and discriminating, or simply conventional, in its enthusiasm for all things Greek and Latin? The purpose of this chapter is to clarify the effect of his upbringing upon his religious maturity, by following closely his use of one Greek and one

Roman source, Homer and Horace. *The Liberty of Prophesying* (1647) is justly celebrated as Taylor's plea for religious toleration. Was such a generous ecumenical spirit learned by taking to heart the huge, dark, alien religion of the Homeric age and the mysteries of imperial Rome? Or was he so used to translating the classical gods into Christianity, that he did not notice the paganism? For he let it slip in *Holy Dying* that he was intolerant of other faiths like Islam.

HOMER'S *ILIAD* AND *ODYSSEY*

Only infrequently did Taylor refer to Homer's characters by name. In the wedding sermon, *The Marriage Ring*, he distinguished between the loveliness of a good wife and the meretricious glamour of Circe:

> when *Circe* had turned *Ulysses* companions
> into hogs and monkies by pleasures
> and the inchantments of her bravery and luxury[1]

For *The Foolish Exchange*, preached on the text: 'What shall a man profit if he gain the whole world and lose his own soul?' he produced a scorching description of hell-fire and despair, warning his listeners to take care lest for some trifling, inconsiderable gain in this world, they should end in such torment. Not even for Helen of Troy, he declared, could it be worth exchanging the kingdom of heaven.

> Was this the face that launch'd a thousand ships,
> And burnt the topless towers of Ilium?

was already a catch-phrase.[2] Taylor interrupted his sermon to press his preferred theory about the Trojan War:

> Although Homer was pleased to complement
> the beauty of Helena to such a height
> as to say it was a sufficient price for all the evils
> which the Greeks and Trojans suffered in ten years.
> Yet it was a more reasonable conjecture of Herodotus,
> that during the ten years siege of Troy
> Helena for whom the Greeks fought,
> *was in Egypt, not in the city,*
> because it was unimaginable but that the Trojans
> would have thrown her over the walls
> rather then for the sake of such a trifle,
> have endured so great calamities[3]

Then his sermon went on to use Helen of Troy as an allegory:

> We are more sottish then the Trojans,
> if we retain our Helena, any one beloved lust,

> any painted Devil, any sugar'd temptation,
> with (not the hazard but) the certainty
> of having such horrid miseries, when God speaks from heaven
> full of arrows steeled with wrath, headed and pointed,
> and hardned with vengeance

When Taylor, in his sermon *Via Intelligentiae*, preached to Dublin University in 1661, wished to show that nothing makes fools of us but our own vices, he explained that what really put out the eye of Polyphemus was:

> the sweet Wine that *Ulysses* gave to the *Cyclops*[4]

Direct reference to Homer's characters like this is uncommon.[5] Liberally sprinkled throughout Taylor's work are snatches of the Greek text of *Iliad* and *Odyssey*, as likely as not untranslated.[6] He is a very reliable translator.[7] There are obvious stock quotations among these Homeric references. Taylor's discourse *On Obedience*, included in *Great Exemplar*,[8] is rounded off with a famous tag. The ghost of Achilles utters a warning to Odysseus:

> Better a poor man's slave alive, than king among the dead.[9]

Also well-known was the Greek quotation about Helen in *The Foolish Exchange*:

> No reason to feel angry
> that the Trojans and the armoured Greeks
> have suffered so long all because of a woman like her.
> She is remarkably like the immortal goddesses to look at.[10]

The wiliness of Odysseus,[11] the fore-knowing of Zeus,[12] and the uneasiness of Agamemnon's crown[13] are also referred to by familiar quotations. Coleridge noticed the opulence of Taylor's erudition.[14] What is difficult to guess is how much of it was common coin. Not every reference he made to Homer can be classified in that way.

That classical Christian education which Jeremy Taylor received, the continuation of Christian Platonic humanism promoted by Colet and Erasmus, and thought to be especially characteristic of England,[15] was not suspicious of ancient religious ideas. The relation of Christianity to the Homeric pagan world was not approached as a difficulty which might prove insuperable. Then, as now, the epic heroes seemed not to be inscrutable, but astonishingly accessible. If Taylor not only quoted Homer but plundered his source without any sense of incongruity, then that might be said to illustrate an unquestioned Christian attitude to pagan learning, that it was useful spoils.

Along with the Hebrew Bible's idea of holy war, and its insistence on *herem* (blotting out the enemy and his possessions to avoid infection) there are some practical words of advice about booty in the book of Deuteronomy, chapter 21, verses 10–13 (cf. Numbers 31.18), to the effect that a beautiful woman among the captives may be spared, taken home, her head shaved and her nails pared, and shortly married. Jerome considered this the very picture of the Christian appropriation of pagan literary treasure. Augustine compared it to spoiling the Egyptians (Exodus 3.21f.; 11.2; 12.35f.).[16] Evelyn argued it in his letter to Taylor, 26 April 1656.

Here is an example of plundering. Taylor appealed for perseverance in a holy life,[17] arguing how reckless it would be for a good man to throw it all away. 'Every deadly sin destroyes the rewards of a seven years piety.' Book II of the *Iliad* is quoted, line 297, in Greek:

> *What a shameful thing it would be,*
> *after staying so long, to go home empty-handed!*

Here is what sounds like classical support from Odysseus. But the wily Greek was arguing for a continuation of the struggle to bring down the towers of Troy. The next speaker was Nestor:

> *Let there be no scramble to get home,*
> *till every man of you has raped a Trojan woman,*
> *and has been paid for the toil and groans*
> *that Helen caused him.*

He added menacingly that anyone whining to push off home need only lay a finger on his fine black ship to find himself a dead man. To pare the claws of a passage such as this one, and to transfer it into a Christian home, in which the rewards of patience do not include a permit to ravish the enemy's womenfolk, is a feat of plundering incongruous enough to count as vandalism.

The vow of Nestor to offer to the goddess Pallas Athene the sacrifice of a yearling heifer, broad-browed, uncovered, and never yet subject to the yoke,[18] is not so remote from the Levitical sacrifices of the Hebrew Bible as to disturb Jeremy Taylor, who was used to understanding the term 'sacrifice' in its secondary, spiritual sense. But he noticed more than once that Nestor wished to gain extra divine approval by first *gilding the horns* of the sacrificial animal. Pure gold and gold leaf are mentioned. So, in his sermon about repentance, Taylor commended, with suitable Christian translation, this aesthetic, if expensive, extra:

> repentance is not onely an abolition,
> and extinction of the body of sin,

a bringing it to the altar,
and slaying it before God and all the people;
we must also mingle gold and rich presents,
the oblation of good works, and holy habits with the sacrifice[19]

It is not difficult to appreciate why Jeremy Taylor might have avoided the literal meaning of his Homeric texts. At his consecration sermon in Dublin he felt obliged to claim that the office of a bishop was so important for the unity of the Church, that any bishop impious enough to divide the flock should himself deserve to be hewn limb from limb. He did not mean this literally, but metaphorically. So he politely quoted Odysseus in Greek, who threatens to do exactly that to the suitors who had been besieging Penelope in his house; and echoes the language used when Cyclops is cutting up two of Odysseus' shipmates for supper.[20]

Taylor could completely disregard the context of some of his Homeric gobbets. *The Rule and Exercises of Holy Dying* makes direct and continuous reference to Book XXIII of the *Iliad*, the funeral of Patroclus, with its elaborate preparations on account of the honour due to the dead. The ghostly Patroclus, beloved of Achilles, haunts Taylor's own peroration concerning the Christian care of the departed. His mysterious remarks about perceiving or communicating with those who were our friends but are now at rest, spring out of the nightmare interrogation by Achilles of his dead friend. Certainly Taylor knew every detail of Homer's description of savagery at a funeral, of the atrocities done to the poor, dragged body of Hector, of the butchery not only of sheep and cattle, of dogs, and of horses, but of twelve human prisoners-of-war on the funeral pyre; and then, of the terrific blaze, and the long drawn out excitement of funeral games, with prizes of cauldrons and tripods, livestock and captive women.

Holy Dying is a gentle book. It is remote from noisy wrestlers, and from charioteers churning wild circles on the stiff, grey sand. Taylor was never going to suggest to seventeenth-century mourners at an English funeral the Homeric custom of turning a wake into a sports day. What is regrettable is his indifference to everything in this busy scene of the *Iliad* except the tears of Achilles. He thought them immoderate. So he said so; as if Achilles was an Englishman. Of course, some honour is due. Those Myrmidons of Achilles were right to drive past Patroclus 'and mourn for him as a dead man should be mourned'. But pompous and ostentatious grief was most unbecoming.

As a father weeps when he is burning the bones of a son
who has died on his wedding day
and left his stricken parents in despair,
Achilles wept as he burned his comrade's bones,

moving round the pyre on leaden feet
with many a deep groan[21]

sang Homer. Patroclus was dead and gone. 'This grief is ill-placed and undecent',[22] said Jeremy Taylor. His Christian good sense was reasserting itself; for loud sobbing at a Church of England funeral was not just ungentlemanly, it suggested lack of confidence in the resurrection.

In the same famous essay, but also twice in *Unum Necessarium*,[23] Taylor admired the ability of Odysseus to be the master of natural impulses like weeping, and to keep a stiff upper lip when it is needed. But what is revealed in *Holy Dying* is not just the recognizable assertion of English decorum, but plain evidence of two worlds which do not fit together. The wisdom, humanity, and beauty of ancient pagan writing is also melancholy with the ferocity of its religion. But the entire curriculum of the seventeenth-century school of Dr Perse in Cambridge was Latin and Greek grammar, heroic drama and imperial history, Homeric saga and Roman love poetry. If this was the first furniture for the mind and imagination of an intelligent child like Jeremy Taylor at that school, how was it assimilated into a Christian framework? Was it by a form of censorship, a habit of avoidance, so that a scholar could come to use Book XXIII of the *Iliad* as booty, as a quarry for quotations, without having to wring his hands in amazement at what was being related there with such dread, and such verve?

The cultural and religious discontinuity can be seen at all sorts of odd little moments, as when Taylor appealed, in *Clerus Domini*, to the opening scene of the *Iliad* to illustrate a long-standing respect for the authority of the parson. He referred to the fact that the clergyman, a priest of Apollo, seeking his daughter in Agamemnon's tent, happens to be carrying a golden sceptre. Here is the symbol of recognizable authority derived from a source distinct from worldly sway. Its bearer successfully prays down a plague upon the Greeks and their black ships. The prayers of an Englishman in holy orders may also prevail with God; but it would never do for a Royalist vicar to begin: 'Lord, if it ever pleased you that I burned all the rich thigh pieces of bulls, of goats'[24] nor to go on humbly to implore that Parliament might all catch the Black Death.

When Taylor preached on the mysteriousness of marriage[25] he cited relations between Zeus and his wife. If the *Iliad* reports the Father of the gods sometimes speaking sharply, but refraining from wife-battering,[26] Taylor approved. When Zeus accepts his wife Hera's invitation to sleep with her,[27] Taylor indicated the passionate friendship of man and wife. But the fact that she was beguiling him, to distract his attention from Poseidon's scheme to interfere in the Trojan war, was not mentioned. Taylor's difficulty is that not even Homer thought of the immortal gods as exemplary. Their matrimonial adventures are not related for moral instruction, but for entertainment. O golden Aphrodite, wife of Hephaestos, what fun the deathless Olympians have when they all catch you in bed with Ares, swiftest of the gods![28]

It could be argued that Taylor and his contemporaries entirely appreciated Homer's raids upon Olympian theology, and the amusement it gave all-seeing Zeus to be hoodwinked by Hera at her most seductive. Surely, the wiles of the partners are part of the equipment of matrimony. But in *The Marriage Ring* Taylor preferred to describe an obedient and compliant wife, fit for the Book of Common Prayer, rather than an affectionately intriguing one, in the classical, Homeric manner.

The cultural shift, which shows itself in quotations awkwardly out of context, may not have been so evident to the seventeenth century. Theseus and Hippolyta and all the other Athenian citizens in *A Midsummer Night's Dream* were dressed, as Ronald Watkins puts it, in 'an unequivocally Elizabethan wardrobe . . . Shakespeare habitually worked out his themes in terms of the life of his own day: nor in dress only, but in every circumstance of daily life anachronism is his rule.'[29] When the conspirators in *Julius Caesar* present themselves on a stormy night at the door of Brutus, they are seen by Shakespeare and his audience at The Globe in the 'native semblance' of Catesby and Guy Fawkes: 'their hats are plucked about their ears, And half their faces buried in their cloaks.'[30] It is but one step from the Ides of March to the Gunpowder Plot. The sense that the great authors of Greece and Rome belong to the world of Spenser, and Milton, and Taylor, provide the first objects of imitation, and the sources of their own inspiration and knowledge, was certain to diminish whatever sense they had of the pastness of the past.

Yet there is an elegiac note in the sermon which Jeremy Taylor preached at the funeral of Frances Carbery, which has him admitting how dead the dead past is, and how inaccessible:

> They descend into their Graves,
> and shall no more be reckoned among the living;
> they have no concernment
> in all that is done under the Sun.
> *Agamemnon* hath no more to do
> with the Turks Armies invading
> and possessing that part of *Greece* where he reigned,
> than had the *Hippocentaur* who never had a being:
> and *Cicero* hath no more interest
> in the present evils of Christendom,

> than we have to do with his boasted discoveries
> of *Catilines* conspiracy. What is it to me
> that *Rome* was taken by the *Gauls*?[31]

Sometimes Taylor sees that the ancient world is out of reach; sometimes with features that did not fit in his own world. But there are also resonances in Homer which carry easily across worlds. When Taylor considered the beatitude 'Blessed are the poor in spirit' for his chapter in *Great Exemplar*,[32] he was reminded of Zeus turning his eyes away from the Trojan War to the peaceful lands of the horse-breeding Thracians:

> the lordly *Hippomolgi* who drink mare's milk,
> and the *Abii*, the most law-abiding folk on earth.[33]

Taylor continued:

> Poverty is the sister of a good mind,
> not a meere poverty of possession,
> which intitles us to the blessing,
> but a poverty of Spirit;
> that is, a contentednesse.

Whence has Taylor this inkling of the tented life of the semi-nomadic horse-traders, their frugality and their virtue? Contentedness was, as we have seen, a theme very dear to Jeremy Taylor. But not every Christian who rehearses the Beatitudes thinks of Thracian gypsies.

There is also a sermon of his on the felicity of the temperate man, called *The House of Feasting*. In it he referred to Achilles tossing and turning upon his bed,[34] and provided this contrast:

> If men did know what felicity dwels
> in the cottage of a vertuous poor man,
> how sound his sleeps, how quiet his breast,
> how composed his minde, how free from care,
> how easie his provision,
> how healthfull his morning, how sober his night,
> how moist his mouth, how joyfull his heart,
> they would never admire the noises and the diseases,
> the throng of passions,
> and the violence of unnatural appetites,
> that fill the houses of the luxurious,
> and the heart of the ambitious[35]

In the same paragraph Jeremy Taylor also quoted Horace, Juvenal, Lucian, Plutarch and Seneca (and in the rest of the sermon many other classical writers), all of whom could describe, with accuracy and relish, a condition not strange to the seventeenth century, or now, of:

fellowes coming drunk from a banquet
loaden with variety of follies and filthinesse,
their legs failing them, their eyes red and staring,
cousened with a moist cloud, and abused by a doubled object,
their tongues full as spunges, and their heads no wiser[36]

The comedies and tragedies of human manners are sufficiently perennial for Taylor to consult Homer and the rest not just for eloquence but for veracity. They certainly informed his Christian understanding of sobriety for his primary task in *Holy Living*.

There are signs also of a deeper engagement with Homer, of which the best example comes in *Great Exemplar*, published in 1649. The discourse on the Eucharist[37] gathers something like a pharmacopoeia of comparative remedies, none of which, in Taylor's view, was as good as the Bread of the sacrament.

Christ is known in the breaking of bread;
that it is a great defence
against the hostilities of our ghostly enemies,
this holy bread being like the cake in Gideon's camp
overturning the tents of Midian;
that it is the relief of our sorrows,
the antidote and preservative of souls,
the viand of our journey,
the guard and passport of our death,
the wine of angels;
that it is more healthful than rhubarb,
more pleasant than cassia,
that the betel and lareca of the Indians,
the *moly* or *nepenthe* of Pliny,
the lirinon of the Persians. the balsam of Judea,
the manna of Israel, the honey of Jonathan,
are but weak expressions,
to tell us that this is excellent above art and nature,
and that nothing is good enough in philosophy
to become its emblem.
All these must needs fall very short
of those plain words of Christ;
this is My body.

To explain the reference to *moly* in this catalogue, here is the instruction of Hermes to Odysseus for outwitting the enchantress Circe:

'*Against you her spells will not avail, forbidden by this saving charm I give you. Let me explain your course of action. When Circe strikes you with her long, thin wand, draw the sharp sword that is on your hip, and make for her as if you had a mind to run her through. She will cower, and implore you to be her bed-mate instead: and your best suit is not to spurn this divine paramour but to make the lying with her a lever to free your followers and win kindly treatment for yourself. Be sure, though, that she swears the gods' great oath not to attempt more evil against you lest she take advantage of your nakedness to unman you shamefully.' Upon such explanation the Slayer of Argus plucked from the ground the herb he promised me. The gods call it Moly, and he showed me its nature to be black at the root with a flower like milk. It would be difficult for men and mortals to dig up Moly; but the gods can do anything.*[38]

Taylor quoted the last two sentences of this excerpt only, and left them in Greek. Does he expect us to know all about moly, in the way we might know that wild garlic is supposed to be an effective precaution against vampires? He was saying, of course, that the Eucharist is better than the old folk-tales.[39]

He uses a word like *nepenthe* because this was the way Helen, home from Troy, spiked the wine with an opiate to relieve sorrow.[40] As he compiled his magical herbal which cannot compare with the plain words of Christ, Jeremy Taylor reminded himself of the loveliest of women and the drugged wine, of the splendid bed of an enchantress and the bathing and anointing of a weary Odysseus, and the banquet following. That the Eucharist is better than all the golden tales of the *Odyssey* is not said wistfully; it is Christian worship prevailing with the help a powerful classical imagination.

The landscape of this imagination was not altogether private. At precisely the same time Claude, working in Rome where he had lived since 1627, could not keep up with the demand to paint such life-like pictures of the legendary world.[41] His *Narcissus and Echo* was painted for an unidentified English patron in 1644. A reason for studying the way in which Homeric quotation arises in Taylor's writing is to discover if his prayer and meditation dwell at all in the morning light and the evening light of such classical landscapes. In his sermon to Dublin University, Taylor, who was just as ready to quote from Ovid as from Homer, found room for the Latin tag about Narcissus: *Tua te fallit imago* (Your own reflection deceives you). But everything which Taylor wrote reflects the beauty and the virtues of the ancient world.

Of some importance, then, is the fact that Taylor could distinguish himself from this classical scene. Over the question of Original Sin he is modern. In *Deus Justificatus*[42] he wrote that:

> *Adam* might with just reason lay the blame from himself,
> and say as *Agamemnon* did in *Homer*, But I was not to blame.
> *It was Zeus and Fate and the Fury who walks in the dark.*[43]

The significance of this reference to the *Iliad* is that it properly accuses St Augustine, and subsequent Calvinist teaching about predestination, not just of pessimism, but of paganism. It is in Agamemnon's tragic world, where Zeus and Fate and the Furies hold sway, that a theory of predestination might be suitably be argued:

> It was not I that sinned, but it was fate or a fury,
> it was God, and not I, it was not my act,
> but the effect of the Divine decree,
> and then the same decree may make us sin,
> and not the sin of *Adam* be the cause of it.
> But if a liberty of will made *Adam* sin,
> then this liberty to sin being still left to us,
> this liberty and not *Adams* sin is the cause of all our actual.

In the treatment of Adam and Eve, Taylor's theological step away from Augustine is also exhibited in the Book of Common Prayer. It is not in a penitential liturgy about human frailty but in the Marriage Service where the Church of England remembers to celebrate our first parents. This emphasis is significantly different from *Paradise Lost* (1667). The puritan and very penetrating voice of John Milton declared the tale in Genesis to be:

> Of Mans First Disobedience and the Fruit
> Of that Forbidden Tree, whose mortal tast
> Brought Death into the World, and all our woe

But for Taylor, and for the Prayer Book, the point of the tale is the shout[44] with which Adam welcomes Eve. They are made for each other; intended to cleave together. 'Therefore shall a man leave his father and his mother and cleave unto his wife.' The Prayer Book directs: '*Then shall the Priest join their right hands together, and say*, Those whom God hath joined together, let no man put asunder.' This is a quotation from Mark 10.9, the one place in the gospels where Jesus is portrayed referring to the story of Adam and Eve.

When Adam and Eve were turned out of the Garden, what was lost, said Taylor, were *the privileges* of Eden; that is to say, dreaming innocence and immortality. Adam and Eve were returned to their natural condition. They were not deformed, or turned into crocodiles. They were beautifully human:

> Our excellent bodies, and usefull faculties,
> the upright motion, and the tenacious hand,[45]

all illustrate the miracles of the divine mercy. They had not lost their first blessing, which was each other.[46] They had not lost the wedding ring. Nor had they lost all freedom of choice; and that is how it remains with us, he thought; naked, childish, ignorant, unreasonable, but not incurable.[47] There remains in us

> a naturall freedom of doing good or evill,
> great inclinations to some good.
> And if God has snatched that from us
> and makes us bound to be sinners, where is his goodness?
> Where is our liberty? Where is our Nature?
> What is become of all Lawes, and of all Vertue and vice?
> If by the fall of *Adam* we are so wholly ruined
> that we cannot do any good, but must do evill,[48]

shall we excuse ourselves by blaming Adam, poor man? Shall we

> entertain our sins infallibly,
> and never part with them,
> upon pretence that they are natural and irresistible?[49]

So much for Zeus, Fate and the Furies! The practical possibility of the programme Jeremy Taylor issued as *Holy Living* depends upon genuine human freedom. The same freedom is needed to make Heaven and hell intelligible.

By inspecting his use of Homer, it is now possible to discern Taylor's sophistication. Some of his quotations are stock;[50] some are misplaced illustration; but some are apt and evocative, and some are critical. Homer might not be given an authority comparable to the authority of the Bible. But, especially in the Christian interpretation of the Hebrew Bible, Taylor was accustomed to a long tradition of patience and ingenuity in understanding uncongenial verses in Holy Writ. The Benedictine Rule, which guides the Church of England's recitation of the whole Psalter, invites worshippers who expect to retain the angry and protesting psalms and curses to acquire some cultural agility. The *Iliad* could be treasured in much the same way; rare and unavoidable, of unruly strength, full of barbarous theology and poetry, fiercely demanding to be heard for itself, a source of inspiration.

OTHER CLASSICAL SOURCES

Taylor considered that

> the wisest persons, and those who know how to value and entertaine the more noble faculties of their soule and their precious houres, take more pleasure in reading the productions of these old wise spirits, who preserved naturall reason and religion in the midst of heathen darknesse ... then the triflings of many of the latter Schoolemen, who promoted a petty interest of a family, or an unlearned opinion, with great earnestnesse, but added nothing to Christianity but trouble, scruple and vexation. And from hence I hope that they may the rather be invited to

love and consider the rare documents of Christianity, which certainly is the great treasure house of those excellent morall and perfective discourses, which with much paines and greater pleasure we find respersed and thinly scattered in all the Greek and Roman Poets, Historians, and Philosophers.

Of the classics, Taylor wrote to fifteen-year-old Christopher Hatton in a dedication for the *Grammar*, a text-book for the school set up in Llanfihangel by Nicholson, Wyatt and Taylor in 1647: 'These sadnesses which cloud many good men at this present, have taught us all, that nothing can secure a happinesse or create one, but those inward excellencies, which like diamonds in the night sparkle in despight of darknes.'

From the indexes of the indefatigable Charles Page Eden it is possible to make an estimate of Taylor's own preferences. If frequency of quotation is any guide, the books within his arm's reach would have included Aristotle's *Nicomachean Ethics*, Seneca's *Letters*, Plutarch's *Lives*, the *Iliad* and *Odyssey*, the *Odes* of Horace and Virgil's *Aeneid*. Cicero is easily the most frequently quoted of Taylor's Latin texts; Aristotle, Homer and Euripides the favourites in Greek. Other important sources included Plato, Herodotus, Sophocles and Aeschylus; Martial, Juvenal, Ovid, Plautus and Tacitus. The Fathers and Doctors of the Church were, of course, his mentors in ransacking the pagan classical library before him. His classical library did not end there. Reginald Heber noticed that it was hard to point out any author of eminence with whom Taylor was not acquainted. In the exuberance of his citations, complained Heber, 'he more than once refers to obscure stories in ancient writers, as if they were of necessity as familiar to all his readers as himself'.[51]

THE *ODES* OF HORACE

How a classical education affects religious maturity can be detected in the prominence of the pagan *Odes* of Horace in a Christian sermon on the Lord's Prayer. In his Discourse XII, *Prayer (Great Exemplar)*, Jeremy Taylor used 91 quotations, which are shared roughly equally between three sources:

pagan classical authors (34)
biblical quotations (32)
Christian authors (25)

but if we pick individual writers quoted at least three times:

St Luke (3)   St Matthew (4)
St Gregory (3)   St Paul (5)

Plutarch (3)   St Augustine (5)
Juvenal (3)   Horace (11)

the pre-eminence of a pagan lyrical poet in an essay about the Lord's Prayer is striking. What has Horace to contribute to the English liturgical habit of very frequent repetition of the Lord's Prayer?

Taylor thought that the Lord's Prayer belonged to the present, and rejoiced because of it, and practised the presence of God accordingly. Life is short. Give us this day. But the Latin poet Horace is famous for coining the phrase 'Life is short' (*vitae summa brevis*, a line from the poem *Solvitur acris*). So when Taylor wrote about 'our daily bread',

> we may be confident of the Divine providence
> and not at all covetous:
> for therefore God feeds his people
> with extempore provisions,
> that by needing allwayes,
> they may learn to pray to him;
> and by being still supplyed,
> may learn to trust him for the future,
> and thank him for that is past,
> and rejoyce in the present[52]

he backed up what he was saying with quotations from three poems[53] of Horace, entirely in sympathy with Horace's advice to be happy in the present moment, good-humoured when life is bitter, and incurious about an inconceivable future. Taylor was right to attach 'Give us this day our daily bread' to 'Take no thought for the morrow'. But his Latin illustrations come from some wildly romantic poetry. For Horace, 'be ye not anxious for the morrow' implied 'gather ye rosebuds while ye may'. His poem ends by urging a wayward, wanton Lydia to fasten her lovely hair behind in a neat Spartan bun, and to hurry on down with her lyre.[54]

What did Taylor think of Horace's prayers? As for making vows to the gods, said Horace in *Tyrrhena regum*, to make a panic-stricken vow to the gods when the mast starts groaning under a storm from the south-west, that was not his style.[55] Taylor, also cautious of vows, approved. But he was unhappy with Horace's description of the typical petition of a pagan money-grubber:

> *In his prayer to the beautiful goddess of Profit,*
> *he barely moves his lips for fear of being overheard.*
> *O, that she would make it possible for him to cheat*
> *while appearing scrupulously fair!*
> *And keep his fiddles and falsifications in the dark!*[56]

Taylor commented: 'The old Heathens prayed to their God for such things which they were ashamed to name publikely before men, and these were their *private prayers*, which indeed they durst not for their undecency or iniquity make publike.'[57] Then he explained what is proper for Christian prayer. About the deficiencies of ancient religion he was trenchant:

> For the holy JESUS,
> coming to redeem us from the bottomlesse pit,
> did it by lifting us up out of the puddles of impurity
> from all these vanities
> (glasses and beads and trifles fit for an American Mart)
> JESUS hath redeemed all his Disciples,
> and not onely thrown out of his Temples
> all the impure rites of *Flora* and *Cybele*,
> but also the trifling and unprofitable ceremonies
> of the more sober Deities, not onely vices,
> but useless and unprofitable speculations,
> and hath consecrated our Head into a Temple,
> our understanding to Spirit, our Reason to Religion,
> our Study to Meditation;
> and this is the first part of the Sanctification of our Spirit.[58]

He did not think the whole of Horace was trifling and unprofitable. In explaining those same words 'Give us this day our daily bread' he called to mind, from *Otium divos*:

> *To live well is to be content*
> *With little; only the family salt-cellar*
> *Shining silver on a bare table;*
> *With neither care nor greed*
> *To drive away good dreams.*

Here, like a Latin grace which descends at supper time on a polished Jacobean table, where the family treasure sits elegantly on the dark board, pagan verse enters the Christian household of an English school-boy. The food is simple. There is enough to live on. It is good to be humble. Sleep is blessed with quiet and contentment, without fear, without longing. Contentment is primarily a classical, and only then a Christian virtue; but at this moment Jeremy Taylor took the words of his beloved poet and lifted them into the heart of his daily prayer.

These examples of quotation from Homer and Horace in the work of Jeremy Taylor suggest a critical intimacy with the whole classical library more profound than a baroque taste for ornament; they show a love for ancient *virtus* and *pietas* which was contrasted with the quarrelsome

Christianity of the Civil War. The ordered, moral direction of a happy and holy life, simply expressed in *Holy Living*, might be considered thoroughly classical. There are times when Taylor has so misused his sources, or swallowed them, or mistaken them in their Christian appropriation, that it remains doubtful if he could have fully appreciated what Tertullian[59] described as the *demonic* horror of paganism and Homeric religion. The name of St Perpetua, who was thrown to the wild beasts in Carthage arena rather than give official worship to demons (the Roman gods), stood in the Calendar of the Book of Common Prayer. Nevertheless, the religious sensibility *common* to Homer and Sophocles, Horace and Cicero, and to Jeremy Taylor's Church of England is no longer plain to our society, in which Greek, Latin and Divinity are hardly known by anyone.

3

Political Holy Living

JEREMY TAYLOR'S *Holy Living* might well be expected to reflect its
time. It was written soon after the execution of Charles I, when the
assault upon a Royalist Church was to continue for a decade before
the restoration of the monarchy and the Anglican establishment.
'We cannot discern what comes hereafter' is one of Taylor's favourite
quotations from Horace. The attempt to attack and reform the
Anglican tradition was going to fail. Evidence of the stubborn religious
conservatism[1] of English parish life must have been obvious to Taylor
and his Royalist friends. None of them could take it for granted, however, that Parliament was in fact going to be unable to get rid of
bishops, or of the continued use of a set Prayer Book, or even finally
to dislodge something as light as Christmas decorations (lighter than
Vanitie itself) from England. Jeremy Taylor did not quietly get his
parsonage back at this time, as some other 'obnoxious ministers' had.
He treated the official banning of the Prayer Book as an opportunity
to construct new liturgy in its place, and to publish it; an achievement
not appreciated by the Anglican Commission appointed to revise the
Prayer Book for its re-issue in 1662.[2] But all the time Taylor believed
that God so 'disposed all things and all chances . . . by secret and un-
discernible ways bringing good out of evil'[3] that he was able to make
of the disarray of the Church the very condition for *living in the presence
of God*. What about disorder in the State?

What came first in *Holy Living* was an appeal to the conscience of the
individual. The managing of one's personal habits – temperance,
chastity, humility, modesty and contentment – were the important rules
to sort out; but no one could stop there, in virtuous isolation. Next was
the obvious recognition that to live in the presence of God implied
attempting to deal justly in society as well, coaxing civil relationships
between the powerful and the powerless, protecting a rule of law, and

not putting up with tyranny or rebellion. The righteous citizen and the pious prince needed each other to be law-abiding; and that is how they were to be characterized. Here was Taylor's direct indication that to live a holy life was not a private aspiration for the serious-minded, but a political programme. It was being addressed to a society. Holiness was a social infection. To live and to become holy could not be realized by the living, unless there was some measure of public agreement among them, about the ways they treated one another, what was lawful, how they were to be governed.

His chapter on Christian justice is short. It was composed at the end of the decade which had seen the destruction of much of the fabric of an ordered society: monarchical rule, the House of Lords, the Anglican Church, its bishops, its ecclesiastical jurisdiction. An eye-witness of the confusion of popular iconoclasm, class antagonism, and armed conflict, he was not alarmist. He would set out at length to demonstrate the foundation of law and order in the conscientious application of Natural and Divine Law, in what he regarded as his most important work, *Ductor Dubitantium* (1660). Here, in *Holy Living* (1650), came concise reasons for being obedient, rather than rebellious, towards lawful authority, and for superiors being responsible; for probity in the conduct of business and commerce, and in the honouring of debts. It was clear to him that dishonest trade practices were symptoms of an immoral society just as much as civil disorder, cruelty to children, or oppressive taxation. Jeremy Taylor considered these matters briefly in turn.

OF CHRISTIAN JUSTICE 1:
LAW-ABIDING SUBJECTS

He did not immediately explain why we should obey the civil magistrate or the rules of the Church. He simply appealed to the New Testament: 'The powers that be are ordained of God.'[4] But his real starting-point was that the keeping of the rules of a lawful authority is an important *conscientious decision* for everyone. He noted some cases in which the law of the land might be disobeyed: if it was seen to conflict with the law of God; if strict adherence to the letter of the law frustrated the real intention of the law; if the machinery for reasonable dispensation had broken down; if customary flouting of a law showed it to be ineffective. Sometimes an appeal to a higher court might be appropriate; but the real upholder of law was one who submitted even to its unjust censure without complaint, suffered its punishments, not merely patiently, but contritely. Being sorry and asking for pardon was a very important part of obedience to law. Such reverence for the law, rather than continually looking for ways of getting round it, or criticizing and disparaging the officers of the law, was imperative.

> He that ever felt, or saw, or can understand
> the miseries of confusion in publick affairs, or amazement
> in a heap of sad, tumultuous, and indefinite thoughts,
> may from thence judge of the admirable effects of order
> and the beauty of government.

The person of the monarch, the ministers of the Crown, one's parents and spiritual guides or clergy, all classed together as our superiors, were to be revered and protected, not assaulted or reviled, but treated with honour. This was a pious duty of the law-abiding citizen, even if such authoritative figures turned out to be disappointingly unreliable:

> If the prince or parent fail of their duty,
> we must not fail of ours;
> for we are answerable to them and to God too,
> as being accountable to all our superiours,
> and so are they to theirs:
> they are above us, and God is above them.[5]

The picture of an obedient, law-abiding citizen was emerging, in which the idea of obedience and non-resistance clearly owes something to the monastery and the Rule of St Benedict.[6] Indeed, in a curious appendage to this section, Taylor described *degrees* of obedience: an actual but grudging obedience; a cheerful and willing obedience (*obedientia sine mora*) in which the will is surrendered; and, supremely, an uncritical, unquestioning obedience, in which common sense itself is set aside. Jeremy Taylor is usually suspicious of any sort of fanaticism. He would have agreed that unquestioning obedience to the orders of a superior officer would not serve as a defence in the Nuremberg Trials. Jeremy Taylor prized the *reasonable, thinking* tradition of the Anglican Church. Perhaps the conviction that

> By obedience we are made a society[7]

and can be distinguished from a heap of flies 'who do what they list, and are incapable of laws, and obey none' made him put a value upon uncritical obedience as 'a complicated act of virtue' for a country which had been caught up in civil war. The best citizen, he thought, by such unswerving obedience would be showing his love:

> For when he hath given up his understanding
> to his prince and prelate,
> provided that his duty to God be secured by a precedent search,
> he hath also with the best,

and with all the instruments in the world,
secured his obedience to Man.[8]

If the basis of law and order is understood to be religious, and therefore
suitably expressed by an attitude of pious deference to a hierarchy of
authorities descending from God, is a sermon about the duties of subjects
sufficient? It may 'give a very misleading impression unless it is set beside
a sermon from the same author setting out the duty of kings'.[9] Jeremy
Taylor expected the king and the ministers of the Crown of a law-
abiding nation to preface their responsibilities with the declaration: As
God is my judge! How did he estimate these responsibilities?

OF CHRISTIAN JUSTICE 2:
DEFECTS OF KINGSHIP

The duties of the monarch are very shortly enumerated. It could be
said that Taylor was saving up what he had to say about the head of
state for a hundred pages in Book III of *Ductor Dubitantium*. There he
would discuss the right of kings, and whether the Crown could ever be
said to be above the law; he would examine supreme and coercive
power, and its rejection, rebellion, and whether resistance was lawful;
he would consider the king's authority in relation to the Church. The
deceptively modest remarks made in *Holy Living* are interesting because
they were being composed when everyone in England was staring at
an empty throne. Suddenly, even shockingly, monarchy had turned into
an option for discussion; not that everyone was capable of arguing
about classical models of a republic, based on Athens or pre-imperial
Rome, or of comparing monarchy to the constitution of Venice or the
United Provinces of the Netherlands. The historical judgement that any
1650 opinion poll in England would have been decidedly in favour of
returning at once to the Stuart monarchy is entirely plausible.[10]

A former royal chaplain might be supposed qualified to put forward
a view of what would be ideally fitting for a king's conduct of the affairs
of state; but Jeremy Taylor's summary *can also be read* as what went
wretchedly wrong in the government of his master Charles I, and what
at least must be imperative for any future king. Taylor would not admit
criticism of the sovereign, although he had no doubt watched in continual frustration the wonderful ability of Charles to rub people up the
wrong way. *Holy Living* gives a tantalizing glimpse of that dire reign, as
well as of the loyalty of an observant preacher at court, contemplating
his future dissertation on the working of conscience, but not always able
to inform the stiff conscience of his employer.[11] Taylor would write in
Ductor Dubitantium:

Conscience is like a King
whose power and authority is regular,
whatsoever counsel he follows;
and although he may command fond things,
being abused by flatterers, or misinformation,
yet the commandment issues from a just authority,
and therefore equally passes into a law;
and we may no more disobey our Conscience
commanding of evil things
than we may disobey our King
injoyning things imprudent and inconvenient.[12]

Some of the motives of those who took up arms against the Crown and its dignity are reflected in what follows.

Whether a determination to rule without Parliament should be called the personal rule[13] of Charles, or years of tyranny,[14] it was clear to Jeremy Taylor that tyranny would not do, but only the passing of royal laws which had general and popular consent:

For he that enforces a law upon a people
against their first and public apprehensions,
tempts them to disobedience,
and makes laws to become snares and hooks to catch the people,
and to enrich the treasury with the spoil, and tears,
and curses of the commonality,
and so multiply their mutiny and their sin.[15]

It must be clear that there were Royalists who were not champions of absolute monarchy or arbitrary government. Jeremy Taylor, like Sir John Strangeways,[16] assumed a rule of law which went back a very long way, defining and qualifying power; so that:

Ancient privileges, favours, customs
and acts of grace indulged by former kings to their people,
must not without high reason and great necessities
be revoked by their successors,

always remembring
that the interest of the prince and the people
is so infolded in a mutual embrace,
that they cannot be untwisted
without pulling a limb off,
or dissolving the bands and conjunction
of the whole body.[17]

The king must be in control of his executive. The ministers of the Crown must not take the law into their own hands, or excuse the monarch from his duties, especially a lazy one. Princes

> must be severe exactors of accounts
> from their delegates and ministers of justice.

Charles delegated so much of his state correspondence to his secretaries of state, that 'it seems reasonable to conclude that compared to any other Tudor and Stuart monarch a higher proportion of acts done in Charles's name were done either without his knowledge or initiative'.[18] He was indolent, short of patience, and not really interested in state papers, unless it was church, or foreign, affairs. The absence of parliament was serious; but a bored attitude to routine government, avoidance of privy council meetings, a preference for court and for the pleasures of hunting were 'a publick scandal and displeasure'. Diligent administrators like Coke and Laud might not always have regretted the inattention of the head of state; they were serving a master 'who knew not how to be or to be made great', observed Laud later on, in the Tower.

It was the duty of the king to make the law easy of access, not harsh, and not corrupt.

> an ease to the people, not an instrument of vexation;
> the shortest and most equal ways of trials appointed,
> fees moderated and intricacies and windings
> as much cut off as may be

The ambition of reformers, and the high expectation of the Parliament of Saints, to reclaim from the 'tortuous, ungodly jungle' of English law short, plain paths to justice, was shared by Taylor. It was the aim to simplify canon law which inspired his *Ductor Dubitantium*. The disgrace of church courts was as keenly felt by Anglicans as by their opponents. The intolerable abuse of ecclesiastical jurisdiction is well described by Christopher Hill;[19] his attention to the popular rejection of oaths[20] is also adumbrated in Jeremy Taylor's short summary:

> Princes must not multiply publick oaths
> without great, eminent and violent necessity,
> lest the security of the king become a snare to the people,
> and they become false when they see themselves suspected,
> or impatient when they are violently held fast:
> And if security of kings can be obtained otherwise,
> it is better that oaths should be the last refuge.

Taylor was vividly aware of the obsessive anxiety of Charles I about the loyalty of his subjects; but he also had something to say firmly about royal patronage:

> Places of judicature ought at no hand
> to be sold by pious princes.

Bribery is less punishable
when bribery opened the door by which they entred.

Had Taylor the name of Sir Charles Caesar in mind? What Holdsworth indicates is that Mountague paid for the post of Chief Justice of the King's Bench, and that Richardson gave money for his post of Chief Justice in 1626. But 'It is quite certain that the Mastership of the Rolls was sold to Sir Charles Caesar in 1639'.[21] He goes on to illustrate the prevailing corruption with the case of Henry Yelverton made attorney-general, who although he refused to improve on Sir James Lea's bid of £10,000 for the job, told the king privately that if there was no mention of any sale for the post, he would give the king £4,000 in ready money, and received a royal hug.

Arrangements made for royal revenue by the Stuarts, and the way it slid into a racket, are described by Charles Wilson.[22] The cost of king-ship might always be said to have built-in extravagance; but public provision for monarchical government had a long history of inadequacy. The poverty of the Crown has to be included among the indirect causes of the Civil War.[23] Whatever deal the Stuarts struck with the Commons by way of supply and subsidies, they were continually looking for extra-parliamentary revenue. How to exploit assets from the feudal past, in the management of Crown lands, or in the manipulation of the royal prerogative in relation to the defence of the realm, in exploiting customs duties and taxes on trade, in granting patents, monopolies and charters, were consuming interests, in which, it may be fairly said, they got in so deep, 'they drowned themselves'.[24] The financial pickle was not all their fault. Landowners and men of business showed no alacrity for rational reform of the tax system. If the king farmed out the collection of dues, the sudden efficiency was felt as extortion, and the scramble for such a farming concession by courtiers and officials, as an example of the country's affairs being sold as a bargain to the highest bidder. Merchants wealthy enough to assist an insolvent monarch with problems of cash flow could expect some recognition for services, and thus was created that most famous allegory:

> A Fair wherein should be sold all sorts of vanity . . . at this fair are all such merchandise sold as houses, lands, trades, places, honours, preferments, titles . . .[25]

Where Taylor indicates the sale of judicial appointments, Conrad Russell speaks of 'a trend to the privatisation of law enforcement',[26] and Christopher Hill turns to an expressive title of John Warr's, *The Corruption and Deficiency of the Laws of England*, published in 1649.[27] Tanner estimated that corruption began with the Purged Parliament of the

Commonwealth; but John Seldon remarked on the way Charles I was willing to rid himself of judges who disagreed with him, and to appoint those who saw eye to eye with him: 'what judges cann be made to doe wee all knowe.'[28] Since the sale of offices was plainly illegal, Jeremy Taylor's singling out of this abuse by the head of state is an indirect, but grave, insinuation. But when we read that

> Princes must in special manner be guardians
> of pupils and Widows,
> not suffering their persons to be oppressed,
> or their estates imbezelled,
> or in any sense be exposed to the rapine of covetous persons

the unspoken regret that Charles was incapable of being a father to his people becomes more obvious:

> Princes must be fathers of the people,
> and provide such instances
> of gentleness, ease, wealth and advantages
> as may make mutual confidence between them;
> and must fix their security under God in the love of the people,
> which therefore they must with all arts of sweetness,
> remission, popularity, nobleness and sincerity
> endeavour to secure to themselves.

Jeremy Taylor was quite sure that clergymen, unlike kings, should not seek popularity, but gain the love and respect of their parishioners by sheer diligence and devotion to the task. But the unpopularity of Charles, on principle disinclined to win the love of his people, was folly. The king needed warm, popular approval, not the beguiling make-believe of a court masque. He needed the self-confidence to be gentle. He needed to be known as a sincere statesman, not as an untrustworthy politician. When Taylor instanced the recklessness of his imaginary prince keeping, among his favourites on the payroll, 'vicious persons, which are publickly and deservedly hated' and 'kept in defiance of popular desires',[29] whom did he really have in mind? Buckingham? Strafford? Windebank? He did not tell us. Instead he wrote this prayer for that circle round the ruler:

> Bless all his friends,
> relatives, confederates, and lieges;
> direct their counsels, unite their hearts,
> strengthen their hands, bless their actions.
> Give unto them holiness of intention,
> that they may with much candor and ingenuity
> pursue the cause of God and the King.

> Sanctify all the means and instruments of their purposes,
> that they may not with cruelty, injustice, or oppression,
> proceed towards the end of their just desires;
> And do Thou crown all their endeavours
> with a prosperous event,
> that all may co-operate to, and actually produce,
> those great mercies which we beg of thee;
> honour and safety to our Sovereign,
> defence of his just rights, peace to his people,
> establishment and promotion to religion,
> advantages and encouragement to learning
> and holy living[30]

Prayer is what is looked for in Jeremy Taylor, not political commentary; sermons, not court gossip. His remarks about kingship in *Holy Living* have remained undisturbed and disregarded. The reflection within its pages of an execution on a cold day in Whitehall has become invisible. The reticence of the author, his clothing of criticism under generalization, and even by platitude (as when he insists that justice must be impartial, or that to indulge in merciful sentencing would scandalize victims of crime) shows a Royalist balancing loyalty and candour. But that *Holy Living* includes a contemporary and close estimate of the chief faults of Charles I in the judgement of an intelligent and sympathetic supporter is hardly to be doubted.

OF CHRISTIAN JUSTICE 3: PARENTS AND CHILDREN

Jeremy Taylor's starting point in any debate about family life would be that a child's upbringing and education spring out of parental love and example, and that the tender care of such a creature, from being a babe-in-arms, to finding suitable adult employment *and a spouse*, are all part of parental responsibility. To treat the provision of play-groups, nursery education, school places, youth employment and training schemes, as matters for *political* argument and solution, he might have welcomed as signs of the emergence of a just society. To estimate what role today's parents exercise in their offspring's choice of a partner to set up house with, might have filled him with consternation. But he would also have noticed the extraordinary shift of emphasis, as if responsibility was being leached away from the parents, and with it, the heart of the matter, the discovery of family love. He did not come to the subject with a *theory* of parental authority, as John Locke would, a generation later. (Locke was a boy at Westminster School when Charles

I was executed in Whitehall.) Locke was anxious to provide a reasonable argument for the philosophical idea of human equality, and realized that infancy had to find a place in the discussion.

> Children, I confess, are not born in this full state of equality, though they are born to it. Their parents have *a sort of* rule and jurisdiction over them when they come into the world, and for some time after, but it is but a temporary one.[31]

That we are born free is more important to Locke than that parents have power over their children. His essay concerns the subjection of minors and the limits of paternalism. It is humane, but shrewdly different from Taylor's loving expectations of family life, as a physically intimate communication. Locke pondered political and parental government; Taylor celebrated breast-feeding.

His brief headings in *Holy Living* start with the New Testament. He applied Ephesians 6.4:

> Fathers, provoke not your children to wrath;
> Bring them up in the nurture and admonition of the Lord.

Part of a New Testament household code, it is prized in modern scholarship for the shift in attention, from the breathless expectation of the end of all things, to long-term plans like raising a family, and hum-drum matters of curriculum.[32] Its tone, which Taylor could as well have found in Seneca as in Paul's letters, of disciplined but kindly education in which harsh correction of the young has no part, was given more amiability by Taylor. He agreed on the importance of securing the religion of the young; but his way of achieving this shows an admirable lightness of touch:

> season their younger years
> with prudent and pious principles,
> make them in love with virtue,
> and make them habitually so
> before they come to chuse
> and discern good from evil
>
> while they are under discipline,
> they suck in all that they are first taught

Of course they will need good teachers and good company; just as they need baptism, catechism, confirmation. But it is the example of their parents which is essential:

> and all those instances of charity
> which usually endear each other,
> sweetness of conversation,

affability, frequent admonition,
all significations of love and tenderness,
care and watchfulness,
must be expressed towards children,
that they may look upon their parents
as their friends and patrons,
their defence and sanctuary,
their treasure and their guide.[33]

Fanny, the wife of his patron Richard Vaughan, the Earl of Carbery, whose hospitality and friendship at Golden Grove was so valuable to Jeremy Taylor that the Church of England will always be in debt to the excellent woman, died 9 October 1650.[34] He preached the funeral sermon, very conscious that she had loved listening to him, and that she had been able (even very good preachers need this) to gather up his words 'from the ground, where commonly such homilies are spilt, or scattered in neglect'. She had ten children, and died of the eleventh. She had been an exemplary mother:

she was in the flower of her age,
spent less time in dressing, than many servants;
she was of a most noble and charitable soul;
a great lover of honourable actions,
and as great a despiser of base things;
hugely loving to oblige others,
an excellent friend,
as a Wife, she was chast and loving,
fruitful and discreet, humble and pleasant,
witty and complyant, rich and fair;
as a Mother, she was kind and severe,
careful and prudent,
very tender, and not at all fond,
a greater Lover of her Childrens Souls than of their Bodies

her prudence in the managing her children
was so singular and rare,
that when ever you mean to bless this family,
and pray a hearty and profitable prayer for it,
beg of God. that the children may have those excellent things
which she designed to them,
and provided for them in her heart and wishes,
that they may live by her purposes,
and may grow thither,
whither she would fain have brought them.

She lived as we all should live,
and she died –
as I fain would die[35]

Edmund Gosse described that last sentence of Taylor's as 'one of his most perilous outbursts of mortuary splendour'.[36]

In the proper exercise of love, women were not all like Fanny Carbery, but quite likely to pamper their children. Taylor put it:

> These soften them with Kisses and imperfect Noises,
> with the Pap and Breast-milk of soft Endearments,
> they rescue them from Tutors,
> and snatch them from Discipline,
> they desire to keep them fat and warm,
> and their Feet dry, and their Bellies full;
> And then the Children govern,
> and cry, and prove Fools and troublesome,
> so long as the Feminine Republick does endure.
> But Fathers, because they design
> to have their Children wise and valiant,
> apt for Counsel or for Arms,
> send them to severe Governments,
> and tie them to Study, to hard Labour,
> and afflictive Contingencies.[37]

This is a piece of utterly conventional Stoicism; Taylor quoted Seneca in the margin. But he also gave a tick to classical Roman matrons for breast-feeding their own babies rather than employing wet-nurses. In *Holy Living*, the nursing of children is 'the first, and most natural, and necessary instance of piety which mothers can shew to their babes; a duty from which nothing will excuse, but a disability, sickness, danger, or publick necessity'. Those words summarize what appeared in *Great Exemplar* (1649) as Discourse I, *Of nursing children in imitation of the Blessed Virgin-Mother*.[38] It is a curious, flimsy homily from the pulpit in Uppingham in his salad days as a married priest. First he embroidered the Infancy Narratives:

> she suckled him,
> and bound him in her arms and swadling bands,
> and when she had represented to God
> her first scene of joy and Eucharist,
> she softly laid him in the manger,
> till her desires and his own necessities called her
> to take him, and to rock him softly in her arms;
> and from this deportment
> she read a lecture of piety and maternall care
> which mothers should perform
> toward their children when they are born,
> not to neglect any of that duty
> which nature and maternall piety requires.

JESUS was pleased to be born of a poor mother
in a poor place, in a cold winters night,
far from home, among strangers,
with all the circumstances of humility and poverty;
and no man will have cause to complain of his corse robe,
if he remembers the swadling clothes of this holy childe;
nor to be disquieted at his hard bed
when he considers JESUS laid in a manger;
nor to be discontented at his thin table,
when he calls to minde the King of heaven and earth
was fed with a little breast milk.[39]

Since it is part of the natural law, argued Taylor awkwardly, that what is instinctive among mammals should be natural for us, the mother who nourished her infant in the womb should expect to nurse it when it was born. What were the two 'exuberant fontinels' for? Were they 'needless excrescencies'? It could almost be called an unnatural vice to seek a wet-nurse instead of what nature provided. He was shrewder when he claimed that mothers risked alienating their child's affection. Derelict children, as he called them, loving their substitute-mothers with a natural intimacy, because of the 'longer communication of constituent nourishment', could only be expected to be polite to their real mothers after that, if not downright provocative. Then he tried to stampede his fashionable parishioners by warning them of what a child might digest in the milk of a careless or a coarse nurse: 'peevishness', 'low and base demeanours', 'stubbornness'. You could be sure that such 'distemperatures may pass in the rivulets of milk, like evil spirits in a white garment', faster than anything virtuous, or noble. How improvident it was to allow your child to suck imperfection from a vicious breast! It is not often that Jeremy Taylor blundered about so ludicrously. His knowledge of infection was negligible, of course. A wet-nurse incubating smallpox or chicken-pox would have been infectious; a nurse with impetigo would have been contagious; a tipsy one would certainly supply sufficient alcoholic toxicity to act as a sedative. The baby would be sleepy rather than bad-tempered. A wet-nurse who smoked tobacco would threaten the child with respiratory infections. But communicable diseases like TB can be distinguished from moral delinquency. Bad language is not in the milk, but in the nursery chatter, if the nurse has the habit of swearing. (Earlier this century when nurse-maids were not unheard of, Venetia Wingfield Digby, aged three, had a nurse and Irish groom, and a toy fox. If anything got spilt or broken, Venetia immediately fingered the culprit, in her imitative brogue: 'Bogger that foxy!')

It is true that the seventeenth-century puritan was still taught to think with Augustine that Original Sin was sexually transmitted in concupiscence; and that *purity* had always been fundamental in religion. Jeremy Taylor was ready to dispute with Augustine, but he was clearly very keen to protect breast-feeding for the innocent formation of mutual family love, in which he thought mother's care, rather than nannies' and nursery-maids', came first. No doubt Phoebe Taylor, and Lady Hatton, and Frances, Countess Carbery, were all enthusiasts for natural breast-feeding too.

It was the parents who were also going to provide education, a Christian up-bringing, and job training for their children:

> education and employment,
> good trades, arts, or learning,
> to defend themselves against the chances of the world,
> that they may not be exposed to temptation,
> to beggary, or unworthy arts
> that also is part of the duty
> we owe to God for them.

Young unemployment had to be faced by parents. It was not someone else's problem, a crisis for the Board of Trade (first created in 1650, the year *Holy Living* was published), or something to be shrugged off as a consequence of recession in overseas markets.

Taylor was writing, however, at a time of real and prolonged economic difficulty for England, and for the nation's export trade, especially of undressed woollen cloth to Northern Europe. Charles Wilson[40] shows how *explanation* of economic depression was becoming less superstitious; there was less in terms of grievous Visitation (plagues, unseasonable weather and bad harvests), more about the Balance of Trade. What was at issue were strongly mercantile interests: takeover and monopoly, manipulation of currency and foreign exchange, European market rivalry, dislocation of trade by war, especially by Anglo-Dutch disputes at sea. (Fifteen years after *Holy Living*, Admiral Sir George Ayscue was telling Pepys: 'the warr and trade could not be supported together – and therefore, that trade must stand still to give way to that.'[41]) If to market competition is added a long slow rise in the seventeenth-century population of England, and a decline not only in the price of wool, but of barley, and then of wheat, and the effect upon small cultivators of large-scale capitalist development of the countryside in enclosures, fen drainage and forest clearance, then rural parishes everywhere would find themselves with a labour surplus. Urban growth could only digest some of the unskilled poor. As George Herbert had seen it:

The great and national sin of this Land he esteems to be Idleness; great in itself, and great in Consequence. For when men have nothing to do, then they fall to drink, to steal, to whore, to scoff, to revile, to all sorts of gamings. Come, they say, we have nothing to do, let's go to the Tavern, or to the stews, or what not . . . it concerns the Commonwealth, that none should be idle, but all busied . . . All are either to have a Calling, or to prepare for it.[42]

Charles I might have been genuinely sorry about the poor and about the widening gap between his rich and his poor subjects; but his granting franchises to big developers pauperized small farmers. The burden of care of the unskilled, out-of-work labourer driven off the land, and of the urban poor, remained with private philanthropy; but Wilson detects a shift which 'economic opportunism' now brought to the religious inspiration of almsgiving. Why should the labour of the poor be wasted? Benefactions increased for rehabilitation and training and enterprise. It is interesting to see that Jeremy Taylor, when he addressed almsgiving in his next chapter in *Holy Living* (in this book, Chapter 5), neglected neither the religious motive nor the social amelioration. He ran through the customary list of corporal and spiritual alms; and then added:

> Erecting publick schools of learning;
> Maintaining lectures of divinity;
> Erecting colleges of religion and retirement
> Finding employment for unbusied persons,
> and putting children to honest trades.
>
> Give, looking for nothing again;
> that is, without consideration of future advantages;
> Give to children, to old Men,
> to the unthankful, and the dying,
> and to those you shall never see again;
> for else your alms or courtesy is not charity,
> but traffick and merchandize.[43]

The parents' interest in their childrens' choice of a marriage partner is included. They must provide; they must take care with the question of religion; they must look for affection and love, not forcing the children to choose according to the parents' wish (nothing could be more injurious):

> Better to sit up all night, than to go to bed with a dragon.

Parental consent is discussed in *Ductor Dubitantium*, its legal place in classical Roman law and Old Testament tradition, and thence to canon law, and into Christian marriage liturgy, 'carefully to this day observed in the Church of *England*', in which the bridegroom and the bride 'should be presented to the Priest *by their Parents*'.[44] Taylor complained:

> But then according to the nature of all good laws
> and manners running down the hill,
> this thing never left running
> till children had leave to despise their Parents,
> and marry when and where they pleased.[45]

Taylor produced a moderating position to honour both the liberty of those who marry, and the transparent interest of the parents, and the family, and the rest of society, as witnesses. What is striking today is that even in the most thoughtful discussion of Christian marriage, *The Marriage Bond* by Helen Oppenheimer (1976) and *Marriage* (1990) by the same author,[46] the families of the bridegroom and the bride *have become invisible*. Consent, except in the case of a party to a marriage being an infant, is of no interest to the law. Has that element in the whole negotiation, parental love and concern, been relegated to romantic fiction? But in *The Most Excellent and Lamentable Tragedy of Romeo and Juliet*, and in *Pride and Prejudice*, it was a living issue. Who giveth this woman, Juliet, to be married to this man, Paris, but her father Capulet? And who, in the audiences of The Globe (*c.* 1594), would have questioned their belief in the right of the parents to arrange such things, or would have disturbed the plot of 'a pair of star-crossed lovers' whose deaths 'bury their parents' strife'? Arranged marriages, today a curiosity of the cultural patterns of certain ethnic minorities and immigrant communities in Britain, are not a feature of secular society. The category of a 'mixed marriage', especially between Protestants and Catholics in Northern Ireland, is usually perceived as a sectarian threat, rather than an ecumenical opportunity.

It was Taylor's conviction that children should be able to look to their parents as friends, defence, and treasure, which, he thought, gave parents a head-start as marriage counsellors to their own young. He ruled out arranged marriages, and wrote a whole book for Protestants and Catholics to demonstrate the way out of religious bigotry. If he had had to consider the high incidence of divorce, and of remarriage, there can be little doubt that he would have *extended* the responsibility of parents, to be real allies to their children and their grand-children, able to sympathize, to absorb acrimony, and to welcome the possibility of a fresh marriage after the breakdown of the first; and to bear their children's griefs, to suffer in their consciences for others, for others' vows broken, and to begin to share Christ's intercession.

When Jeremy Taylor turned to the love which husbands must give to their wives, he filled the margin with six lines from the *Odyssey*, untranslated. It is the contention of Edmund Gosse that the popular success of *Holy Living* was a direct consequence of Taylor's long holiday from an academic library. Homer, at least, must have been on the shelves at Golden Grove. Here, then, is salty Odysseus, having abandoned Calypso's raft, and cast naked ashore just where Nausicaa washes the clothes, making his introduction with that clumsy branch of leaves in front of him:

> to you may the Gods requite all your heart's desire; husband, house, and especially ingenious accord within that house: for there is nothing so good and lovely as when man and wife in their home dwell together in unity of mind and disposition. A great vexation it is to their enemies and a feast of gladness to their friends; surest of all do they, within themselves, feel all the good it means.[47]

Poor Nausicaa! When Odysseus has bathed and changed, and has been given (by patient, invisible Pallas Athene) that little touch of star quality, wide-eyed Nausicaa, having seen most of him already, is now quite sure she would like to marry him.

Taylor also quotes a speech of Achilles about men loving and cherishing their wives; but this time it concerns his quarrel with Agamemnon over the captive Briseis, in *Iliad*, Book IX. Neither had married the girl. So here the Greek footnote is not well suited (as was noticed in the last chapter) to Taylor's direction that husbands and wives

> must be complicated in affections and interrest,
> that there be no distinction between them of *mine* and *thine*.
> their goods should be as their children
> not to be divided, but of one possession and provision:
> whatsover is otherwise, is not marriage, but merchandise.[48]

Taylor concluded that a master's responsibilities towards his household servants, and the duties of teachers and guardians to pupils and children, were also paternal, governed by the same advice he had given to parents.

OF CHRISTIAN JUSTICE 4: BUSINESS ETHICS

Commercial sharp practice is part of the world where *Holy Living* has to be worked out. In the middle of the seventeenth century there had been three consecutive bad harvests, 1647–49. Which chandlers were 'retaining corn', as Taylor put it, to inflate prices in the commodities market? Whose clerks were regularly catching out the customers with long contracts in small print? Which dealers equivocated over trade descriptions? Were the great London-based overseas trading companies exploiting monopolies against the public interest? And who was responsible for encroachments upon common property, notoriously in the enclosure of common land?

The context of a 1650 publication on business ethics would be an awareness of what was happening to the price of salt and soap, for example, now that they were in the hands of monopolists who had found a way of getting round the law of 1624 against monopolies. (Immediately Jeremy Taylor would be reminded, of course, of Lysimachus and the Tragasean salt scam, to complicate matters in the classical margin.) There had been extension and increase of custom duties on exports and imports, and other government interference in trade and industry, as well as in agriculture and transport. But English sea-borne commerce had grown; the ship-money fleet was not just a grievance; it was a success. It was not clear that future Parliamentary taxation would be a lighter burden. There had been the War. Some had lost everything; but there had been profiteers. Was one of the economic consequences of the War a rise in real wages, the first since Henry VII?

Taylor was not hatching an economic theory or a bourgeois political philosophy. From Paris in 1651 would come *Leviathan* (and what a cheerful commentary it is on John Evelyn, that the long entry in his diary for 7 September 1651 which begins: 'I went to visit Mr. Hobbs' retails no philosophical conversation, but the grandstand view he had from Thomas Hobbes' window in Paris of the entire cavalcade of Louis XIV on its dazzling way to Parliament. Perhaps such a spectacle itself was seen as the epitome of political science, or a lively illustration of *The Principles of Christian Politiques*). Whereas Hobbes needed absolute sovereign power to regulate the City and the conduct of business in the whole commonwealth, and to correct 'the lucrative vices of men of trade or handicraft; such as are feigning, lying, cozening, hypocrisy, or other uncharitableness', Taylor's appeal was to the conscience. He could imagine a commercial world without cheating, where debts were honoured. The practice of the presence of God inspired it. He could envisage a trader with a reputation for fair-mindedness being trusted for the right price. He could see neighbourliness playing its part when goods were sold on credit, and where risk was calculated; that to drive a hard bargain might be legal but invited rapacity; that wages should be paid promptly, not because delay was illegal, but because it was mean to do otherwise. The rule of thumb about buying cheap and selling dear worked if it was kept within bounds, and if those who were making the bargain were matched in experience, so that the tiro was not taken advantage of. Favourable terms to special customers should only refer to cases of generosity to the poor. To keep promises, especially the inconvenient ones, was essential.

He was reflecting the tradition of the righteous entrepreneur of the Hebrew Bible, of Job, and the excellent Boaz, for example, and the prophetic teaching against deceitful scales. It has been suggested that when he spoke up for employees – 'Detain not the wages of the hireling' because it 'grinds his face till tears and blood come out' – he was reminding Lord Carbery that chaplains are embarrassed unless their tiny stipends are paid on the dot. But it is the biblical tradition and the parables of Jesus, like the Labourers in the Vineyard, which echo in his argument:

> Let no Man for his own poverty
> become more oppressing and cruel in his bargain,
> but quietly, modestly, diligently, and patiently
> recommend his estate to God,
> and follow its interest, and leave the success to Him:
> For such courses will more probably advance his trade[49]

Not only is the Unmerciful Servant (Matthew 18.21–35) in the background of this piece of advice, but the Unjust Steward (Luke 16.1–8) also. When he was facing poverty, the unjust steward did not oppress his firm's debtors, but diligently followed its interest by offering substantial discounts, gaining friends; and was congratulated by his rascally employer for advancing his trade.

Taylor does not complete his short and apt advice without a word about professional, medical and legal fees. Not just charging for services they cannot render,

> Physicians must not meddle with desperate diseases,
> and known to be incurable,
> without declaring their sense before-hand;
> that if the patient please,
> he may entertain him at adventure,
> or to do him some little ease.
> Advocates must deal plainly with their clients,
> and tell them the true state and danger of their case;
> and must not pretend confidence in an evil cause:

The candour invited here belongs to any discussion *today* about good practice. Only the syntax and the vocabulary remain in the seventeenth century; but prose which can use the alliteration and assonance of 'client, case, cause' has already transcended that limitation.

OF CHRISTIAN JUSTICE 5: MORALS AND
JURISPRUDENCE

Zacchaeus was in Jeremy Taylor's mind when he began to think about restitution. The sequence of events in this story of the chief tax collector in St Luke's gospel (Luke 19.2–10) is admirably summarized by Christopher Evans:

> As an enunciation of conversion, or as a sign of it having taken place ... Zacchaeus solemnly, before *the Lord* as witness, makes a double profession of intent, the first part of which (*the half of my goods I give to the poor*) goes far beyond what was expected for charity, and the second part of which (fourfold restoration of what had been fraudulently gained) goes beyond the requirement of the law, which was the amount plus a fifth (Lev 6.5).[50]

In *Unum Necessarium*, Taylor, who also noticed that Zacchaeus far exceeded what might have been required – 'he was tied only to the payment of one fifth part above the principal' – called this 'an excellent fruit of repentance, and a part of self-judicature'.

> These are the fruits of repentance,
> which grow in Paradise
> and will bring health to the Nations,
> for they are a just deletery to the state of sinne,
> they oppose a good against an evil;
> against every evil;
> they make amends to our *Brother exactly*;
> and to the *Church competently*,
> and to *God acceptably*,
> through His mercy in Jesus Christ.
> These are all we can doe in relation to what is past[51]

But what he had to say about indebtedness and restitution in *Holy Living* sounds much more like chapter headings for a possible textbook of the law of Tort than a homily on sin and repentance. For he lumped together, without any extended discussion, the payment of debts with what a law-court would call variations in capacity, instances of accidental injury and compensation, damage limitation, contributory negligence, trespass, nuisance, the extinguishing of liability by death, enticement of a spouse, damages in respect of fatal accident, defamation, false imprisonment, writ of ravishment (now obsolete); and he concluded in one long rush:

> By proportion of these Rules,
> we may judge of the obligation
> that lies upon all sorts of injurious persons;

the sacrilegious, the detainers of tythes,
cheaters of Mens inheritances,
unjust judges, false witnesses and accusers,
those that do fraudulently or violently bring Men to sin,
that force Men to drink, that laugh at and disgrace vertue,
that persuade servants to run away,
or commend such purposes,
violent persecutors of religion in any instance;
and all of the same nature.[52]

To this assembly of torts (and I suppose encouraging a runaway servant might be considered to be actionable in the seventeenth century) Taylor gathered an assortment of sinners. Then he added another sort of debtor, those who owe *a debt of gratitude* to their friends and benefactors, and should know not to forget to repay a good turn, nor to neglect the duty of love, service and prayer for them. So here is a fine mixture of liability, crime, sin, and good manners in a few paragraphs. It leaves the impression of someone rapidly going over what is meant when we say that we ought to pay our debts, and the sooner we pay them the better. It is true that he will compose a treatise, *Unum Necessarium* (1655), on the doctrine and practice of repentance, and an even bigger one, *Ductor Dubitantium* (1660), on the foundation of law. Here, in an exhilarating way, he storms into territory described by moral theology and jurisprudence, not in order to show that law can enforce morals, but to commend the justice required by a holy life both as sane, entirely within our reach, and, as in the case of Zacchaeus meeting Jesus, coming from the heart.

The just society, its government and its law-abiding citizens, notice that influence, counsel, argument, persuasion and exhortation are not excluded from politics and the exercise of power. How does Christian opinion get a hearing, or get its way with the State? Before examining the third strand in *Holy Living* (rules about devotion; Chapter 5), it will be pertinent to see what Jeremy Taylor thought about relations between Church and State. *Holy Living* with its strictures on the monarch had just begun but had not finished an account of Christian politics.

At the end of the first chapter I argued that Jeremy Taylor was defining holiness afresh in English religious tradition. What was striking was the confident and pragmatic appeal to personal values and the reform of manners that would not be lost on a puritan. He was looking for awe and innocence, and for common sense. He pointed to physical health and moderation, to sexual love and marital fidelity, to being realistic about ourselves and not nosey about others, and to being even-tempered in a tight spot. Those were the qualities needed for a start in a holy life. To this he added the political and commercial definition of holiness, the life of the holy city, in which government, law and order, and public life, all reflected the active, loving concern of good parents.

4

Merely spiritual power

ACCORDING to George Rust in the funeral sermon, Jeremy Taylor had great skill in civil and canon law.[1] He was alluding to two folio volumes published in early June 1660, and presented to Charles II, *Ductor Dubitantium*. Tucked away in this large-scale proposal for the reformation of English moral argument is a discussion on Church and State, in particular the relationship between the law of the land and the ecclesiastical courts. It was being written when no such relationship could be presumed for the Church of England. On Christmas Day 1655 John Evelyn wrote:

> This being the last day, after which Cromwell's proclamation was to take place that none of the Church of England should dare either to preach or administer sacraments, teach schoole, and cetera, on paine of imprisonment or exile. So was this the mournfullest day in my life I had seene, or the Churche of England herselfe since the Reformation; to the greate rejoicing of both Papist and Presbyter.[2]

Taylor was eventually persuaded by his friends to accept voluntary exile in Ireland. But he was still in England in 1657 when Evelyn noted: 'Dr Taylor shew'd me his MSS. of Cases of Conscience, or Ducto Dubitantium, now fitted for the presse.'[3] A year later he made this entry in his diary: 'There was now a collection for persecuted and sequestr'd Ministers of the Church of England, whereof divers are in prison. A sad day! The Church now in dens and caves of the earth.'[4] Edward Conway's country house at Portmore on the Lisburn shore of Lough Neagh in Ireland was planned by Inigo Jones. Nothing remains of this mansion where Jeremy Taylor was conveyed in 1658 to complete his book in safety. But it must be supposed to have been one of the more elegant and salubrious caves of the earth for a sequestered minister ejected from office by Parliament to hide in.

Two decades earlier Taylor had been promoted by the Archbishop of Canterbury, William Laud; but he did not share his political instinct about the place of the Church in the State. For both, Church and State stood together. Taylor described it as one hand helping the other – 'and both are lift up to God'. But for Charles I, in partnership with Laud, a working relationship in which 'it is almost impossible to tell precisely who was doing what'[5] was establishing *the identity* of Crown with Church. If the Christian King (in Council, 12 November 1630) decided to deal with food shortages in the realm, at least in the capital, by ordering a fast on Fridays for his subjects, and no business for his inn-keepers that night of the week, Laud would be quite content for the ecclesiastical courts to deal with consequent fast-breaking as a criminal offence. He expected State sanction in return for all his liturgical arrangements, and for uniformity of worship in the English Church, with suitable punishment, fines and imprisonment, for breaking such canon laws.

There was an obvious affront to religious freedom here: part of the impetus of *The Liberty of Prophesying* and of *Ductor Dubitantium* was the need to be honest about the power of the Church and the ambition of the State to coerce religion. If the man in 'a practised double act' with the monarch was the Archbishop of Canterbury, then conviction politics, disposing of any conflict between the interests of Church and State, was likely to gather to itself very impressive power. It makes sense not to describe either Charles I or William Laud as a martyr. But *to that exclusive cause, the Anglican kingdom*, martyrs they were. Afterwards Jeremy Taylor sat down to write a constitution in which the Church has no power at all in the State except spiritual power. This admirable and genuinely religious proposal was published exactly at the time of the Restoration. But it was disregarded. The leaders of the Church of England trusted to be restored to power, to Laudian power, if that was possible.

Ductor Dubitantium is not a new proposal. The Erastian principles it accepted had already been discussed and defended by Richard Hooker in *Ecclesiastical Polity*. If common boundaries for a State and its Church can be imagined, then the administration of justice cannot be divided 'as if there were two sorts of justice, the one for Seculars and the other for Church-men'.[6] And because, as Taylor insisted again and again, 'Religion is no pretence to Regalities', meaning that Christianity can never claim to exercise coercive power, the civil magistrate must always be supreme in ecclesiastical as well as in secular causes.

Thus the Church hath power to command us
to be devout in our prayers, to be charitable to our Brother,

> to forgive our enemy, to be heartily reconcil'd to him,
> to instruct the ignorant, to follow holiness,
> and to do justice, and to be at peace with all men.[7]

> the Church makes no absolute laws
> her legislative is wholly a ministry of grace and godliness,
> not of Empire and dominion.
> For the difference is this:
> Civil laws *oblige* in publick and in private,
> for reason and for Empire,
> when the cause ceases and when it remains,
> when the breach is scandalous and when it is not scandalous.
> But the Canons of the Church oblige
> only for their reason and religion,
> for edification and for charity,
> when the thing is useful to others or good in itself.
> But the authority it self being wholly for these purposes,
> is a ministry of religion,
> but hath in it nothing of Empire,
> and therefore does not oblige for it self and by it self,
> but for the doing good, and for the avoiding evil.[8]

Since the Crown cannot be supreme in the realm unless it has all the power of government, the clergy, just like lawyers and soldiers, must be servants of the Crown. The bishop bears no sword of his own. The New Testament admonition that a bishop must be no striker[9] confirmed for Taylor the very picture of spiritual government. The bishop has no power of the sword. He governs 'by arguments and reason; by fear and hope, *by preaching*'.[10] In his two Visitation sermons, *The Whole Duty of the Clergy*, and in the pamphlet *Rules and Advices to the Clergy of the Diocese of Down & Connor* Taylor made no secret of the sheer gift given to the preacher to captivate those who listened to the sermon; and, therefore, of the awful responsibility that goes with preaching: 'to minister Gods Word unto the People is the one half of his great Office and Employment.'[11] So, the merely spiritual power of the bishop, under the Crown, was sufficient for Taylor; because he was quite sure that '*there is an Empire in preaching*'.[12] He spoke of 'commanding in the name of God' and of being direct. 'Some things are so clear and obvious, so necessary and confess'd, that he who neglects them is condemn'd by himself.' But this is not power as the world knows it. 'It compels those who are willing to be compell'd; that is, it does not compel at all, and therefore is but improperly an act of Jurisdiction.'[13]

The Crown always had a special interest in religion because it is a great instrument of political happiness, a view which Taylor traced back to Homer.[14] Since the force of religious conviction can be subversive, religion is a weapon which a wise sovereign must hold firmly if he is not to be knocked on the head by it. The credulous citizenry, an easy prey to every sort of superstition and bogus religion, needs wise civil government as a remedy. How can a nation be godly and quietly governed, unless the turbulence of strange, new religions is restrained by the law of the land? The Emperor of pagan Rome was also *pontifex maximus*, supreme in his religious title as well as in his imperial power. In a Christian society the Crown has a similar double role, representing Christ's deputy in the exercise of that kingdom, power and glory, which is expressly denied to any other pontiff or minister of religion.

Taylor argued that such royal power was not arbitrary; its purpose was the defence of the Church and of all the king's subjects in their service of God. But if 'the supreme judgement and the last resort is to the Prince, not to his Clerks'[15] what would happen if the established Church were to be shackled to a prince like the Emperor Nero? Or like Cromwell? The Erastian theory would not be modified. When time was running out for Charles I, before his execution he gave his watch to his chaplain, Jeremy Taylor, who inscribed on its plain, gold dial: *Nescitis horam*. But Taylor indeed *did not know the hour* when monarchy would be restored, or if it ever would be; or if the Church of England could ever be re-established. Nevertheless he repudiated rebellion against government, whatever its legitimacy, and however it might treat the Church. It was plain to him that the Church could argue with but not defy the State. But there is a deeper reason. 'Religion thrives as well in a storm and in persecution as in sun-shine.' God had granted

> another Oeconomy for religion,
> the way of the Cross, and the beaten way of humility,
> and the defensatives of mortification,
> and the guards of self-denial,
> and the provisions of contentedness,
> and the whole spiritual armor,
> and prayers and tears,
> and promises,
> and his holy spirit,
> and these are infinitely sufficient to do Gods work,
> and they are infinitely the better way.[16]

His description of the religious economy, the way of the Cross, the merely spiritual power, is typical of Jeremy Taylor, who includes here the virtue of contentment, about which, as we have seen, he had much to say in *Holy Living*. His armoury also has the very important hendiadys 'prayers-and-tears' in it, which is a weapon from the Eastern Orthodox spiritual tradition, valued, for example, in *The Discourses* of Symeon the New Theologian, and on the seventh rung of John Climacus' *Ladder of Divine Ascent*. What informs his essay about the place of an established Church in the realm is not primarily a political or a legal interest; it is the continual awareness that *prayer* is what really matters to the State, its ruler and subjects, and that it has a priority over important issues of power and justice. That the power of prayer is not coercive, but has a better authority, is not always plain to those who are interested in ruling the roost.

Merely spiritual power is not merely ineffective. 'As the Civil power hath authority in Ecclesiastical matters, so the spiritual power hath a share in the legislative.'[17] Wise government might be expected when the supreme power listened to its spiritual advisers. But Taylor admitted there was also considerable force in the conscientious decision of the Church to suspend its own action, and to use its liberty, for instance, to refuse to baptize or, more especially, to refuse to communicate. The abuse of the power of excommunication, its use in trivial cases, and its callous exploitation in bishops' courts simply to raise revenue, had been challenged by reformers from Wyclif onward.[18] It was Jeremy Taylor's aim in writing *Ductor Dubitantium* to provide an English alternative to the mediaeval tradition of Catholic legalism. 'It was necessary that Cases of Conscience should be written over a-new, and established upon better principles, and proceed in more sober and satisfying methods.'[19] Ecclesiastical censure Taylor reckoned to take up at least half of the whole corpus of Roman canon law. He believed that without relinquishing the prerogative of the bishop to declare someone 'to be out of the way of salvation, and unworthy to receive the holy mysteries', canon law about excommunication should be reduced to a few simple rules, chief of which was that it could not make sense for the national Church to excommunicate the head of state, nor to inflict such a sentence upon anyone without the consent of the State. Again he underlined the difference between the power of the Church and coercive state power, pointing out that the secular magistrate who discovers too late that he had condemned the innocent to death is not like the excommunicating bishop whose sentence 'is harsh as the noise of Peacocks, but does no more harm'.[20]

Part of the force of spiritual rules should be their simplicity:

> What God had made plain, Men have intricated,
> and the easie commandment is wrapped up in uneasie learning
> the very title of canon law was *Concordantia Discordantiarum*
> a tying of contradictions together in one string
> so that there is a wood before your doors,

> and a labyrinth within the wood,
> and locks and bars to every door within that labyrinth,
> and after all we are like to meet with Unskilful guides.[21]

Simple rules were not a threat to freedom. He supposed that the Eucharist, for example, was founded upon the divine command: 'Do this in remembrance of me.' So it was entirely proper for canon law to prescribe the doing of the Eucharist: it enshrined a divine command, and must be obeyed. But the *manner* of celebrating the Eucharist should be allowed all the liturgical freedom which Taylor detected in the New Testament, and which he gladly traced to the common sense and proper liberty of the apostolic community.

> For of all Men in the World
> they would least put a snare upon the Disciples,
> or tie fetters upon Christian liberty.
> But in Divine Commandments,
> and in what were the appointed ministries of grace,
> they were but the mouth of Christ
> and Ministers of his holy spirit;
> and in those things
> what they told the Churches
> is our law for ever.[22]

The nerve of Taylor's advice was that canon law and religious customs 'can become religion if they be the outward act of an inward grace; as giving money to the poor . . . made religion by the grace within'.[23] So his concluding judgement was forthright:

> Ecclesiastical laws must serve religion,
> but must never pretend to be religion.[24]

Jeremy Taylor was resisting the claim, both Roman and Calvinist, that Church law could realistically be independent of, or superior to, the law of the land. The Crown's supremacy, and its government of the Church, was not a threat. It was a defence of Christianity. Harshly dealt with by such a State, the Church would have to be content to be persecuted. The strong appeal of any spiritual law, with its utter lack of coercion, and with its emphasis upon grace, underlies the importance of conscientious Christian judgement, which is the whole theme of *Ductor Dubitantium*.

Is this arrangement, a national Church tied to the secular State, a practical possibility? Could the establishment of the Church of England survive? The formula of being bound to a secular Parliament not all of whose members were themselves C of E would not frighten Jeremy Taylor. But what if the Department of Social Security quietly adjusted a Christian description of marriage and family life, a description which

Jeremy Taylor put at the heart of *Holy Living*, so as no longer to distinguish partners living together from spouses, and children born in wedlock from those who are not? Put the other way round, is it possible for those who find the principle of remarriage in church for divorced people unacceptable to belong to a *national* Church when the nation has made up its mind differently about divorce and remarriage?

At a time when divorce was a rarity, an established Church might get away with refusing to dispense from vows and not allowing marriage to those who had been divorced and whose former spouse was still alive. Today this Church is established in a nation where divorce is reckoned to affect nearly half of all marriages, and remarriage is frequent (for there remains 'in men and women a wonderful desire of marriage', said Jeremy Taylor). Between a sect with an unyielding theological opinion that remarriage is adultery and a national Church which fulfils a civic duty to marry those citizens who present themselves, it is possible to put Jeremy Taylor's understanding of canon law. Only for 'great reason and necessity' could a national Church avoid matrimonial failure and dismay by pretending that some church regulations were in fact religion. It is the advantage of an established Church to represent the realm of unhappy, unsuccessful marriages and family breakdown, and to be found among the deserted, and the cheated, and the unfaithful. Utterly reliable compassion, which the Church exists to provide, ought to be well known to those seeking remarriage. A marriage discipline for Anglicans which was charitable and easy need not be antinomian; nor should it have to rely upon annulment as a remedy. A national Church could not be content to think that the divorced are entitled to a national Register Office. Marriage has spiritual needs which the civil magistrate is not competent to satisfy. The merely spiritual power of a national Church is best expressed in hope, and in overwhelming hospitality towards those for whom a divorce has brought woe and acrimony, and another chance to marry.

The character of an established, national Church which inspired Taylor was one which would not be able to excuse itself when the civil magistrate promoted equality for women. It should be impossible to frame state law seeking equal opportunities for women without inviting the state Church to review its own employment and management policies. It would be laughable to decry such a Church for yielding to secular fashion in making up its mind to ordain women, and to consecrate them as bishops. A *national* Church can hardly be anything if it is not secular. For such a Church (which usually expects that the-powers-that-be are ordained of God) to refuse to reflect the law of the land about women's employment would be heresy.

In a national Church all who live in the land are parishioners, and their offspring can claim the ministry and protection of the Church. Any attempt to restrict the membership of the national Church by admitting to baptism only those who believe must be mistaken. Infant baptism copes with the unselfconscious faith of being born and included in the Establishment. Such a Church has to ask itself if it is ever at liberty to refuse baptism or to discourage anyone who asks for it. The policy of a national Church would never be to pick and choose which citizens of the nation might be said to deserve it; all sorts and conditions of citizens in all sorts and conditions of belief would always be welcome; because baptism is awash with grace.

For Jeremy Taylor grace started with the mercy of God. There was no grace except grace to sinners. He described that as the first sermon of Jesus, and (as he usually did in biblical meditation; see Chapter 6, 'The great employment') he put together the good news of the first sermon in Luke's gospel, its lesson of release, recovery and liberation (Luke 4.14–22) with the account of the sermon in Mark's gospel (Mark 1.14f.): Jesus came into Galilee, preaching the gospel of God, and saying 'The time is fulfilled, and the kingdom of God is at hand; *repent*, and believe the gospel' (cf. Matthew 4.17). Jesus 'began his Office with a Sermon of Repentance . . . of grace and favour . . . not Works . . . but remission of sins . . . the grace he hath purchased for us, that is our sins for his sake shall be pardoned'.[25] Saved by the grace of God, we are enabled, by the continual gift of the Spirit, to grow in grace as a new creation, in the imitation of Christ who is full of grace. The rest of what Jeremy Taylor had to say about grace can be found in his Whitsunday sermons *On the Spirit of Grace*, and especially in two sermons (published with 25 others for the summer half-year in 1651) entitled *Of growth in grace, with its proper instruments and signs*.[26] They are dedicated to Richard Vaughan, Lord Carbery, after the death at Golden Grove of his wife Frances.

In the seventeenth century St Augustine's passionate interpretation of St Paul's teaching on grace and nature was still the opinion every theologian started with. Its development in strict Calvinism, not without warm argument, about the scale of human depravity, the limits of almighty patience, and the qualifications for admission to redemption (would it be members only?), about predestination, and whether grace could be resisted (even though it was necessary?), kept the Protestant dons of Cambridge busy when Jeremy Taylor was a student. Professor Jakob Hermensen of Leiden, known as Arminius, had died just seventeen years earlier. Those who took the cause of Charles I against Parliament, against Presbyterian order, and against absolute predestination, are sometimes labelled Arminian. But Jeremy Taylor never referred to Arminius. He read Augustine; and he read Cassian, Augustine's contemporary, and he read everything else.

The significant contribution which Taylor made was to treat the word grace as synonymous with the Holy Spirit. His Whitsunday sermon is not a description of the mechanics of an *impersonal* power which might or might not be irresistible, but of the presence of God himself, the Spirit of grace, as 'the best friend', as 'the best relative' anyone could imagine; caring as parents care for their children, or as a friend prevails upon a friend. 'Whosoever hath the Spirit of God lives the life of grace.' With Augustine he agreed that it is essentially a matter of delight to ask God to 'prevent and follow us'. God prevents us, when, for example, the Spirit of grace moves us to pray. But everyone who prays is a fellow-worker with God. And here Taylor quoted Cassian:

> It is a sign our prayers will be heard, when the Holy Spirit moves us to pray with confidence, as if quite unconcerned about receiving what we ask.[27]

It is tempting for present-day Anglicans in a secular culture to think that faith was easier in the past. But Taylor contrasted his own century with the beginning of the Christian era, when he supposed there were 'multitudes overcome by grace, and passionate with zeal'. Household codes for the conduct of Christian life are a regular feature of New Testament letters. They are the canon law of the early Church.

> Piety was so universall
> that it might well be enjoined by *Saint Paul*
> that *if a Brother walked disorderly*,
> the Christians should avoid his company;
> they were not to endure so much as *to eat with*,
> or *to salute a disorderly brother*, and ill-living Christian:
> But now if we should observe this canon of Saint Paul,
> and refuse to eat, or to converse with a fornicatour,
> or a drunkard, or a perjured person, or covetous,
> we must also *go out of the world*;
> for a pious or a holy person is now as rare,
> as a disorderly Christian was at first:[28]

It seemed plain to Taylor that faith was something that was alive and on the move. Religion did not stand still. 'If it does not grow better, it grows much worse.'

> *But grow in grace*; Thats the remedy,
> and that would make us all wise and happy,
> blessed in this world, and sure of Heaven.[29]

What follows is an admirable description of the formation and development of moral character. Growth was measured from the first instance of regret in a hardened sinner who has been used to thinking himself none the worse for his sin. 'But when the grace of God begins to work upon a mans spirit, it makes the conscience nice and tender.' Stages of growth in grace were marked by the stirring of good resolutions, the discovery of the 'first deliciousnesses of religion' and of virtue made easy by habit; of the good life becoming not so laborious, nor driven 'like Pharoahs charets with the wheels off', but rolling along as irresistibly as sea-waves upon the strand. The stewardship of time, the mastering of passion, were further signs of advance towards the condition when 'Vertue is like *hunger and thirst*, it must be satisfied or we die'.[30]

Taylor's psychological description of a state of grace and the maturing of moral character is not held up by awkward questions about the Spirit of grace *interfering with* human freedom. He was providing a picture of the growing freedom of human virtues. It was promoted by lively illustrations, claimed as evidence of the Spirit at work. He picked out, for example, the attractive habit of listening meekly to criticism without making excuses, and not being prickly about one's reputation. He warned those who had enough sense to avoid eating forbidden fruit, but still allow themselves *to kiss the apples of paradise*. Small sins unravel holy purposes. Growth in grace was not only shown in greater resistance to temptation, but in the ability not to be caught out suddenly by unpremeditated sin. He liked the way grace spreads through character. Something was lacking in a grace which is 'apt for prayer and close-fisted in Almes, sound in Faith and dead in Charity'.[31]

Although the signs of grace were as obvious 'as eating and drinking are signs of life' they were not to be looked for directly. In fact, lack of self-concern or of any wish to feel satisfaction with one's own virtue was another sign of growing up in the fellowship of the Spirit of grace. What was to be aimed at was not self-improvement, but political justice and proper care of the unemployed. Taylor ended his sermon with the good soul quite unaware that such 'downright endeavours' and 'hearty puposes' would lead to eternal felicity. That is precisely like saying that the Good Samaritan in the parable is the only one who does not know that he is the good Samaritan.

5

Devout Holy Living

PRAYER fills *The Rule and Exercises of Holy Living*. When Jeremy Taylor set out to provide exercises, he obviously thought it possible and practical to sharpen prayer by working on it, like someone maintaining an engine. Spiritual formation involved being ready to learn how; as if grace, acknowledged, for example, in an unrehearsed initiative to pray, and to wonder, and to weep, attracted education. God's gift allowed room for skill, timing, intelligence, patient effort. John Jewell had pictured collaboration between the grace of God and the effort of worshippers: 'The wheel turneth round, not to the end that it be made round; but because it is first made round, therefore it turneth round.'

Taylor began to teach prayer by putting his finger on illiteracy, on the use and abuse of hunger, and on 'the great inequality' of rich and poor. Thus the third part of *Holy Living*, concerning Christian worship, was as enterprising and unmysterious as the first part, which began with the overcoming of drug addiction, or the second part, which included the separation of powers to prevent Government interference with the judiciary.

THE BIBLE AND ILLITERACY

The best source of prayer and of worship was the Bible. It had better be read. *Attentiveness to the word of God* was all that was necessary. The phrase would need sorting out, in case the word of God and the text of Scripture were not the same thing. But what about those who could not even read? It is fairly certain that in Jeremy Taylor's England less than half of adult males, and a much smaller fraction of women, could sign their names.[1] More could read than write: signing one's name, however, is not a very advanced sign of literacy.

There are many that cannot read the word,
and they must take it in by ear,
All the doctrine of salvation is plainly set down there,
that the most unlearned person, *by hearing it read,*
may understand all his duty.

Set apart some portion of thy time,
and if it be possible, every day read
or hear some of it read.

God, by hearing us speak to him in prayer,
obliges us to hear him speak to us in his word.[2]

Taylor was not obscurantist. There were those who regretted the Reformation, who wished that English Bibles, printed in huge quantities cheaply, could be collected up again, translated back into Latin, and kept under lock and key. A hundred years earlier these cautious friends of Henry VIII had caught Tyndale and killed him. But his English translation escaped. It was not strangled and burnt; it became the authorized language of King James' Bible. To try and guard the text from the vulgar eye and ear was no longer even possible. Was God unable to look after his own truth, except by the help of scholars under the direction of a magisterium? Jeremy Taylor saw that the plainness of the Bible and its availability, that it was bursting with radical ideas which threatened the worldliness of the *status quo*, were not embarrassments to holy living. If it was the mark of a Protestant family to read it round the table, why should that put off a High Church Cavalier? The only thing Taylor found regrettable was the illiteracy of his friends. When God made Adam and sent him out of Paradise, explained Taylor, he did not deprive him of speech, or of

the rare invention of letters, and the use of writing,
God gave us these when he made us[3]

Taylor was optimistic about a literate Christian faith. He preached as if he demanded a literate congregation, though he was far too good at it to leave the unlettered behind. (Witness his advice to preachers to speak 'usefully and affectionately' to those with least understanding, and to use 'primitive, known and accustomed words'.[4]) His own free-school upbringing, his part in founding a school, Newton Hall, in Llanfihangel Aberbythych,[5] his momentous solution to the problem of Irish sectarianism, the reconstruction of university education in Dublin, which he called *Via Intelligentiae*,[6] the way of understanding, testify to more than an enthusiasm for learning.

Unmediated access and intimacy in being *able to read the word of God* (rather than just to hear it, or to recite it, or to snip out a little strip of *Torah* to fasten closely to the left forearm, a touchingly eloquent, illiterate use of the Hebrew Bible) is at the heart of prayer in the tradition of Pharisaic Judaism and the synagogue, which was the religious formation of Jesus.[7] St Luke's picture of the reading aloud of the *Haftarah* by Jesus in the synagogue at Nazareth (Luke 4.16–30)[8] was referred to by Taylor:

> we may be instructed by the same religion
> amongst the Jews and Christians:
> Reading and meditating the law was the religion of the Jews
> upon their feasts and Sabbaths.
> They met in their Synagogues,
> and they heard *Moses* and the Prophets read and expounded:[9]
> there they did all the actions of Natural religion;
> there they taught piety and holiness,
> justice and government, Oeconomical and Political;
> and the measure of things good and bad and indifferent[10]

'The general effect of modern biblical studies has made it difficult, some would say impossible, to make a direct identification between the Word of God and the written words of the Bible.'[11] One of the implications of this, pointed out by Tom Baker, is that our studies and our prayers may forcibly be kept in watertight compartments. Jeremy Taylor would have hated to think of literacy and learning threatening piety like that; somehow Reason and traditionally sacred Scripture had to make friends, if the word of God was to leap down from Heaven. The following chapter in this book considers what Taylor described as 'the great imployment' of our lives, biblical meditation. Suffice it to say that he did not separate private, secret prayer from Bible study, or from hearing it read out in Church. God had to be able to speak in his word to those who could not read. The more informed the attentiveness was, and the more literate, the more he supposed that God's word would bless human imagination. To get at the word of God, his advice was to read the plainest parts of the Bible, especially the gospels and psalms, to be ready to learn it off by heart, and to get the scholarly help of a spiritual director.

The advance in critical studies (the comparison, for example, of typical Qumran interpretation of biblical passages, preserved in the Dead Sea Scrolls,[12] with early Christian claims upon a biblical passage like Isaiah's good news for the poor) would fascinate Jeremy Taylor. The biblical *ignorance* of a sophisticated secular society today which does not even take in the Bible by ear, would astonish him. What sort of engine for prayer could serve instead? Would astronomy and poetry do?

THE FAST AND THE USE OF HUNGER:
(A) JOHN MILTON

It is important to compare Jeremy Taylor with John Milton, his contemporary. Milton was five years older than Taylor; but they overlapped as university students at Cambridge. Milton was extremely critical of his university, argumentative, and unpopular, and wondered why he had ever left London. Taylor was not only quick, he was very much at home, and was promoted. In the year in which Milton was writing pamphlets against episcopacy (*Reason of Church Government*, 1642) Taylor was awarded his DD in defence of bishops, *Episcopacy Asserted*. Milton took a swipe at the clergy in *Lycidas*:

> The hungry Sheep look up, and are not fed

but Taylor set out to inspire them (see Chapter 8). Taylor was Chaplain in Ordinary to Charles I; Milton was Latin Secretary to Oliver Cromwell during the Commonwealth. From different sides they can be found tackling the same subjects. In *Comus*, Milton describes chastity, very elegantly, as a virgin goddess. In *Holy Living*, Taylor, with better insight, claims chastity for married love. Taylor always makes more sense and less poetry than Milton. Both were intent upon liberty of conscience, and on human freedom (Milton in *Areopagitica*, Taylor in *Liberty of Prophesying*) but Taylor thought liberty went with Christian unity; Milton thought it needed plenty of diversity and schism.

In the year that Jeremy Taylor died, *Paradise Lost* was published by John Milton, and Heaven and hell began to disappear into a metaphor. Milton is not responsible for this shift in theology; he was reflecting it. He provides a marvellous contrast to Taylor, all of whose good moral sense referred to values which do not shift, but are essential, eternal, and real. The absolute necessity for Heaven and hell in Taylor's scheme of *Holy Living* and *Holy Dying* is discussed in a later chapter. Here to begin with is how Milton treated fasting.

Tertullian had regretted that Adam was unable *uni arbusculae jejunare*, 'to fast from one little tree', and was consequently punished *tormentis atque suppliciis inediae*, 'with the torments and penalties of hunger'. The remedy which Tertullian proposed to his enthusiastic friends was sometimes to treat food like poison, and to put up with hunger as the antidote, as if 'hunger might rekindle the salvation' lost by Adam's one bite of the apple.[13]

This is exactly the theme of John Milton's *Paradise Regained* (1670), a reliving and reversing, by Jesus, of Adam's temptation:

> *Eden* rais'd in the wast Wilderness (I.7)

It is plausible that Milton was much more interested in Virgil than in Tertullian; the poem has 'a georgic form, a georgic style, a georgic theme . . . the praise of the temperate, disciplined frugal life'.[14] But hunger so whistles through Milton's account of the temptation of Jesus, that it is difficult to read the poem without feeling ravenous.

Paradise Regained begins with God's plan to conquer sin and death by humility: 'His weakness shall o'recome Satanic strength' (I.161). Jesus, led into the wilderness, 'hunger'd then at last / Among wild Beasts' (I.309f.). Satan, disguised as 'an aged man in Rural weeds', explains that anyone alone in that place dies of hunger and drouth. Those who dwell like him in the wilderness

> Live on tough roots and stubs, to thirst inur'd
> More then the Camel (I.339f.)

He tempts Jesus (in Milton's shrewd version of the temptation, with its echo of the miracle of the Feeding of the Five Thousand) to use compassion in turning stones to bread:

> save thy self *and us relieve*
> With Food (I.344f.)

Not deceived by the Arch Fiend's disguise, Jesus enlists the example of Moses and Elijah:

> Man lives not by Bread only, but each Word
> Proceeding from the mouth of God: who fed
> Our Fathers here with Manna; in the Mount
> *Moses* was forty days, nor eat nor drank,
> And forty days *Elijah* without food
> Wandred this barren waste, the same I now (I.349–54)

This speech is a fine anticipation of one of Milton's master-strokes, the food fantasy dream. When Jesus rebukes Satan for lying, 'For lying is thy sustenance, thy food', Book I of *Paradise Regained* concludes excitedly:

> Satan bowing low
> His gray dissimulation, disappear'd
> Into thin Air diffus'd: for now began
> Night with her sullen wing to double-shade
> The Desert, Fowls in thir clay nests were couch't;
> And now wild Beasts came forth the woods to roam.
> (I.497–502)

Milton shows such admirable use of the gospel of St Mark's very few words about the temptation (he will return to Mark for the ending of his poem) and such familiarity with the Psalter, that reservations which may be entertained about *Paradise Lost,* cannot obscure his biblical cunning in this poem.

Milton accurately described the use of fasting prayer, when Jesus

> tracing the Desert wild
> Sole but with holiest Meditation fed
> Into himself descended (II.109–11)

Satan, meanwhile, has returned to his gloomy consistory (is not hell full of archdeacons and ecclesiastical lawyers?) to decide that even the most persuasive *sexual* temptation imaginable will not work on this subject.

> And now I know he hungers where no food
> Is to be found in the wide Wilderness (II.231f.)

Will Jesus weaken, perhaps, at the prospect of power and glory? Jesus, who now really feels 'the sting of Famine', tells himself that he is

> fed with better thoughts that feed
> Mee hungring more to do my Father's will. (II.258f.)

Then Jesus dreams 'as appetite is wont to dream'; and with original and artistic insight, Milton recapitulates the sleep of Adam in Paradise (the Lord God had whetted the appetite of Adam for an help meet for him, caused him to sleep; and Woman was taken out of Man sleeping); but now he fastens on food, not on sexual longing. The device, Jesus dreaming of the ravenous ravens of Elijah, incorporates traditional Christian exegesis of the forty days fast, for example Chrysostom's 'both Moses and Elias anticipating Him',[15] but the psychological accuracy of fasting and dreaming is impressive. When Jesus dreams, he dreams the Bible, and the marvellous restraint of the birds not to eat the food they were bringing to the hungry prophet in the Wadi Kerith.[16]

Satan whisks in his magical banquet, by courtesy, one might say, of *The Faerie Queene* (where, incidentally, *sexual* temptation is also explicit), complete with forbidden food, and the smell of it; but Jesus could as readily himself 'Command a Table in this Wilderness' (II.384). Satan's 'progressive frustration and loss of control over himself' is contrasted with Christ's 'kingship over the self'.[17] Northrop Frye's regret that 'it is essential to Milton's plan that Christ should be able to see every card in Satan's hand'[18] issues in the claim that the drama is without suspense, and that Jesus must lose sympathy for not being human enough to collapse under temptation. But Milton believed that Jesus 'the glorious Eremite' was genuinely subject to temptation (cf. Hebrews 2.17f.; 4.15).

His dramatic structure has two surprises in store. First is the marvellous juxtaposition at the final temptation, in the Lukan order, when Jesus is placed on the pinnacle of the Temple:

> Tempt not the Lord thy God, he said and stood.
> But Satan smitten with amazement fell (IV.561f.)

Milton has combined Luke 4.12, from the temptation narrative, with Luke 10.18, 'I saw Satan, as it had been lightning, fall down from heaven' (William Tyndale). It is decisive. Satan crashes finally. Although the extended Temptation stories in Luke and Matthew are much closer to *midrash* than to a historical narrative, yet their scriptural status and detail gave Milton much more artistic confidence and theological direction than the unscriptural tradition of the harrowing of hell. As a 'scripturally authorised version of the descent into hell'[19] the baptism and testing of Jesus, like the trials and renunciations of every newly baptized Christian, seemed to him to be perfectly real.

The rescue of Jesus from his 'uneasie station' on the pinnacle of the Temple, his setting down in a 'flowry valley' and before him spread

> A table of Celestial Food divine,
> Ambrosial, Fruits fetcht from the tree of life,
> And from the fount of life Ambrosial drink (IV.588–90)

reclaims St Mark's little account, with huge interest, to regain Eden and to satisfy every sort of hunger.

The fast is the saving work of Jesus acted out, and evil overcome. The uses of the fast for clarification, and for recognition of what is disguised or ambiguous, and for descending into oneself, are well observed. The effects of hunger, its pangs, fantasies, even its unsteadiness, which Milton created by a ruinous night of Satanic foul weather,

> nor slept the winds
> Within their stony caves (IV.413f.),

before the final temptation on the pinnacle of the Temple, and the spiteful

> to stand upright
> Will ask thee skill (IV.551f.)

are genuine experiences of fasting. By making his version express the whole work of salvation so dramatically, Milton has only erred by lifting the story out of reach. His Christ is not exemplary but inimitable. Jeremy Taylor thought we could, and should, copy the fast of our Great Exemplar.

THE FAST AND THE USE OF HUNGER:
(B) JEREMY TAYLOR

In *Ductor Dubitantium* (1660) Jeremy Taylor illustrated what he meant by obedience to canon law, and freedom under it, by examining the Christian tradition of the Lenten rule of fasting. He was convinced that this ancient discipline was not restrictive, but a loving response which found its expression in the liberty of conscience. Fasting for forty days was an old and undeniable custom of the Church. Since it was strictly imitative, derived from the gospel narratives of the temptation of Jesus in the wilderness, the Lenten fast could count as divinely commanded. Thus it was entitled to the place it had in canon law. But 'under the Gospel we fast by the love of Vertue, and the choice of our own will, rather than by the coaction of any Law'.[20] Prudentius is cited with approval:

> *A rule of fasting is laid upon all;*
> *it is free and unrestrained.*
> *not driven by straight-laced anxiety,*
> *merely the willingness to do it.*

Continual reference to classical authors, both pagan and Christian, remained Taylor's habit. On fasting, he consulted the Fathers with particular thoroughness, especially Tertullian's *De Jejunio*, of course, but also Cassian, concluding that they were

> very shie of receiving any load of ordinances
> and burdens to their consciences,
> as soon as ever they had entred
> into the liberty of Christians.
> They did all that reason and all that love would require:
> but if love was the parent of their observations,
> they would do them in love, and not in necessity,
> lest they should be again intangled in a yoke of bondage.[21]

Then, with irony and antithesis, Taylor launched one of the most eloquent attacks on Church legalism ever written:

> It is enjoyn'd
> not that we fast totally; but that we fast so:
> you may dine, if you will eat at the Merchant's hours,
> after twelve or one of the clock,
> but you may not eat flesh;
> you may eat sweet-meats, the most delicious fish,
> the Sturgeon, and the Scarus, the Lamprey and the Oyster,
> the Eel and the Salmon, and all the delicacies of Nature,
> so you do not touch the fillets of a Veal, nor eat an Egge.

Now what can be the meaning of this?
For if fasting and abstinence be the thing required,
this is nothing of it.[22]

It was plain to Taylor how scrupulosity and superstition could bring sensible rules about fasting into ridicule. Nice questions about avoiding a *meat* knife to cut *bread* with in Lent, or 'whether a Cook that dresses meat for sick persons may lawfully lick his fingers' are 'an exact parallel with the practice of the Pharisees in that folly which our Blessed Saviour reprov'd'.[23] He did not intend to turn canon law upside down. But he had a keen sense of what was bogus in the tradition, and what trespassed upon ordinary, perfect, Christian liberty:

They exorcise salt and water to cast out Devils;
they give Verses out of the Psalms or Gospels to charm Witches;
they ring the bells to appease tempests,
and very many more such ridiculous devices.[24]

As with Milton, Jeremy Taylor's study of the temptation of Jesus is profound. Just under half of the first part of *Great Exemplar* is devoted to it, with its cognate themes of austerity, baptism, and infant baptism. He will return to Christ's fast at the end of the second part. His straightforward paraphrase and harmony of the gospels include the choice of Matthew's order of temptations. The temptation '*upon the battlement of the Temple*' Taylor thought 'silly and weak'; but the sight of all the kingdoms of the world was 'an admirable Map'. Jesus '*was led by the* good *Spirit to be tempted by the* evil [spirit]'; his temptations were likely to be immaterial 'in words and *Idea's*. *Jesus* was not a person to be affrighted with an ugly phantasm.' He showed that retreat is needed from active life, especially by teachers, to give room for the vacancy of prayer; and that

he had by a forty days Fast done penance for our sins,
and consigned to his Church the Doctrine and Discipline of Fasting
in order to a Contemplative life,
and the resisting and overcoming
all the Temptations and allurements of the Devil,
and all our ghostly enemies.[25]

As if muskets are unforgettable, what is also significant about his meditations on the temptation narratives in the New Testament (he called them Considerations) is the residue of the Civil War, never far from his imagination. 'Hard battels' await those who have begun to serve God. To be 'engaged in an action or course of life that is full of Temptation and empty of comfort' may be accepted as a blessing. Since Christ absorbed the full malice of the assault of Satan,

we may know to whom we owe the happinesses
of all those hours and dayes of peace
in which we sit under the trees of Paradise,
and see no serpent encircling the branches.[26]

The Devil is alwaies prompting us to change our Stones into Bread,
for he knows that the ascetick Tables of Mortification
and the stones of the Desert are more healthfull
then the fulnesses of voluptousness and the corn of the valleys.
He cannot endure that we should live a life of austerity;
if he can but get us but to satisfie our senses
and a little more freely to please our naturall desires,
he then hath *a fair field* for the battle;
but so long as we force him to fight in hedges and morasses,
encircling and crowding up his strengths into disadvantages,
by our stone walls, our hardnesses of Discipline
and rudeness of Mortification,
we can with more facilities repell[27]

As for being tempted with kingdoms, those '*who by injury and usurpation
possess and invade others rights*' should ask themselves 'if the condition be
first to worship the Devil'.

And we may observe
that *Poverty, Praedestination* and *Ambition*,
are the three quivers from which the Devil drew his arrowes
which (as the most likely to prevaile) he shot against *Christ*;
but now he shot in vain,
and gave probation that he might be overcome;
our Captain hath conquered for himself and us.
By these instances we see our danger,
and how we are provided of a remedy.[28]

His advice on the manner of fasting (Discourse XIII in *Great
Exemplar*)[29] commended the fast before receiving the Eucharist, so long
as it did not overturn charity. As an exercise in mortification, fasting
was not as realistic as habitual temperance. Fasting assists prayer. He
quoted St Bernard: 'prayer is the wings of the soul' and he added
'fasting is the wings of prayer'. He warned against getting too fond of
the instrument, and of becoming anorexic. The fast must not violate
health.[30] It must be reasonable, not 'accidentally criminal'. It was all
about prayer, not about diet:

to have no dinner, and that day to run on hunting,
or to play at cards, are not handsome instances of sorrow,
or devotion, or self-denyal. It is best
to accompany our fasting with the retirements of religion,

and the enlargements of charity,
giving to others what we deny our selves.[31]

An instruction of the Elizabethan Church that the wealthy ought, in fasting, 'to abate and diminish the costliness and variety of their fare, and increase therewith their liberality and alms towards the poor' was included in *The Order for the general Fast* issued in 1563; so was the injunction against spending the day of fasting 'in plays, pastimes, or idleness, much less in lewd, wicked or wanton behaviour'.[32]

The fasting regime in *Holy Living* is succinct. The aim for prayer was 'that the spirit might be clearer and more angelical'. To serve repentance, the fast should be 'short, sharp, and afflictive'; but the mastery of passions, sexual problems included, was assisted by a gentle diet of continual fasting. He reiterated that it was important to be whole-hearted:

For a Man must not,
when he mourns in his fast, be merry in his sport;
weep at dinner and laugh all day after;
have a silence in his kitchen and musick in his chamber;
judge the stomach, and feast the other senses.[33]

it is called the nourishment of prayer,
the restraint of lust, the wings of the soul, the diet of Angels,
the instrument of humility and self-denial,
the purification of the spirit.[34]

His plain eagerness to commend fasting is not matched by his attention to feasting. Did he have to explain the duty of a feast to anyone? How to throw a party? His sermon *The House of Feasting* was about eating and drinking much too much. It should not be held against him. For those who had by this time learned in holy living about temperance, and what a festival Holy Communion is, anticipating a banquet in Heaven, what more was there to be said? Taylor provided an exquisite passage at the end of *Holy Living* on preparing for the Eucharist, on the duty of penitence, and of the joy of the day when the Eucharist is celebrated. Three great books would be furnished, *The Real Presence* (1654) on eucharistic doctrine, *Unum Necessarium* (1655) on repentance, and *The Worthy Communicant* (1660).

TEACHING ON PRAYER

Taylor's *Holy Living* is also a compendium of prayers. For every topic discussed, he wrote a suitable prayer, and collected them at the end of each chapter. There are some sixty of these prayers, together with alternative forms of Office for morning and evening and midday, and some special devotions. They are on the whole quite dull. That must be deliberate. Jeremy Taylor was capable of sustained brilliance in writing, of directness and of wit, nerve, style, and confidence. But it is quite clear that when he prayed he did not intend to show God how eloquent he was. He is correct, formal, long-winded, courtly in a hieratic way. He wished his friends to pray, not to be engaged by the interesting voice of Jeremy Taylor. It is a self-effacing exercise of his, quite difficult to accept, and not to be disappointed by; because some prayer really does need intensity, short and piercing, personal eloquence. Some prayer is a great cry. Some thanksgiving is so blissful that it needs to rebound upon the persons praying, with blessedness in the words themselves. Taylor preferred, as he put it, to be 'grave' in his liturgical offerings, calm, modest and impersonal. There is a touch of the obsequiousness he reserved for the dedications of his books, when the Cambridge barber's son was deferring to grandeur.

There are prayers for temperance, health and chastity, for humility, contentedness and obedience, for spending time well, for a holy intent, for faith, hope and charity. There are prayers for use at special times of difficulty: in temptation, under threat of invasion or conquest, in sickness, in mourning, in a storm at sea; and prayers at other times, before a long jouney, before Bible study, before fasting, on feast days, on a birthday, on Sunday, during Holy Week (this is a litany, and it is head and shoulders above the rest), and before the Eucharist. There are prayers for the use of particular individuals: widows, virgins, spouses, parents, kings, employers, merchants, debtors, invalids; and intercessions to be offered for ourselves, for the Church, the leaders, the clergy, for parents and mothers-to-be, friends, patrons and benefactors, for the sick and dying, for casualties and refugees of war. Thanksgivings are included: for deliverance from peril, for the birth of an heir, for safe delivery in childbirth, for victory, for harvest, at Christmas and on festive days. There are also acts of love and forms of confession. Even this bald inventory may be said to indicate some seventeenth-century priorities.

What he wished to convey as a teacher was that prayer was both remarkable and easy. Those who faced their backwardness in praying, who were customarily nervous of long prayer and glad when it was over, should learn

> to speak to the eternal God, to run to him as a Father,
> to lay open our wants, to complain of our burthens,
> to explicate our scruples, to beg remedy and ease,

the prayers of Men have saved cities and kingdoms from ruine:
Prayer hath raised dead Men to life,
hath stopped the violence of fire, shut the mouths of wild beasts,
hath altered the course of nature,
caused rain in *Egypt*, and drought in the sea,
it made the sun go from west to east, and the moon to stand still,
and rocks and mountains to walk;
and it cures diseases without physick,
and makes physick to do the work of nature,
and nature to do the work of grace,
and grace to do the work of God,
and it does miracles of accident and event;
and yet prayer that does all this,
is of itself nothing but an ascent of the mind to God,
a desiring things fit to be desired,
and an expression of this desire to God as we can,
and as becomes us.[35]

Learning to ask for the right things, for the gifts of the Spirit, for what was necessary, for what was innocent; having the confidence to be importunate and persistent in praying, 'in bed, on horseback, every where' (*practising the presence of God* is another way of speaking of ceaseless prayer); being wary of many words; working for what was being prayed for, 'the body of our prayers is the sum of our duty'; attending to posture; uniting prayer to the prayers of others 'like a well-ordered army', this is all practical advice. So is his help for wandering thoughts, as in these short imperatives: use prayer to assist prayer; reduce the prayer; begin the prayer again; even if the prayer was not attended to, get the Amen right; it helps attention to pray silently; it helps not to lead such a busy life – why should God attend to those prayers not thought worthy of *your* attention? Similarly, his remedies for tediousness of spirit are simple and practical: to seek economy, variety (try *singing* the prayer instead), and interruption; to get used to praying without expecting consolation in it, and to prefer that; to turn a habit of prayer into second nature; to fasten upon the Last Things, because death and destruction are not boring.

THE RULES OF MERCY

Dear Jeremy Taylor! There are many times in his huge output when it is possible to glimpse something of the character of the author. But he is so much at home in mercy, that his short chapter *On Alms*, in its joyful simplicity and warm-heartedness, its high good humour and vivacity, befriends the reader unconditionally. It is where prayer has become a deed; it is where love is on fire to rescue the poor. It is not

a scheme for putting right the inequality of the world; but it recognizes
that the great prayer of *Holy Living* is a work of mercy. What a treat it
is to read that, after all, 'Cheaters and robbers cannot give alms'; that
filthy lucre (money gained immorally) has to be repented of; that a
national lottery is improved if some of the proceeds are distributed to
charitable causes, but for the lottery enthusiast

> it were better yet, that he lay by so much
> as he is willing to lose, and let the game alone,
> and by giving so much alms traffick for eternity[36]

and that a national lottery should not be replacing, as an 'intermedial',
one's own direct involvement in a charitable cause!

> if you converse in hospitals and alms-houses,
> and minister with your own hand
> what your heart hath first decreed,
> you will find your heart endeared and made famillar
> with the needs and with the persons of the poor,
> those excellent images of Christ.[37]

Everyone who ever found prayer difficult should read the cheerful
news that money is devotion; and that when one gives, one should give
quickly, 'he gives twice that relieves speedily', and that one should 'give,
looking for nothing again', and that some fasting from customary afflu-
ence and extravagance will secure the money that is needed. Practical
advice about dealing with beggars, about not patronizing, about not
being too poor to help ('If thou hast no money, yet thou must have
mercy') is so steeped in experience, so overwhelmingly generous and
happy, so tender-hearted, that Taylor's own thread-bare condition as an
evicted clergyman in a time of persecution becomes part of the joke:

> The best objects of charity
> are poor housekeepers that labour hard
> and are burthened with many children;
> or gentlemen fallen into sad poverty,
> persecuted persons; widows; and fatherless children,
> putting them to honest trades or schools of learning.
> And search into the needs of numerous and meaner families:
> For there are many persons that have nothing left them
> but misery and modesty.

> I am not ignorant that great variety of cloaths
> always have been permitted to princes and nobility,
> and others in their proportion;
> and they usually give those cloaths as rewards to servants,
> and other persons needful enough.[38]

With these words suddenly Jeremy Taylor himself is revealed, not in his own attire, but in items passed on from Richard my Lord Carbery's wardrobe, a patron as useful as an Oxfam shop.

Bubbling energy for acts of loving-kindness puts to shame envy, and anger, and covetousness. With special clarity, Taylor described how only almsgiving was able to rescue such failings. Thanks to Taylor, almsgiving came to be associated with the eucharistic offertory. 'Taylor was one of the pioneers in rediscovering the importance of this part of the liturgy . . . At the Restoration, the revised English Prayer Book followed Taylor in having a presentation of the alms.'[39]

6

The great employment

TEN years after the publication of Jeremy Taylor's *Holy Living*, persecution ended. Here is what John Evelyn wrote in his *Diary*, 29 May 1660:

> This day his Majestie Charles II. came to London after a sad and long exile and calamitous suffering both of the King and Church, being 17 yeares. This was also his birth-day, and with a triumph of above 20,000 horse and foote, brandishing their swords and shouting with inexpressible joy; the wayes strew'd with flowers, the bells ringing, the streets hung with tapistry, fountaines running with wine; the Maior, Aldermen, and all the Companies in their liveries, chaines of gold, and banners; Lords and Nobles clad in cloth of silver, gold, and velvet; the windowes and balconies well set with ladies; trumpets, music, and myriads of people flocking, even so far as from Rochester, so as they were seven houres in passing the Citty, even from 2 in the afternoone till 9 at night.
>
> I stood in the Strand and beheld it, and bless'd God. And all this was don without one drop of bloud shed, and by that very army which rebell'd against him; but it was the Lord's doing, for such a Restauration was never mention'd in any history antient or modern, since the returne of the Jews from the Babylonish captivity; nor so joyfull a day and so bright ever seene in this Nation, this hapning when to expect or effect it was past all human policy.

Taylor had returned from Ireland. Now he was sent back again to be a bishop in Ulster, and entrusted with an impossible task: to reconcile the immigrant Scottish crofters, who were Presbyterian, and the native Irish families, who were Catholic, with the Restoration Church of England, which he expected to be 'plain, honest, pious, simple, prudent, and charitable'. His solution to the ecumenical deadlock would be to weaken sectarian prejudice by providing better Irish education. But at once he encouraged the new clergy of his diocese of Down and Connor to put

The Rule and Exercises of Holy Living into practice. As teachers of prayer, they were told to 'teach his people the use, practice, methods and benefits of meditation or mental prayer', to 'draw out for them helps and rules for their assistance in it; and furnish them with materials, concerning the life and death of the ever blessed Jesus, the greatness of God, our own meanness, the dreadful sound of the last Trumpet . . .'[1]

There is a stupendous description of the last Trumpet in the first of his Advent sermons. It is drawn from his living through the terror of bubonic plague in Cambridge,[2] when he was a university student at Caius College. The house he was born in was just across the market-place from Caius, near Trinity Church, where his father Nathanael was sometime Churchwarden. Colleges locked their doors to keep out the plague, and were unwilling to let anyone in or out. Jeremy Taylor was a sizar, a student who worked his way through college. He would be the sort of person who might be sent on an errand in perilous times. He might have asked to be allowed to go to his own sad family's funeral.

> He that stands in a Church-yard
> in the time of a great plague,
> and hears the Passing-bell perpetually
> telling the sad stories of death,
> and sees crowds of infected bodies
> pressing to their Graves,
> and others sick and tremulous
> and Death dress'd up in all the images
> of sorrow round about him,
> is not supported in his spirit
> by the variety of his sorrow:
> and at Dooms-day,
> when the terrors are universall,
> an intire Kingdome of fear;
> and amazement is the King of all our passions,
> and all the world its subjects,
> that shrieke must needs be terrible,
> when millions of Men and Women at the same instant
> shall fearfully cry out, and the noise
> shall mingle with the Trumpet of the Archangell,
> with the thunders of the dying and groaning heavens,
> and the crack of the dissolving world,
> when the whole fabrick of nature shall shake
> into dissolution and eternall ashes.[3]

In *Holy Dying* Taylor directed: '*every Night we must make our Bed the Memorial of our Grave, so let our Evening Thoughts be an Image of the Day of*

Judgment.[4] But his first concern for his Irish flock, and his own original contribution, was not so doom-laden; it was directed to biblical meditation on the life of Jesus, in order to imitate it.

TEACHING ON MEDITATION

He was quite certain that everyone is capable of this form of mental prayer. He did not treat meditation as a beginner's exercise only, which the more proficient would soon be leaving behind for stages of contemplation. Unlike George Herbert, he did not fasten upon the religious experiences which might be reported in prayer. He made no attempt to describe them in the subtle ways which Herbert employed; nor did he recommend seeking for religious experiences. Meditation began with reflection, thinking about Jesus, and then, going and doing likewise. His teaching can be found in Discourse III of *Great Exemplar*, summarized by the prayer which concludes it:

> Holy and Eternall JESUS,
> whose whole life and doctrine was a perpetuall sermon
> of holy life, a treasure of wisdome and a repository
> of Divine materialls for meditation,
> give me grace to understand,
> diligence and attention to consider,
> care to lay up, and carefulnesse to reduce to practise,
> all those actions, discourses, and pious lessons
> and intimations by which thou didst expressly teach,
> or tacitely imply, or mysteriously signifie our duty:
> Let my understanding become as spirituall
> in its imployment and purposes,
> as it is immateriall in its nature:
> fill my memory, as a vessell of election
> with remembrances and notions highly compunctive,
> and greatly incentive of all the parts of sanctity.
> Let thy holy Spirit dwell in my soul,
> instructing my knowledge,
> sanctifying my thoughts,
> guiding my affections,
> directing my will in the choice of vertue,
> that it may be the great imployment of my life
> to meditate in thy law
> to study thy preceptive will,
> to understand even the niceties of
> and circumstantialls of my duty,
> that ignorance may neither occasion a sinne,

nor become a punishment:
take from me all vanity of spirit,
lightnesse of fancy,
curiosity and impertinency of enquiry,
illusions of the Devill,
and phantastick deceptions:
let my thoughts be as my religion,
plain, honest, pious, simple, prudent, and charitable;
of great imployment and force
to the production of vertues and extermination of vice,
but suffering no transportations of sense and vanity,
nothing greater then the capacities of my soul,
nothing that may minister
to any intemperances of spirit,
but let me be wholly inebriated with love,
and that love wholly spent
in doing such actions as best please thee
in the conditions of my infirmity
and the securities of humility,
till thou shalt please to draw the curtain
and reveal thy interiour beauties
in the kingdom of thy eternall glories:
which grant, for thy mercies sake
O Holy and Eternall JESU. Amen.[5]

The purpose of meditation is a happy life, said Jeremy Taylor. He reiterated it. Meditation drives to practice. It issues in holy living. It is like opening windows to let in the sun and the wind. Its effect is blessedness. The meditation must get into performance, into a rule, into duty, into the obligation to act virtuously. If the end of meditation is love, and not thought, it is the love of virtue. It is a desire for good deeds, rather than a desire for devotion. It is set upon the 'acquist of virtue'.[6] The effect of the sublimest meditation is a good life, not abstractions, but good works, a universal correction of our life and manners.

So plain is the moral point of prayer, it seems, so energetic for justice and sobriety, so intent upon doing well, that the therapy of preaching oneself a homily, based upon the gospel narratives of Jesus, and bent on moral improvement, seems to have taken the place of prayer as an address to God. Taylor did not apologize for that; we should set out to imitate the sanctity of Jesus, our great example. As he explained to Christopher Hatton of Kirby Hall, to whom *Great Exemplar* is dedicated: 'When interest divides the Church' and religious disputing is likely to go on for ever, 'it was not here, that GOD would have mans felicity to grow.'[7] Not argument, but only a holy life will land us in Heaven.

He offered his patron, as a meditative scheme, a new history in English of the life and death of Jesus, with this prayer:

> *Holy JESU,*
> *since thy image is imprinted*
> *on our nature by creation,*
> *let me also express thy image*
> *by all the parts of a holy life,*
> *conforming my will and affections*
> *to thy holy precepts;*
> *submitting my understanding*
> *to thy dictates and lessons of perfection;*
> *imitating thy sweetnesses and excellencies of society,*
> *thy devotion in prayer,*
> *thy conformity to GOD,*
> *thy zeal tempered with meekness,*
> *thy patience heightened with charity,*
> *that heart, and hands, and eyes,*
> *and all my faculties,*
> *may grow up with the increase of God,*
> *till I come to the full measure*
> *of the stature of CHRIST;*
> *even to be a perfect man in Christ Jesus;*
> *that at last in thy light*
> *I may see light,*
> *and reap the fruits of glory*
> *from the seeds of sanctity*
> *in the imitation of thy holy life,*
> *O blessed and holy Saviour JESUS Amen.*[8]

To present his continuous narrative of Jesus, Taylor claimed to have followed 'the design of Scripture'.[9] His attempt to harmonize does not accord with the critical use of the Bible today; but, in his hope to follow a design, something quite intricate was happening.

Consider his treatment of the call of Levi, narrated by three gospels:[10]

A while after JESUS went again towards the Sea, and on his way, seeing *Matthew* the Publican sitting at the receipt of custome he bad him follow him. *Matthew* first feasted JESUS, and then became his Disciple. But the Pharisees that were with him, began to be troubled, that he eate with Publicanes and sinners. For the office of Publican though among the Romans it was honest, and of great account, and *the flower of the Roman Knights, the ornament of the city, the security of the commonwealth was accounted to consist in the society of Publicans,* yet amongst both the Jewes and Greekes, the name was odious, and the persons were accursed; not onely because they were strangers that were the chief of them, who tooke in-to them some of the nation, where they were imployed; but because the Jewes especially, stood upon the charter of their nation and the priviledge of their religion, that none of them should pay tribute, and also because they exercised great injustices and oppressions, having a power unlimited, and a covetousnesse wide as hell, and greedy as the fire or the grave. But JESUS gave so faire an account concerning his converse with these persons, that the Objection turned to be his Apology, for therefore he conversed with them: because they were sinners; And it was as if a Physician should be reproved for having so much to doe with sicke persons, for therefore was he sent, not to call the righteous, but sinners to repentance, to advance the reputation of mercy above the rites of sacrifice.

But as the little bubbling and gentle murmurs of the water are presages of a storme, and are more troublesome in their prediction, then their violence; so were the arguings of the Pharisees symptoms of a secret displeasure, and an ensuing warr, though at first represented in the civilities of Question and scholasticall discourses, yet they did but forerunne vigorous objections, and bold calumnies, which were the fruits of the next summer.

Jeremy Taylor has taken the three gospels (Mark, Matthew, Luke) and has begun to plait them together as three strands, including details peculiar to each evangelist. 'A while after' is taken from Luke; 'JESUS went again towards the Sea' comes from Mark; 'seeing *Matthew*' is chosen from Matthew (rather than the name 'Levi', in Luke, or 'Levi the son of Alphaeus', in Mark); 'the Publican' is from Luke; and so on. He has not chosen *one* of the three gospel narratives. He was trying to tell the story which he thought all three were telling, including those particular details from any of them which the other accounts might be supposed to have overlooked, or to have forgotten. No one wishing to compose a harmony of the gospels would like to leave anything out. It did not occur to Taylor that Matthew may have had designs upon Mark's text in front of him, to abbreviate it, for instance; and to improve it, in order to replace it.

But the differences between the texts intrigued Taylor. Where one gospel writer had something which the others did not, Taylor wondered about it. In Mark and Matthew, the Pharisees ask why Jesus ate and drank with publicans and sinners. Only in Luke does it say: 'the Pharisees and their scribes *murmured* against his disciples.' (In the Greek text, the word for 'murmured' is *egongoozon*, a rude, onomatopoeic word.) Taylor was held up by *egongoozon*. He pondered it. He produced the bubbling of water before torrential rain, the rumbling of foreboding, for his paraphrase.

Thus it is possible to catch some of the actual process of Taylor's own mental prayer, as it emerged into his writing. The slow work of meditation attended to every scrap of the biblical text in Greek, including the sound of it. It cannot help being accompanied by a *classical* interest, for example, in the word 'publican', which Taylor explained with no less than three references to Cicero, not to mention Xeno and Suidas, in the margin of *Great Exemplar*, to get at different cultural meanings of the word. Compared with any of the three gospel accounts of the call of Levi, Taylor's version is cumbersome. It is also revealing; it shows the classically trained imagination pursuing the voice of the gospel, word by word.

It was not a new method. 'Arise, then, O soul devoted to Christ, and examine diligently, consider attentively and mull over carefully each of the things that are said about Jesus', wrote Bonaventure (1221–74) in his prologue to *The Tree of Life*.[11] In the sources of Jesuit tradition, there should be a place for Ludolf of Saxony's *Vita Christi* (Strasbourg and Cologne, 1474) which, it is said, Ignatius read after the siege of Pampeluna (1521) recovering from his leg wound, and by which he was inspired to hang up his sword. Taylor's directions for meditation were learnt from Ignatius, especially in the confident use of the imagination to enter and sympathize with scenes in the gospel.

In watching with Jesus at Gethsemane 'by a fiction of imagination' the attentive soul 'fears in the midst of CHRISTS agonies, it hears his groans, it spies *Judas* his Lanthorn afar off, it follows JESUS to *Gabbatha*, and wonders at his innocence and their malice, and feels the strokes of the Whip, and shrinks the head, when the Crown of Thorns is thrust hard . . .'[12] Anyone who can read the Passion narrative and spy Judas' lantern afar off, needs no better assistance than this from Jeremy Taylor.

Great Exemplar is full of this imaginative confidence. Taylor depicted the *Gloria in excelsis Deo*, from St Luke's story of the nativity, as a crescendo of blessed choristers singing their Christmas carol, and teaching the Church a hymn:[13]

> But as light, when it first begins to guild the east,
> scatters indeed the darknesses from the earth,
> but ceases not to increase its flame
> till it hath made perfect day;
> so it happened now
> in this apparition
> of the Angel
> of light,
> he appeared
> and told his message,
> and did shine, but the light arose

higher and higher, till midnight was as bright as mid-day;
for suddenly
there was with the Angel
a multitude of the heavenly host:
and after the Angel had told his Message in plain song,
the whole chorus joyned in descant,
and sang an hymn to the tune
and sense of
Heaven

Taylor knew that meditation was as strange to his readers as the 'undiscovered treasures of the Indian hills'. He recognized that it was sheer lack of practice in meditating which led to boredom and failure; that good intentions could 'set with the evening sun'; that prayer would be dull and difficult unless imagination brought the colour and focus of pictorial imagery to what was abstract; and that wandering attention, darting from one subject to another, needed restraint.

He distinguished meditation from thinking. It is quite possible to think about hell, and whether real flames can torment the discarnate soul. But unless this enquiry leads to avoiding hell and practising virtue rather than vice, it could be called research, but not meditation. He would not wish Religious Studies or the Sociology of Religion to be confused with prayer. Nor did he think profound thinkers specially suited to meditation. He was conscious of prayer being impeded by the speculative, scholarly interest, of which he himself was capable. The simple understanding of the uneducated impressed him. Meditation was for everyone.

AVOIDANCE OF MYSTICISM

To be distracted by spiritual ecstasy reminded him of Atalanta and the golden apples;[14] and although he referred to the mystical description of the traditional spiritual journey in three stages, and could put his finger at once upon characteristic features of it (beginners in the purgative way were to consider the Fall, sin, and wrath: 'if these nettles bear honey, we may fill ourselves; but such sweetnesses spoil the operations of these bitter potions') he argued that at each stage the important issue is the virtuous behaviour it inspires. In fact all talk of ascending up 'as high into the mountain as you can' was misleading, when prayer should *descend* into the personal working out of the design of a good life.

About unspeakable things, like the perfection of God, and what is called contemplative union, it is encouraging that such a chatterbox as Jeremy Taylor should be lost for words:

To behold
the glories and perfections of GOD
with a more direct intuition
is the priviledge of Angels,
who yet cover their faces
in the brightness of his presence:
For beyond
this I have described,
there is a degree so exalted
it consists in unions and adherences to GOD;
it is a prayer of quietness and silence,
a meditation extraordinary,
a discourse without variety,
a vision and intuition
of divine excellencies,
and immediate entry
into an orbe of light,
a resolution
of all our faculties
into sweetnesses, affections
and starings upon the Divine beauty;
and is carried on to
ecstasies, raptures,
suspensions,
elevations,
abstractions,
and apprehensions beatifical.

the soul
is like a Virgin invited
to make a matrimonial contract.
Thus it is said.[15]

It was a perilous route in which piety could be mistaken, thought Taylor. It would be safer to refer to God's perfection *reflected*, in the goodness of creation, and in righteous deeds. The gospels had nothing to say about this secret union, or how to achieve it; so it could not be required of anyone. With the help of Plato, he put a question mark against the incoherence of ecstatic experience. Pretence, illusion, and madness might be the explanation. 'I will not say that all violencies and extravagancies of a religious fancy are illusions, but I say that they are all unnatural, not hallowed by the warrant of a revelation, nothing reasonable, nothing secure; I am not sure they ever consist with humility . . .'[16]

Here, then, is a teacher as talkative as Teresa of Avila, and as poetic as John of the Cross, evidently shy of the English mystical tradition which appeared with the first expression of prayer in English. *Incendium Amoris* and the English epistles of Richard Rolle (d. 1358), *The Cloud of Unknowing, The Scale of Perfection* by Walter Hilton (d. 1396), and *The Showings* of Julian of Norwich (d. 1416) did not mean as much to him as the Latin of Thomas à Kempis (d. 1471) whose *via purgativa* and *via illuminativa* in the *Imitation of Christ* underlie Taylor's discourse. It can be safely assumed that no copy of Julian of Norwich was available to him, but was preserved by Augustine Baker in exile with English Benedictines in the Low Countries and France.[17] But had he read *The Cloud of Unknowing?* Taylor made considerable use of the spiritual tradition of the Eastern Orthodox Church which lies behind *The Cloud of Unknowing.* He quoted the German Augustinian canon Hugh of St Victor; but not the English Augustinian Walter Hilton. Taylor's characteristic use of alliteration

> Pity poor mankind whose portion is misery

echoes that love of words with the same initial letter which can be found in the prayers of Richard Rolle 300 years earlier:

> His lufsum lyf was layde ful low[18]

It is difficult to imagine Taylor, the friend of Davenport and Chillingworth,[19] quite ignorant of all this material, even if some of it had been excluded and suppressed by censorship and royal proclamation, and some had only survived in Catholic houses abroad. The challenge to live a just, sane, and orderly life in a society where the sharing of religious values was vehemently disputed, was bound to persuade him that the pursuit of religious feelings, devotional love and contemplative ecstasy had little to do with real holiness.

In her discussion of Catholic devotional literature of the sixteenth and seventeenth centuries, Helen White argued that it was Fr Augustine Baker who rescued the English mystics when they had been largely forgotten at home. But mysticism could also be misleading, as she indicated in the work of a disciple of Augustine Baker, Dame Gertrude More who wrote *The Holy Practises of a Diuine Lover, or The Sainctly Ideots Deuotions* (Paris, 1567). Towards mysticism and quietism every Church and sect of the time developed cautious attitudes; for they were haunted by problems of the authenticity of the 'inner light' and other private revelations.[20] So if as a young master of prayer[21] Taylor loved not the rare works of fourteenth-century English mysticism, and was later on to describe what must be a plain rule for the last of the Anglicans, he deserves to be taken seriously in claiming: 'There is no such thing as the unitive way – save onely in the effects of duty, obedience' and suchlike 'precise virtue'.[22]

Contemplative prayer was not ruled out. In his comments on the infancy narrative of Matthew, he allowed the contemplative life to the Magi:

> When they had paid the tribute of their offereings and adoration, *Being warned in their sleep by an Angel not to return to Herod, they returned into their own countrey another way*, where having been
>
>
> satisfied with the pleasures of Religion,
> and taught by that rare demonstration
> which was made by CHRIST,
> how Mans happinesse did nothing at all consist
> in the affluence of worldly possessions,
> or the tumours of honour;
> having seen the Eternal Son of GOD
> poor and weak, and unclothed
> of all exteriour Ornaments,
> they renounced the World
> and retired empty
> into the recesses of Religion
> and the delights of
> Philosophy.[23]
>

Besides offering contemplation as a *retirement* vocation, Taylor recognized the *wilderness* of John the Baptist as a place where contemplation served training, before a working-life in society:

> the *Baptist*, while he was in the wilderness, became the pattern of solitary and contemplative life, a School of Virtue, and Example of sanctity, and singular austerity: so at his emigration from the places of his retirement he seemed, what indeed he was, a rare and excellent Personage . . . In the Wilderness his company was Angels, his imployment meditations and prayer, his temptations simple and from within . . . and all this besides the innocencies of his silence, which is very great, and to be judged of in proportion to the infinite extravagancies of our language . . . And yet after all these excellencies the Spirit of GOD called the Baptist forth to a more excellent ministry; for in *solitude* pious persons might go to Heaven by the way of prayers and devotion; but in *society* they might go to Heaven by the way of mercy and charity . . . *John* the Baptist united both these lives[24] . . . Jesus reconcil'd both.[25]

GEORGE HERBERT AND JEREMY TAYLOR
COMPARED

Cambridge rhetoric is what unites Herbert and Taylor. There is a generation gap. In the year that Jeremy Taylor was christened at Trinity

Church, 1613, George Herbert graduated at Trinity College, Cambridge. Both became university lecturers in rhetoric. By the time Taylor had completed his Cambridge schooldays, and had begun as a college student at Caius, Herbert had been Public Orator to the University for some years. Jeremy Taylor did not expressly imitate Herbert's language and style, as other young poets did, notably Henry Vaughan. He simply breathed the same Cambridge air of old classical humanism in which English had found its tongue.

> Let foreign nations of their language boast,
> What fine variety each tongue affords:
> I like our language, as our men and coast:
> Who cannot dress it well, want wit, not words.[26]

On his death-bed, it is said, George Herbert sent his poems to his friend Nicholas Ferrar.[27] It is this collection which still lies at the heart of the Anglican tradition, even if it is more treasured on the shelves of English literary criticism[28] than in church today. But more than his prose manifesto on pastoral ministry in Bemerton, *A Priest to the Temple or The Countrey Parson*, his poetry does persist. Henry Purcell and John Blow, as well as other seventeenth-century composers (Jenkins, Wilson, Playford), immediately set Herbert's words to music. Some poems live on in the repertoire of popular English hymns:

> Let all the world in ev'ry corner sing,
> *My God and King.*[29]

This bounding hymn is not entirely typical of Herbert. There is such nervous elegance in his work, such fine contrivance, that one comes to accept a characteristically artificial intricacy. Keble regretted that Herbert 'hides the deep love of God which consumed him in a cloud of precious conceits'.[30] But Herbert's 'utmost art' arises from a wish not only to make a poem dance in a very few words, but for wit and epigram to make a figure in its execution. Here is a neatly turned package of eucharistic doctrine:

> Love is that liquor sweet and most divine,
> Which my God feels as blood; but I, as wine.[31]

That is not insincere; it is ingenious. He knew that the shape, melody, and material of a poem had to go beyond ingenuity. He wanted his lines to be unavoidable, and to pounce on us:

> Man stole the fruit, but I must climb the tree.[32]

That line pounces because we all know about Adam in the book of Genesis. There is another masterpiece (standing at the beginning of the history of Christian poetry in England), *A Vision of a Rood*:

> Then the young warrior – it was God Almighty – Stalwart,
> resolute, stripped himself; climbed the high gallows,
> Gallantly before the throng, resolved to loose Man's bonds.[33]

Herbert had discovered how to fit all the (Hebrew) story about Adam *and* the (Anglo-Saxon) perilous prowess of Christ climbing Calvary, with alliteration, into ten monosyllables.

What T. S. Eliot spotted is how difficult it is for anyone who wants to write religious poetry not to dissemble: 'setting down what he would like to feel rather than . . . what he really feels'.[34] He admired Herbert for being honest. It is a gift to the Anglican spiritual tradition that Herbert's poems are so emotionally direct, and theologically so unblinking.

Some of the peripheral poems, however, especially when he was stringing together moral proverbs outside the threshold of *The Temple*, are disappointing. The escape from old habits in old company feels like drudgery. Even *Pilgrim's Progress* gets wearisome. In the same way George Herbert set out, in his *Church Porch*, to offer moral precepts – like Polonius in *Hamlet*. Not bogus, it was the sort of good advice that won't be listened to, and that doesn't really expect to be.

W. H. Auden said of Herbert: 'His poetry is the counterpart of Jeremy Taylor's prose: together they are the finest expression we have of Anglican piety at its best.'[35] Jeremy Taylor's moral introduction in prose is gripping. He is capable of making righteousness sound interesting, and that is the starting-point of this study. But contrast Herbert, casting the same into verse:

> Lie not; but let thy heart be true to God.
> Thy mouth to it, thy actions to them both:
> Cowards tell lies, and those that fear the rod;
> The stormy working soul spits lies and froth.
> Dare to be true. Nothing can need a lie:
> A fault, which needs it most, grows two thereby.
>
> Fly idleness, which yet thou canst not fly
> By dressing, mistressing, and compliment.
> If those take up thy day, the sun will cry
> Against thee: for his light was only lent.
> God gave thy soul brave wings; put not those feathers
> Into a bed, to sleep out all ill weathers.[36]

What is wrong with the cheerful imagery about stifling the angelic soul in a feather-bed? It has not grasped how demoralizing unemployment is. It shares the anxiety of the book of Proverbs.[37] Old Testament subsistence economies had no room for laziness, or for sluggards turning upon their beds. One of the ways of dealing with the unemployed was to poke fun at them: 'The sluggard says, There is a lion outside!'[38] Herbert showed in *The Countrey Parson* that he was aware of the problem of unemployment in his parish. He offered, especially to the young capable of university education, practical proposals which are intelligent and sympathetic. But he did not really know what it felt like to be idle.

There is also in George Herbert what it is tempting to call silliness, an engaging, droll simpleness or *Giddinesse*.[39] It lies close to his special skill in piety. It is neatly described by Stephen Sykes, in his essay on Herbert, as 'a sense of one's own comic absurdity'.[40] Herbert wrote a poem for Trinity Sunday, with that title (and he said, elsewhere, that it was the very effort and concentration of creating and writing, and succeeding in writing, a poem which brought him to be most aware of God; and, it might be supposed, made him most vulnerable). A poem about Father, Son, and Holy Ghost, would be a poem about creator, redeemer, sanctifier. As a jolly poet he was capable of rhyming mud and blood and good:

> Lord, who hast form'd me out of mud,
> And hast redeem'd me through thy blood,
> And sanctifi'd me to do good;

It is the same comic, religious vitality which informs his striking description of the Bible, as the book where 'Heav'n lies flat', or of the human heart, which God is ready to catch before we have got our eyes properly open in the morning:

> My God, what is a heart?
> Silver, or gold, or precious stone,
> Or star, or rainbow, or a part
> Of all these things, or all of them in one?
>
> My God, what is a heart
> That thou shouldst it so eye, and woo,
> Pouring upon it all thy art,
> As if that thou hadst nothing else to do?[41]

Notice the vocative. The poetry of George Herbert is most often directed to God. It has to be overheard, and puzzled over, as eavesdroppers puzzle over the intimate, private language of telephone conversations. '*Herbert* speaketh *to God* like one who *really believeth a God*, and whose business in the world is most *with God*' was Richard Baxter's famous opinion.[42]

Herbert did not publish these poems; but left his friend at Little Gidding to decide if they might 'turn to the advantage of any dejected poor soul'. As with *Preces Privatae* of Lancelot Andrewes, the privacy of the work helps to guard what is authentic and revealing. For Herbert shared with the Psalmist a need to write laments. (That is why 'Let all the world in ev'ry corner sing' is not typical.) Whoever is drawn into prayer confident of God's love, mercy and protection, has also to learn to live, at least some of the time, by faith alone, when hope is dismayed; to discover what it is like, not just to be depressed by the inner weather (inner weather is Aldous Huxley's name for the subject of Herbert's poetry) but what it is like to be afflicted in the soul by the first law of theology, which is that God is unimaginable.

> When my devotions could not pierce
>   Thy silent ears;
> Then was my heart broken, as was my verse:
>   My breast was full of fears
>   And disorder.
>
> My bent thoughts, like a brittle bow,
>   Did fly asunder:
> Each took his way; some would to pleasures go,
>   Some to the wars and thunder
>   Of alarms.
>
> As good go anywhere, they say,
>   As to benumb
> Both knees and heart, in crying night and day,
>   *Come. come, my God, Oh come,*
>   But no hearing.
>
> Oh that thou shouldst give dust a tongue
>   To cry to thee,
> And then not hear it crying! all day long
>   My heart was in my knee,
>   But no hearing.
>
> Therefore my soul lay out of sight,
>   Untun'd, unstrung,
> My feeble spirit, unable to look right,
>   Like a nipt blossom, hung
>   Discontented.
>
> Oh cheer and tune my heartless breast.
>   Defer no time;
> That so thy favors granting my request
>   They and my mind may chime
>   And mend my rhyme.[43]

Here is that melancholy admission, which a *secular* love poet would have aimed at his elusive and unresponsive mistress, that his love did not smile upon him. A prayer which will not rhyme for him, until the end of the final stanza, is an extraordinarily eloquent *and patterned* description of the plight of disabling spiritual darkness. Writing a poem had come to be assumed as a subtle, and sometimes quite obviously life-giving, colloquy with God, which Herbert wished he could rely on, and indeed fly to, whenever he needed reassurance. But now he is baffled, as much creatively, by his own difficulties as a writer, as theologically, by the perceived absence of God from his prayer. And this is the same poet whose sonnet got the whole world of praying into fourteen lines:

> Prayer the Church's banquet, Angels' age,
> God's breath in man returning to his birth,
> The soul in paraphrase, heart in pilgrimage,
> The Christian plummet sounding heav'n and earth;
> Engine against th'Almightie, sinners' tower,
> Reversed thunder, Christ-side-piercing spear,
> The six-days world transposing in an hour,
> A kind of tune, which all things hear and fear;
> Softness, and peace, and joy, and love, and bliss,
> Exalted Manna, gladness of the best,
> Heaven in ordinary, man well drest,
> The milky way, the bird of Paradise,
>
> Church-bells beyond the stars heard, the soul's blood,
> The land of spices; something understood.[44]

A world of Bible and Prayer Book reference is stored in the compression of these lines. But what about those church-bells? If he had written 'Church-bells *beneath* the stars heard', there would be no imaginative difficulty. Hearing them ringing for evensong after sunset, coming to church on Christmas night, these are common enough experiences. But his phrase is suddenly and awesomely beyond this world. Just as Henry Vaughan started off:

> I saw Eternity the other night[45]

as if we might say: 'I saw the beginning of the universe in the morning paper, from the Hubble telescope', so 'Church-bells beyond the stars heard' claims the dimensions of the universe to be parochial, domesticated by the English method of bell-ringing.

In the biblical poetry of complaining prayer, Job exasperated his comforters by insisting he was not to blame for being abandoned by God. George Herbert did not need persuading. Part of the trouble, he knew, was his own sinfulness:

> My thoughts are all a case of knives
> Wounding my heart[46]

But he was also aware that it is hard to pray. His poem called 'The Pilgrimage' goes:

> I travel'd on, seeing the hill, where lay
> My expectation.
> A long it was and weary way.

He thinks he has reached the end; but he is disappointed:

> I fell, and cried, Alas my King;
> Can both the way and end be tears?

That discovery, that prayer might get worse, marks out George Herbert from most religious poets, and deserves T. S. Eliot's top mark for honesty. He explored empty prayer:

> Then will I trust, said I, in him alone.
> Nay, ev'n to trust in him, was also his:
> We must confess that nothing is our own.
> Then I confess that he my succor is:
> But to have nought is ours, not to confess
> That we have nought. I stood amaz'd at this.[47]

Here is the best seventeenth-century route into the negative way of Walter Hilton, *The Cloud of Unknowing*, and St John of the Cross. It is an expression of spiritual maturity which is blessedly Anglican, rare, and flawless.

It would not do to think he was gloomy,[48] a finely sensitive but neurotic musician, a clergyman who suffered a lot of ill-health because his real vocation was so plainly literary. What he wrote could be purely happy:

> I struck the board, and cried, No more.
> I will abroad.
> What? Shall I ever sigh and pine?
> My lines and life are free; free as the rode,
> Loose as the wind, as large as store.[49]

> I got me flowers to straw thy way
> I got me boughs off many a tree:
> But thou was up by break of day,
> And brought'st thy sweets along with thee.[50]

The simplicity of George Herbert's poems is deceptive. Such precise expression of individual religious experience is not elementary; nor was it intended as a manual through which to *progress*, from a beginner's affirmations into growing obscurity and mysticism. What is trustworthy is that the loneliest of his reports and his brightest doxologies are mixed unevenly. Helen White spoke of 'the ordered meditations of Herbert'.[51] But his attempt to provide order should not conceal the fact that confident hymns are continually being interrupted by uncertainty and distress. That is what praying may be like, some ardour next to a lot of anguish.

> Soul's joy, when thou art gone,
>   And I alone,
>   Which cannot be,
> Because thou dost abide with me,
>   And I depend on thee;
>
> Yet when thou dost suppress
>   The cheerfulness
>   Of thy abode,
> And in my powers not stir abroad,
>   But leave me to my load:
>
> Oh what a damp and shade
>   Doth me invade!
>   No stormy night
> Can so afflict or so affright,
>   As thy eclipsed light.[52]

There is a paradox: a spirited description of a dispirited priest. But, if it is a true description of divine hiddenness in the love of a longing soul, now nervous, now grateful, but never sure that the uncertain light will not become night altogether, how can such praying be commended, or Herbert's obsession with it? The relationship being depicted in these poems is insufferable; it is a mysterious form of unrequited love.

Herbert is a master of *affective* prayer, prayer of feeling, or as Richard Baxter put it best: *Heart-work*. Emotional strength is what is needed for that; a vivid and imaginative love, generosity about whatever is sublime, and a soul that is made of leather; that is, a capacity for the shocks and wounds and utter dismay of such an imprudent talent. Affective prayer is not something to grow out of. But it can be threatened by self-pity. The extinguishing of affective prayer is very painful, and quite difficult to recover from. But it is a bolder sort of prayer than contemplative patience, which really has very little expectations of any kind from prayer, and is consequently often counted as the more serious, as the better 'Engine against th'Almightie'.

An aesthetic conspiracy is at work in affective prayer, because the glory and beauty of God is what inspires it. You can guess that *poets* are interested in George Herbert, not only his contemporaries Herrick, Vaughan and Crashaw, 'Thinke you have an Angell by th'wings';[53] but

Cowper, Christina Rossetti, Hopkins, Auden, Eliot and R. S. Thomas. Coleridge thought you had to be a devout Christian to appreciate Herbert;[54] but an important critical interpreter of Herbert is L. C. Knights, who showed that it is possible to love the poems without sharing the belief. 'It is the artist's feeling for *all* the resources of our language that gives to the greater poems of spiritual conflict their disturbing immediacy.'[55]

Spoken prayer occupies such concern for those who have an ear for the beauty of language, that it can threaten the reality of praying. You might say that the flat language of modern prayer books is a shrewd defence against vainglorious prayers which have too much of the artist in them. Gerard Manley Hopkins began 'The Leaden Echo':

> How to keep – is there any any, is there none such, nowhere
>   known some, bow or brooch or braid or brace, lace, latch or
>   catch or key to keep
> Back beauty, keep it, beauty, beauty, beauty . . . from vanishing
>   away?

And the answer is that if you tried to capture God in a poem or a prayer, you would certainly fail.

> Farewell sweet phrases, lovely metaphors.

> Lovely enchanting language, sugar-cane,
>   Honey of roses,[56]

Everyone runs into George Herbert's poetry to see if he has been able to reflect the loveliness of God there, and keep it. But he tells us about *himself*, and shows us that he has a passionate soul. He describes the conflicts there. His candour is a gift to everyone who ever hoped that the service of Christ would be perfect freedom. But in the struggle of this poet, the initiative and the originality of God, which no one can put a finger on, are not just honoured, but, as Izaak Walton might have said, hooked and netted sufficiently, to count as a catch, when there is nothing on the bank to prove it.

To describe the 'verray parfit gentil' and lyrical rector of Bemerton as an Anglican saint is justified, if it is the mark of a saint to know something about the wrath of God. A very short version of Christianity would be that John the Baptist told the wicked to repent; but Jesus told them that God loves them; and that is overwhelming good news.[57] Special friends of God, however, seem sometimes to be afflicted, as if they were allowed to share in the work of Christ's intercession, and even in the travail of the Cross. The wrath of God might mean nothing to the wicked; but to Isaiah, to St Paul, to Perpetua and her companions, to Martin Luther, and to George Herbert, these words register:

Ah my dear angry Lord,
Since thou dost love, yet strike;[58]

Love is swift of foot;
Love's a man of war,
And can shoot,
And can hit from far.

Throw away thy rod;
Though man frailties hath,
Thou art God:
Throw away thy wrath.[59]

The striking literary difference between George Herbert and Jeremy Taylor is obvious: Herbert's simple tongue and sharp, poetic economy, Taylor's melodious, extravagantly talkative prose; Taylor's English stuffed with classical allusion, Herbert's professional skill in Latin verse completely excluded from his English poems.[60] Jeremy Taylor's openly didactic recipe for meditation may be contrasted with George Herbert's private confession. (His chapter in *The Countrey Parson* on 'The Parson Praying' does not teach prayer, but the edifying example of reverend manners in church.)

Both make constant use of everyday imagery and homely illustration to come to terms with what is mysterious. Their common debt to the language of William Tyndale and the English Bible, to Coverdale and Cranmer and the English Prayer Book, is evident. Herbert brings psychological insight to prayer; Taylor practical acumen. Herbert is concise and passionate; Taylor is cheerful. Both are drawn by love into their prayers; Taylor is affectionate, Herbert speaks in 'the tone of one opening his heart to a friend'.[61] What they share most deeply is the astonishment which accompanies distress of the imagination. It appeared at the beginning of this chapter in Taylor's *Sermon for Advent Sunday*, and in Herbert as 'eclipsed light'. It requires explanation.

7

A terrible imagining

IMAGINATION, wrote Taylor, is what Mark Antony seized on, to stir up the people of Rome to revenge the death of Julius Caesar:[1]

> he brought his body to the pleading place,
> he shewed his wounds,
> held up the rent mantle, and shewed them the garment
> that he put on that night in which he won a victory,
> for which his Memory was dear to them.
> He showed them that wound which pierced his heart,
> in which they were placed by so dear a love,
> that he made them his heirs,
> and left to their publick use places of delight and pleasure;
> and then it was natural
> *when he had made those things present to them*
> which had once moved their love and his honour,
> that grief at the loss
> of so honourable and so lov'd a person should succeed;
> and then they were Lords of all,
> their sorrow and revenge seldom slept in two beds.

Where might the seventeenth-century look for an explanation of how imagination can 'stiffen the sinews and conjure up the blood'? The analysis of anger and revenge in Aristotle's *Rhetoric* was studied by the rabble-rousing Mark Antony; but Jeremy Taylor also quoted Aristotle.[2] After all, what other psychological text-book on the human emotions could be found in Taylor's library to compare with Aristotle? High and mighty anger, pity and jealousy in the despotic worlds of Aristotle and Cicero could be applied without difficulty to the English court manners of Charles I. The psychology of Aristotle supplied Mark Antony with what to say after the death of Caesar. To that story in Plutarch Jeremy Taylor turned to illustrate the effect of imagination in prayer.

Meditation produces the passions and desires it intends,
it makes the object present and almost sensible;
it renews the first passions by a fiction of imagination;

So, when it came to meditating on the Passion of Jesus, after the Last Supper:

It passes from the Paschal Parlour to Cedron,
it tells the drops of sweat, and measures them,
and findes them as big as drops of bloud,
and then conjectures at the greatness of our sins;

it fears in the midst of CHRISTS agonies, it hears his groans,
it spies *Judas* his Lanthorn afar off,
it follows JESUS to *Gabbatha*,
and wonders at his innocence and their malice,
and feels the strokes of the Whip,
and shrinks the head, when the Crown of Thorns
is thrust hard upon his holy brows,
and at last goes step by step with JESUS,
and carries part of the Cross,
and is nailed fast with sorrow and compassion,
and *dies* with *love*.

For if the soul be the principle of its own actions,
it can produce the same effects
by reflex acts of the understanding,
when it is assisted by the imaginative part,
as when it sees the thing acted.[3]

Caesar's assassination and Mark Antony's speech had been acted at Shakespeare's Globe Theatre, where a performance of *Julius Caesar* was seen in 1599. (The Globe was burnt down a few weeks before the infant Jeremy Taylor was baptized in 1613. There is no evidence of his attending any theatre, or of his seeing any of Shakespeare's plays.) On stage, however, it is not only the *words* of Mark Antony, but the terrifying action, the violence of 'the torch-lit mauling of Cinna'[4] by the frenzied mob immediately after the speech, which fills the imagination. Can images of extreme violence, even simulated violence, have a place in meditative prayer?

It was not thinking but *looking* which was the first step in meditation for Taylor. The text was to be imaginatively realized, entered into, in order to be taken to heart. This had been the commonest use of the Bible. Much of what is written there still invites it. The form of many of its narratives, in their simplicity and subtlety, is guided by their imaginative appeal, in the interest of story-telling, to elicit wonder or astonishment. A text venerated as 'the lively oracles of God' leads willing eyes, ears and imaginations to attend with a confidence not expecting to be deceived, or to be led astray. So the picturing mind is likely to be active and vulnerable, and unwilling to be delayed by critical exegesis. Liturgies for Holy Week today thrive upon such innocent entering into the reading of the Passion narratives of the gospels. Taylor picked his illustration of Gethsemane and Golgotha from there, as the most obvious and vivid of all material for Christian meditation. But *Great Exemplar*, with these instructions on meditation, published in 1649, may not only be the first of its kind,[5] but the last of its kind. For ever since the middle of the seventeenth century, the unguarded imagination has had to take account of the rise of biblical criticism. Taylor admitted a scholarly reserve about the indiscriminate use of the Bible. The second of his Visitation sermons (1661) was devoted entirely to how his clergy should approach biblical interpretation.

He argued that the duties of holy living are made plain to us by God. So we might expect to find them in Scripture straightforwardly, not in dark corners. That is why he thought the literal sense of Scripture was almost always to be preferred. But

> he that understands nothing but his Grammar,
> and hath not convers'd with men and books,
> and can see no farther than his fingers ends,
> and makes no use of his reason, but for ever will be a child;
> he may be deceiv'd in the literal sense of Scripture;
> but then he is not fit to teach others:
> but he that knows words signifie Rhetorically
> as well as Grammatically,
> and have various proper significations,
> and which of these is the first
> is not always of it self easie to be told;
> and remembers also that God hath given him reason,
> and observation, and experience,
> and conversation with wise men,
> and the proportion of things,
> and the end of the Command,
> and parallel places of Scripture
> in other words to the same purpose;
> will conclude that if we be deceiv'd the fault is our own[6]

If the word of God was not meant to be intricate, equivocal, or doubtful, the problem for biblical meditation, thought Taylor, could be pettifogging scholarship.

So it is in the Books and Expositions of many men; They study, they argue, they expound, they confute, they reprove, they open secrets, and make new discoveries; and when you turn the bottom upwards, up starts nothing; no man is the wiser, no man is instructed, no truth is discover'd, no proposition clear'd, nothing is alter'd, but that much labour and much time is lost;[7]

It is trenchant. But Taylor, intent upon prayer, had all the scholar's disadvantages himself. Unlettered piety he did not despise; but he could not imitate it. Then, as now, there was not a devotional use for him which was not a scholarly use of the Bible. Every advance in the critical understanding of the formation and editing of the New Testament and of the Hebrew Bible, in their historical and cultural settings, he would surely regard as informing and not quenching imagination. All that he would resist would be the sense that the pastness of the past was on the way to making the Bible inaccessible. He was living within the Revolution where the explosive discovery that the printed Bible in English *was and must be* accessible to everyone at last, even to women (and not just to gentlewomen like Anne Askew, martyred at Smithfield 16 July 1546), opened the door that could never be shut again. If Jeremy Taylor had not written *A Discourse of the Liberty of Prophesying* (1647) on the toleration of nonconformist opinion, it would be difficult to resist Christopher Hill's view in *The English Bible and the Seventeenth Century Revolution* (1993) that Anglicans were wholly reluctant to countenance the Bible slipping out of their custody. But the single most important cause for Taylor's flood of books was the fact that he had been ejected from his parish, and prohibited from teaching, and that, for years, parishioners of the Church of England like his, had to read their Bibles and meditate, without the benefit of Anglican bishops and clergy to instruct them on matters of interpretation.

In the Western spiritual tradition there is guarded advice for the exercise of the imagination in prayer. It is not sharply distinguished from day-dreaming, from untrustworthy fantasy, from invention, from wish-fulfilment, and from anxiety. Kierkegaard, as we shall notice, positively welcomed that. Imaginative work was traditionally thought to indicate an immature stage, about as profitable as distraction; something to be patient with, but through which progress can be made into the sort of prayer which does not require imagery at all, and does not continually bump up against the Second Commandment. Suited to certain temperaments, perhaps to artistic ones, this form of prayer might share with music, ritual and icon the nuisance of being interesting for its own sake.

Taylor disagreed with that cautious tradition. He was quite ready to think that *intercession* was not everybody's vocation. But he was confident that looking upon the exemplary figure of Christ in the gospels was. It is like *seeing* the point of a parable, an immediate and inexhaustible inspiration for good life. Why should not meditative imagination be truthful, as well as common to all?

THE BIBLE AND ARTISTIC IMAGINATION: REMBRANDT

Rembrandt was born in a university town, Leyden, in 1606, seven years before Taylor's birth in Cambridge. Most of his working life was in Amsterdam, where he died in 1669, two years after Taylor's death in Ireland. The earliest of Rembrandt's paintings to leave The Netherlands and the first to arrive in Britain were presented by a diplomat to Charles I. As a royal chaplain, Taylor would have met Rembrandt on the walls of the Long Gallery at Whitehall Palace. Thanks to the King's fame as an art collector, the opportunity for Taylor to study the religious imagination of Protestant Europe as well as the artistic tradition of Spain and Italy was staring him in the face.

Abraham's Sacrifice[8] was painted by Rembrandt in 1635. It is very closely concerned with the text of Genesis 22.10–12a:

> And Abraham stretched foorth his hand
> and took the knife to slay his sonne.
> And the Angel of the LORD called unto him
> out of heaven and said
> Abraham, Abraham.
> And he said, Here am I.
> And hee said,
> Lay not thy hand upon the lad.[9]

The composition of one instant is remarkable. It is intended to grasp the eye, and to arrest time. The angel has seized the wrist of Abraham at the moment the sword arm is raised to strike. With his huge, claw-like left hand Abraham is still gripping Isaac's face, forcing the victim's head back to expose the throat. Out of Abraham's right hand the knife, an elaborately fashioned curving blade, its golden handle stuck with amethysts, is falling. The knife is one of those curios with which Rembrandt stuffed his theatrical wardrobe. The hands of bound Isaac are hidden behind him. The light on the torso of the child is dazzling. His eyes, nose and mouth are smothered in his father's hand. The recognizable, human identity of Isaac cannot be looked upon. It has to be concealed, and assimilated to the anonymity of the old man's practised movement of animal ritual butchery. Abraham's hair has immediately turned white, as prescribed in Jewish legend.[10] The wild intensity of

Abraham's staring at the angel must be the look of one caught murdering. The presence and direct gaze of the angel upon the victim is what throws such light on Isaac, and exposes the deed. The painter has learned the Fourth Gospel: 'So God loved the world, that he gave his only begotten Son, to the end that all that believe in him should not perish, but have everlasting life . . . And this is the judgement, that light is come into the world, and men loved darkness rather than light, because their deeds were evil.'[11] The angel has gently raised a little, but not ineffectual, hand of caution. Even the very smallest angel, as Menahem Mendel of Kosov observed, coming and saying: 'Lay not thy hand upon . . .', *must be obeyed.*[12] Behind Abraham is the pot of fire, against a background as dark as Gehenna. Beneath Isaac is the wood for the burnt offering meticulously laid in order.

The angel has a hand on Abraham, who has a hand on Isaac. Rembrandt's painting of hands, his mastery of expression, and the fact that no painter has made so much of the touching of one figure by another with a hand, in many of his compositions, has been well observed.[13] Here the direction of the blessing, the divine promise which is to be conveyed by manual transmission from father to son, is shown, quite intentionally at its most ironical, in Abraham's grasp of destruction.

A full-size copy of this painting[14] was made a year later, probably by Rembrandt himself, perhaps with assistance from a pupil in his work-shop.[15] By a subtle shift the angel has achieved a more emphatic position overhead. The pot of fire has gone. But, as if in answer to every connoisseur's knowing enquiry: 'Where is the-ram-caught-in-the-thicket, then?' a ram is now included, on the left of the picture. The prominence of the arresting angel, and the appearance of the ram, are reassuring; as if we all know the way out of Abraham's nightmare, and can disregard the morality of his being tempted in such a way. But the appalling faith of Abraham is unrelieved in the earlier painting. It is the entire focus of that great work. It is meant to be a terrifying moment of will for Abraham, before any suggestion of a solution, or relief, by way of a substitute burnt offering, is provided. It puts in its place the claim that anything is resolved in this awful story, or could be resolved, by a substitution for the murder. 'Murder is very largely a family affair.'[16] The taut, intersecting arcs, by which Rembrandt stretches out the body of Abraham over this unendurable problem, caught between the childish angel and the angelic child, who are placed in baroque diagonals on the canvas, are powerful expressions of text turned into paint, without any loss of theological seriousness.

It is impossible to say what produced the second version. The pressure of mercantile Calvinist opinion in respectable Amsterdam, complaining

that he had not painted the whole picture; the sense that he might not
be quite orthodox (in fastening upon the terror in Abraham's bleak
determination, the weakness of the angel, and the deadly account of
faith as grim and uncomfortable); even Saskia teasing him, perhaps, to
touch-in the happy ending, all could have been registered by
Rembrandt. If St Luke himself had commissioned the second picture,
there could be no doubt that the first would have received the entire
approval of St Mark.

'Take *Abraham's* faith as your best pattern', wrote Taylor, in his
sermon *Fides Formata*, Faith working by Love:

> When our faith is spoken of
> as the great instrument of justification and salvation,
> take *Abraham's* faith as your best pattern,
> and that will end the dispute,
> because that he was justified by faith
> when his faith was mighty in effect;
> when he trusted in God,
> when he believed the promises,
> when he expected a resurrection of the dead,
> when he was strong in Faith,
> when he gave glory to God,
> when against hope he believed in hope;
> and when all this past into an act of the most glorious obedience,
> even denying his greatest desires,
> contradicting his most passionate affections,
> offering to God the best thing he had,
> and exposing to death his beloved *Isaac*,
> his laughters, all his joy
> at the command of God[17]

It is this passage (rather than his note in *Great Exemplar*,[18] where,
following Augustine, he recalls the tradition that Calvary was where
Abraham had made an altar for the sacrifice of his son) which anticipates
Kierkegaard's treatment in *Fear and Trembling* (1843), another *tour de force*
in imaginative meditation.

THE BIBLE AND POETIC IMAGINATION:
KIERKEGAARD

'Once upon a time there was a man who as a child had heard the
beautiful story about how God tempted Abraham.'[19] Kierkegaard
described his growing enthusiasm for this story, how he understood it
less and less; and forgetting everything else, how his one wish was to

see Abraham, and to be present on the journey to Mount Moriah. He pictured the event in many different ways, not being sure of any of these as solutions, but not dismissing them. He wrote up four of them with characteristic style: Abraham pretending to be mad, so that in terror Isaac would cry out to God for help, but not lose his faith; Abraham, unable to forget what God had demanded of him, becoming disillusioned; Abraham confused, asking God's forgiveness for being willing to forget a father's prime duty, yet not conceding it could be a sin to be willing to offer to God the best thing that he had; Isaac losing his own faith at the sight of his father's despair.

The persistence of attention and the liveliness of imagination which Kierkegaard describes echo Jeremy Taylor's instructions. The comparison of a pile of provisional images, in which the mind's subjective states were making a contribution (confusion, weariness), and the confident anachronisms ('there was joy in Abraham's house when Sara became a bride on their golden wedding day') deal with what Rembrandt also saw in the picture. All help to explain, without a word of jargon, what moves along in meditative prayer.

Kierkegaard wanted to get at the 'shudder' of Abraham's thought. But after these 'compositions of place' (as an Ignatian teacher of meditation would call them) comes Kierkegaard's song of praise for Abraham who believed the preposterous.

> If Abraham had doubted, then he would have done something else, something glorious . . . He would have plunged the knife into his own breast. Venerable Father Abraham! . . . forgive him who would speak in praise of thee, but he will never forget that thou hadst need of a hundred years to obtain a son of old age against expectation, that thou didst have to draw the knife before retaining Isaac; he will never forget that in a hundred and thirty years thou didst not get further than to faith.[20]

Kierkegaard begins to discuss the 'tremendous paradox faith is, a paradox which is capable of transforming a murder into a holy act well-pleasing to God'; and the difference between this and the tragic heroism of Agamemnon, and Jephthah. These two sacrificed their children. We can weep for them, said Kierkegaard; but we cannot weep over Abraham. 'But people are curious about the result . . . they want to know nothing about *dread*. Before the result, either Abraham was every minute a murderer, or we are confronted by a paradox.'

The resolution of Kierkegaard's meditation is fragmentary. But that is less unsatisfactory than it sounds. It flashes with ironic contrasts between the romantic hero and the bourgeois man of faith. It tests the issues of classical tragedies against Abraham's paradox, and notices that even great art will not solve it; and that the New Testament is not relieved of it. There is no way of 'smuggling Christianity in' without exposing the terrible words about having to hate one's own wife and children for the sake of the gospel. The discussion is urgent, because all the time Kierkegaard was attempting to come to terms with the hopeless muddle of his own flight from marriage. (Another title for *Fear and Trembling* would be *Poor Regina!*) But here is a form of prayer which first appeared in Augustine's *Confessions*, an unsystematic but confident recognition that what is immediate and personal is that which is ultimate and serious.

Kierkegaard's prayer is not a transcending vehicle, as if prayer made a raid upon the unknown and infinite. He is coming to himself. 'In all eternity it is impossible for me to compel a person to accept an opinion, a conviction, a belief. But one thing I can do: I can compel them to take notice.'[21] He shares with Jeremy Taylor the directing of meditation into what is practical, immediate and ethical. But what draws his attention to Abraham and his knife, and his tremendous story? One thing that Willmott noted about Jeremy Taylor was that 'the ruling faculty of his mind was a love of the beautiful, but he possessed, in an eminent degree, the element of the terrible'.[22] But the terrible lies in the Bible first of all. Neither Taylor, nor Rembrandt, nor Kierkegaard averted their eyes.

Part of the character of the Bible is its capacity for the horrific. Difficult, dreadful and shameful things can be claimed as part of religious history, and not only of the sacred history and morality of Iron Age tribes. God is not a savage God; but the way to deal with what is atrocious and unthinkable (like the messengers bringing Job news of the death of all his children) is to put it in the religious library, which also contains awe and holiness. There is a Chinese poem:

> The tribulus grows on the wall,
> upon the stain.
> The things done in that inner room
> men cannot name.
>
> The tribulus grows on the wall.
> The stain is old.
> The things done in that inner room
> may not be told.[23]

Here the ominous is actually created by exploiting the convention that what is awful is also unmentionable. But in the Bible the unnameable is given room. Protected thus, it can become explicit, even intelligible (which is particularly inimical to evil, which needs incoherence to be at home in). A problem for a society in which video images of extreme violence are easily accessible is that there is no such safe deposit or dreadful holy place like a Bible to contain them, or to guard the mystery of evil.

When children (or adults for that matter) are repeatedly exposed to images of terror as *entertainment*, they learn that the appropriate response to the suffering of others is laughter. To sustain demand for their imaginative work, film-makers capable of inventing and willing to portray images of extreme violence discover more ingenious forms of brutality. Behaviour which otherwise would have been simply *unimaginable* to them is brought to the attention of children. They are allowed to see victims who have been cast as sub-human, so that they need not be pitied, or as deserving violent treatment. Unlike the grim stories of old, the adult-only video will expect the viewer to identify with the perpetrator, not with the victim.

That children can be wounded in their imagination, that they can become hardened and callous, or sufficiently schooled in hardness of heart to forget what they have seen, that they can mimic aggression and merciless cruelty, and that not every child can rely upon parents with sufficient discretion and responsibility to protect them from watching images of extreme violence, are genuine concerns for a society in which the active, meditative imagination of Jeremy Taylor's prayer was long ago given up for the imaginative passivity of watching videos. They are properly religious concerns; because an imagination is needed for religion.

In *Metaphysics as a Guide to Morals* Iris Murdoch provides her own brilliant synopsis of Kierkegaard, and accuses him of almost making Abraham comprehensible, by turning him into a tragic hero. She prefaces these remarks : 'Art cannot help changing what it professes to display into something different.' (She could have been referring to Rembrandt; but she chooses Goya.) Her point is that art cannot help, whatever its subject, beautifying and consoling. Goya's horrors of war are terrifying but beautiful. Great art is beautiful; whereas the evils and miseries of human life are not beautiful or attractive or formally complete. 'How can such a terrible planet dare to have art at all?'[24]

Rembrandt was able to produce a beautifying and consoling *copy* of his picture. He first made a great work of art which did not beautify or console or change anything. He showed what the Bible showed, how awful it was for an angel to tempt and restrain Abraham from infanticide. He showed this man whom not even the troubled poet Kierkegaard could understand, and showed him in wonderful chiaroscuro. He did not solve Abraham's business on a mountain, or relieve him of religious madness. An angel (a conventional religious sign, part of 'the ambiguous conspiracy'[25] between art and religion) is different from God, who cannot be displayed. But the text supplied the angel, not Rembrandt. Angels are remarkable for their beauty. Rembrandt did not change that into something different and less than beautiful.

Taylor was not aiming to turn the bloodthirsty assassination of Julius Caesar into drama, as Shakespeare did. Nor did he set out to get the picture of Abraham's agony painted, which Rembrandt did. Nor did he fasten upon the beautiful story of Abraham's dilemma[26] to present a philosophical paper on paradox, like Kierkegaard. Nor did he look steadily at what is awful for the thrill of it.

Tertullian's diatribe against every future purveyor of images of extreme violence, *De Spectaculis*, sprang from the spectacle of Perpetua and her companions[27] thrown to the lions, and of the gladiatorial shows of the Roman amphitheatre. The rejection of these lewd and enchanting showbiz executions was a sure sign, to his heathen acquaintance, that a theatre-goer had turned Christian. The shows ought to be detested 'if for no other reason than there the cry *Christianos ad bestias* (To the lions!) is daily raised against us'.[28] Tertullian lumped together the *ludi* (the combats), the circuses, the *fabula togata* (rustic farce), *mimus* and pantomime, together with Greek comedy and tragedy, without distinction. In Taylor's day this tradition within Christianity of suspicion of art, and revulsion from it, was sustained by the puritan rejection of the theatre. Smock Alley, Dublin, where Jeremy Taylor's friend Katherine Philips put on her play *Pompey* at the Restoration, could not be far from Vanity Fair:

> And, moreover, at this fair there is at all times to be seen juggling, cheats, games, plays, fools, apes, knaves, and rogues, and that of every kind. Here are to be seen too, and that for nothing, thefts, murders, adulteries, false swearers, and that of a blood-red colour.[29]

Taylor's imagination was fixed upon the example of Jesus Christ crucified. 'Fortunate' is how Iris Murdoch describes Christianity, in being able to be pictured by the great painters. 'The image of the crucified Saviour is more familiar in the west than the most ubiquitous advertising cliche.'[30] 'Western art, so solid and so clear, has helped us to believe'; and 'understanding what art is, its charms, its powers, its limits, helps us to understand religion'.[31] She compares bad art with good art, and indicates an analogy with virtue: 'the artist's discipline includes the *exercise* of virtue: patience, courage, truthfulness, justice.'[32] That matches Taylor's use of meditative imagination for the exercise of holy living. At the end of *Ductor Dubitantium* he wrung his hands over an artist who, wishing to improve his painting of the Crucifixion, and having tied his life-class model on to the cross, stabbed him, in order to catch an authentic dying struggle for his composition.[33]

'The contemplation of suffering is difficult', says Murdoch, and explains why.

> All sorts of illusions crowd in to tempt us. We have to attend in a certain way, if the experience is not to degenerate. We seek escape into passive admiration, ingenious sado-masochistic identification, pleasure that someone else is in trouble and not us ... Contemplation of the suffering of the innocent can be redemptive when the spectator is moved by both guilt and love.[34]

This is a good description of how Jeremy Taylor attended to the suffering of Christ:

> they came to *Calvary*,
> a place difficult in the ascent,
> eminent and apt for the publication of shame,
> a hill of death and dead bones, polluted and impure,
> and there *beheld him* stript naked,
> who clothes the fields with flowers,
> And all the world with robes,
> and the whole globe
> with the canopee
> of Heaven;
>
> There they nailed JESUS with four nails,
> fixed his Cross in the ground,
> which with its fall into the place
> of its station
> gave infinite torture
> by so violent a concussion
> of the body of our LORD
> which rested upon nothing
> but four great wounds[35]

And in this way he preached what he had meditated on:

> He entred into the world
> with all the circumstances of poverty;
> he had a star to illustrate his birth
> but a stable for his bed chamber,
> and a manger for his cradle:
> The angels sang hymnes
> when he was born,
> but he was cold and cried,
> uneasy and unprovided;
> He did good where ever he went,

and almost wherever he went was abused;
He deserved Heaven for his obedience,
but found a cross in his way thither;
and if ever any man had reason
to expect fair usages
from God,
he it was onely
that could deserve that,
or any thing that can be good.
But after he had chosen to live a life of vertue,
of poverty, and labour,
he entred into a state of death;
whose shame and trouble was great enough
to pay for the sins of the whole world:

All that Christ came for,
was, or was mingled with sufferings:
But I need not tell that Jesus, beloved of God
was a suffering person:
His very *promises* were *sufferings*
his *beatitudes* were *sufferings*,
his *rewards*,
and his *arguments*
to invite men to follow him,
were onely taken from sufferings in this life,
and the reward of *sufferings* hereafter.[36]

8

Arresting the sun

INTERCESSION, praying for other people, raised two questions for Jeremy Taylor. The first was when it might be appropriate, and he argued for intercession as a post-communion prayer. The second was more emphatic. Could we assume that everybody was capable of interceding? In a three-part sermon (1653) entitled *The Return of Prayers*, and in *The Worthy Communicant* (1660), he pursued these related ideas, which sprang from what he had called 'The third general Instrument of Holy Living, the Practice of the Presence of God'. Prayer faces eternity. For Taylor that brought Heaven close, and the eternal intercession of Jesus the Son of God.

> Consider that as it cost Christ
> many millions of prayers and groans, and sighs,
> so he is now at this instant,
> and hath been for this seventeen hundred years,
> night and day incessantly praying
> for grace for us that we may repent,
> and for pardon when we do,
> and for degrees of pardon
> beyond the capacities of our infirmities,
> and the merit of our sorrows and amendment;
> and this prayer He will continue till his second coming:
> *For he ever liveth to make intercession for us.* (Hebrews 7.25)[1]

The picturesque estimate of the *quantity* of prayer run up by Christ's work of intercession until Jeremy Taylor's own lifetime throws light on the character of Taylor's prayer. It was generous. He wrote long prayers. He wrote them continually. What he had to say about the practice of the presence of God was not pretended. He lived in the ceaseless prayer of 1 Thessalonians 5.17 as it was taught by the Eastern Fathers.[2] His own many hundreds of prayers and groans and sighs may be recognized as Taylor closely imitating his Great Exemplar.

Not until Westcott's commentary on Hebrews appeared in 1906 did a more sedate account of the high-priestly work of Christ appear. Westcott pointed out that in the Jewish liturgy of the Day of Atonement the high-priest entered the Holy-of-Holies as the representative of an Israel now washed clean by the blood of the sacrifice. 'And simply standing before the Lord he fulfilled his work. No words were spoken: no uttered intercession was made. It was enough that man was there according to divine appointment, to witness in the most emphatic manner to the continued preservation of the established relation of man to God.'[3] To sustain the typology of the Letter to the Hebrews, the presence of Christ *seated at the right hand of God* is in itself perfect intercession. It is certainly less laborious than the toil of a million prayers and tears in the imagination and the hard experience of Jeremy Taylor praying; but the vivid, personal, intercessory struggle which he took as work, and work that God does, is a very lively description of what it is to pray for others. It should not be lost.

THE LANGUAGE OF INTERCESSION

That intercession was an expected feature of every Christian's devotion was not denied by Taylor. His design for the first prayers of the day in *Holy Living*, for example, provided for adoration, thanksgiving, oblation, contrition, petition (in that order) and then:

> hear the Prayers of thy servant
> who is unworthy to ask any petition for himself,
> yet in humility and duty is bound to pray for others.[4]

There follow prayers for the Church, the king, the clergy, for wife or husband, for our children, friends and benefactors, family, and for all in misery. He concludes his instructions for what I have called political holy living with suitable intercessions: by subjects for their ruler, by parents for their children, by teachers for their pupils, by the patronized for their patrons. *Holy Living* ends by including in the same list of intercessions prayers for the sick and dying, and for expectant mothers.

It is impossible to read Jeremy Taylor's liturgical compositions without considering again his use of language. These intercessions flow sonorously. He was not economical. He was garrulous. The phrases are well-turned, balanced, laden with doctrine, with the ornaments and echoes of the English Bible, and with the cadences of the Prayer Book.

> O Thou great shepherd and bishop of our souls
> holy and eternal Jesus,
> give unto thy servants, the ministers

of the mysteries of christian religion,
the spirit of prudence and sanctity,
faith and charity, confidence and zeal,
diligence and watchfulness,
that they may declare thy will unto thy people faithfully,
and dispense thy sacraments rightly,
and intercede with thee graciously
and acceptably for thy servants.[5]

The ministry of Word and sacrament and the work of intercession have been lined up together in that prayer for the clergy. The elegant way of writing might even have concealed from you Taylor's preference to entrust intercession to the clergy. We shall return to this emphasis.

Sometimes a well-considered prayer is pierced by directness and urgency:

Pity poor mankind, whose portion is misery

Eloquence springing from the Civil War and its aftermath takes charge, as in his prayer for the Church of England, Charles II in exile, and glum Royalists:

She is founded on a rock,
but planted in the sea.
O preserve her safe

Relieve all oppressed Princes
defend and restore their rights:
Relieve and comfort all Gentlemen
that are fallen into poverty and sad misfortune.

His prayer 'for all estates of men and women in the christian church' exhibits the long cascade of his fervour, and its melodiousness. It is a compendium of living concern:

O holy God, King eternal
out of the infinite store-houses of thy grace and mercy
give unto all virgins chastity, and a religious spirit
to all persons dedicated to thee and to religion;
continence and meekness,
and active zeal and an unwearied spirit;
to all married pairs, faith and holiness;
to widows and fatherless and all that are oppressed,
thy patronage, comfort and defence;
to all christian Women simplicity and modesty,
humility and chastity, patience and charity;
Give unto the poor,
to all that are robbed and spoiled of their goods,

a competent support, and a contented spirit,
and a treasure in Heaven hereafter:
Give unto prisoners and captives,
to them that toil in the mines and row in the gallies,
strength of body and spirit,
liberty and redemption, comfort and restitution;
to all that travel by land thy Angel for their guide,
and a holy and prosperous return;
to all that travel by sea, freedom from pyrates and shipwreck,
and bring them to the haven where they would be:
To distressed and scrupulous consciences,
to melancholick and disconsolate persons,
to all that are afflicted with evil and unclean spirits,
give a light from Heaven,
great grace and proportionable comforts, and timely deliverances;
give them patience and resignation;
let their sorrows be changed into grace and comfort,
and let the storm waft them certainly
to the regions of rest and glory.

Lord God of mercy,
give to thy martyrs, confessors, and all thy persecuted,
constancy and prudence, boldness and hope,
a full faith and a never-failing charity.
To all who are condemned to death
do thou minister comfort,
a strong, a quiet, and a resigned spirit:
Take from them the fear of death,
and all remaining affections to sin,
and all imperfections of duty,
and cause them to die full of grace, full of hope.
And give to all faithful,
and particularly to them who have recommended themselves
to the prayers of thy unworthy servant,
a supply of all their needs temporal and spiritual,
and according to their several states and necessities,
rest and peace, pardon and refreshment:
and show us all mercy
in the day of judgment.
Amen.

Give, O Lord,
to the magistrates equity,
sincerity, courage and prudence,
that they may protect the good,
defend religion, and punish the wrong doers.

Give to the nobility wisdom, valour and loyalty;
to merchants justice and faithfulness;
to all artificers and labourers truth and honesty;
to our enemies, forgiveness and brotherly-kindness.

Preserve to us
the heavens and the air in healthful influence and disposition,
the earth in plenty,
the kingdom in peace and good government,
our marriages in peace, and sweetness, and innocence of society,
thy people from famine and pestilence,
our houses from burning and robbery,
our persons from being burnt alive:
From banishment and prison,
from widowhood and destitution,
from violence of pains and passions,
from tempests and earthquakes,
from inundation of waters,
from rebellion or invasion,
from impatience and inordinate cares,
from tediousness of spirit and despair,
from murther, and all violent, accursed and unusual deaths,
from the surprize of sudden and violent accidents,
from passionate and unreasonable fears,
from all thy wrath, and from all our sins, good Lord,
deliver and preserve thy servants
for ever.
Amen.

Repress the violence
of all implacable, warring, and tyrant nations:
Bring home unto thy fold all that are gone astray:
Call into thy Church all strangers:
Increase the number and holiness of thine own people:
Bring infants to ripeness of age and reason:
confirm all baptized people with thy grace and with thy spirit:
Instruct the novices and new christians:
Let a great grace and merciful providence
bring youthful persons safely and holily through
the indiscretions and passions and temptations
of their younger years:
And to those whom thou hast or shall permit
to live to the age of a Man,
give competent strength and wisdom;
take from them covetousness and churlishness,
pride and impatience,

fill them full of devotion and charity,
repentance and sobriety,
holy thoughts and longing desires after Heaven
and Heavenly things;
give them a holy and a blessed death,
and to us all a joyful resurrection
through Jesus Christ our Lord.
Amen.[6]

The litany which Jeremy Taylor wrote for *Golden Grove* has much in common with this vast intercession. There he also remembered: 'Pity the lunatics; give life and salvation to all to whom thou hast given no understanding; accept the stupid and the fools to mercy.' He prayed health and fair seasons for the farm worker. For the old he asked piety and perfect repentance, a liberal heart, an open hand, and great religion.[7] If it is customary to take refuge in St Paul's dictum that we do not know how to pray as we ought, and that the Spirit himself intercedes for us with sighs too deep for words,[8] it is also true that they were not too deep for Taylor.

PRAYING AFTER COMMUNION

Jeremy Taylor's argument for intercession as a post-communion prayer was probably set in train by his reading of Cyril of Jerusalem, quoted in one of his earliest essays, *Apology for Authorised and Set Forms of Liturgy* (1647).

> *Directly after receiving the eucharist we pray to God on behalf of those who shared it, for the unity of the Churches and the peace of the world, for kings, etcetera.*[9]

He speaks of intercession as 'the apostolic precept' (1 Timothy 2.1) which, next to the Lord's Prayer, was the first Scripture pattern from which the Church framed her liturgy. But intercession is the work of Christ. The catechism which Jeremy Taylor wrote for *Golden Grove* put it in these words:

Q. When began his priestly office?
A. It began at his death; for he was himself the Priest and the Sacrifice, offering himself upon the altar of the cross for the sins of all the world.
Q. Did his priestly office then cease?
A. No: *He is a Priest for ever,* that is unto the end of the world, and represents the same sacrifice to God in Heaven, *interceding* and praying continually for us in the virtue of that sacrifice, by which he obtains relief of all our necessities.
Q. What doth Christ in Heaven pray for on our behalf?

A. That our sins may be pardoned, our infirmities pitied, our necessities relieved, our persons defended, our temptations overcome, that we may be reconciled to God, and be saved.[10]

Taylor's exposition of the Apostles' Creed, which follows, also referred to Christ's intercession:

> he is always in the presence of his Father
> interceding for us
> There he sits and reigns as King,
> and intercedes as our High-Priest.[11]

And that is the reason for Taylor's instruction in *The Worthy Communicant* for intercession to be made after receiving the sacrament:

> it is also the great sacrifice of the world
> which you have then assisted in, and re-presented;
> and now you being joyn'd to Christ
> are admitted to intercede for others,
> even for all mankinde, in all necessities, and in all capacities;
> pray therefore for all for whom Christ died;
> especially for all that communicate that day,
> for all that desire it, that their prayers and yours
> being united to the intercession of your Lord,
> may be holy and prevail.[12]

In the third of the sermons entitled *The Return of Prayers* he shows us how willing he is to organize prayer, George Herbert's 'Engine against th'Almightie'.[13] Effective intercession needs solemn litanies, days of prayer and fasting, the closest association of prayer with almsgiving, but

above all praying in the susception and communication of the holy sacrament, the effects and admirable issues of which we know not, and perceive not... Our prayers can never be so holy as when they are offered up in the union of Christs sacrifice:

> Then we receive Christ;
> we are, after a secret and mysterious,
> but most reall and admirable manner
> made all one with Christ;
> And if God giving us his Son could not but
> with him give us all things else,
> how shall he refuse our persons
> when we are united to his person,
> when our souls are joined to his soul,
> our body nourished by his body,
> and our souls sanctified by his bloud,
> and cloth'd with his robes,

and marked by his character,
and sealed with his Spirit,
and renewed with holy vows,
and consign'd to all his glories,
and adopted to his inheritance?
When we represent his death,
and pray in vertue of his passion,
and imitate his intercession,
and doe that which God commands,
and offer him in our manner
that which he essentially loves,
can it be that either anything
should be so prevalent,
or that God can possibly deny
such addresses, and such importunities?
Try it often[14]

Anyone persuaded by Taylor's liturgical preference for post-communion intercession will notice that the *Gloria in excelsis Deo*, at that point in the Book of Common Prayer, refers to Christ sitting at the right hand of God the Father, and asks that he should receive our prayer. In Taylor's own version of the Eucharist, post-communion intercessions for Church and nation include:

Send us health and peace,
justice and truth,
good laws and good government;
an excellent religion undivided, undisturbed;
temperate air, seasonable showers,
wholesome dewes, fruitful seasons . . .
With a propitious eye & a great pity
behold the miseries of mankind;
Hear the sighings of the distressed,
the groans of the sick,
the prayers of the oppressed,
the desires of the poor . . .
support the weakness of them that languish
ease the pains of them that are in affliction
Take from the miserable all tediousness of spirit and despair:
Pardon all the penitents,
reform the vitious,
confirme the holy,
pity the folly of young men,
their little reason and great passion,
succour the infirmities and temptations of the aged.

Admit O Blessed God
into the society of our prayers
and the benefit of this Eucharist
our Fathers and Brethren,
our wives and children,
our friends, and Benefactours
all that have desired our prayers and all that need them
all that we have, and all that we have not remembered.[15]

Harry Boone Porter has rightly noticed this unusual place for intercession in the Eucharist.

> It is surprising to urge such prayers at this point, as in all editions of the Book of Common Prayer general intercessions are offered at an earlier point. The classic Anglican arrangement was for all mankind to be prayed for in the litany, just before the eucharistic rite began. Within the latter, only the members of the Church are prayed for. Taylor reverses the logic, and sees the eucharist as the occasion for the most universal intercession.[16]

That Taylor should expect communicants to be immediately enabled to participate in the priestly activity of Christ, and become intercessors for all mankind, gives a clear indication of his belief about what is happening in eucharistic worship. The real presence of Christ in the sacrament has a real effect upon vocation, setting the communicant sufficiently free from self-concern to be able to pray for others.

WHO IS CAPABLE OF INTERCEDING?

A sermon, *The Return of Prayers*, began, in fine disregard of preaching practice, with a pile of negatives. Prayer should be easy. It was

> knotted like the folds of a Serpent; in every stage a huge uneasinesse. At first, wee do not know what to ask; and when we doe, then we finde difficulty to bring our wils to desire it; and when that is instructed and kept in awe, it mingles interest, and confounds the purposes; and when it is forcd to ask honestly and severely, then it *wills* so coldly that God hates the prayer; and if it desires fervently, it sometimes turns that into a passion, and that passion breaks into murmurs or unquietnesse; or if that be avoyded, the indifferency cooles into death, or the fire burns violently, and is quickly spent; our desires are dull as a rock, or fugitive as lightening. Either we ask ill things earnestly, or good things remissley; we either court our owne danger, or are not zealous for our reall safety; or if we be right in our matter, or earnest in our affections, and lasting in our abode, yet we misse in the manner; and either we aske for evill ends, or without religious and awefull apprehensions; or we rest on the

words and signification of the prayer; and never take care to passe on to action;[17]

There was, said Jeremy Taylor, a holiness peculiar to the man, and a holiness peculiar to the prayer, that must adorn the prayer before it can be united to the intercession of Jesus.

What makes prayers work? he asked. What is an effective prayer? What makes someone fit to be an intercessor? He began with the story in the Fourth Gospel of the man born blind. Cured by Jesus, he stood up for him under cross-examination. He was thrown out of the synagogue. Against the insinuation that this miracle was performed by a wicked magician, the man who could now see everything perfectly clearly said: *We all know that God does not hear sinners.* Jeremy Taylor agreed.

Why did every religion have its purification ceremonies? They washed their hands. It signified a washing away of iniquity in order to come pure before God. The trouble with such rituals, said Taylor quaintly, was that they could not see through the 'bottome of their lavatories'. What was *meant* was that they should be cleaning up their souls, never mind sprinkling themselves with water.

So the unclean, the evil, impenitent soul, could not be said to pray, only to profane. A merciless person simply cannot pray. And why should we think that God would not resent such sinners more deeply than we do? Taylor knew how suspicious and unforgiving we can be to one another, and yet expect God's forgiveness. He pointed out that 'Forgive us our trespasses as we forgive them that trespass against us' meant what it said.

> As thy poor brother hath groan'd under thy cruelty and ungentle nature, so shalt thou before the throne of God; thou shalt pray, and plead, and call, and cry, and beg again, and in the midst of thy despairing noyses be carried into the regions of sorrow, which never did and never shall feel a mercy. *God can never heare the prayers of an unmerciful man.*[18]

It may not be obvious that sinners have no recourse to God; but Taylor's attack was that God can no more accept an unholy prayer than listen to a lie, and a wicked person can never utter anything else. To make the beginning of a good prayer, there must be charity. There must be no pretence. Sin destroys purity of spirit. The best argument to move God was for the prodigal to repent and turn back home. The Spirit of God, teaching us how to pray, makes us like himself, in order to make a proper prayer. So we must begin holy living if we expect to be able to pray.

Even the prayers of Taylor's good Anglican friends were liable to be hindered, for instance by their anger:

Prayer is not a fury. Prayer is the peace of our spirit,
the stillnesse of our thoughts, the evennesse of recollection,
the seat of meditation, the rest of our cares,
and the calme of our tempest;
prayer is the issue of a quiet minde, of untroubled thoughts,
it is the daughter of charity, and the sister of meeknesse.
He that prayes to God with an angry spirit
is like him that retires into a battle to meditate

Lukewarmness and apathy could also hinder a devout person's prayer. 'He that is cold and tame in his prayers is a stranger to the secrets of the Kingdome' and the marvellous work of Christ; and does not know what it is to hunger for God. 'Alwaies standing at the gate of wearinesse; coming to God because it is civill to do so . . . Can we expect that our sinnes should be washed by a lazie prayer? *I will not let thee go till thou hast blessed me . . .*' The fervour of Jacob's cry is needed. Cold prayers are 'like the buds of roses which a cold wind has nip'd into death . . . Fall upon your knees, and grow there . . .'

If Christians assembled peevishly or reluctantly for worship, it was bound to impede the prayer of each individual. But when good people prayed with one heart together, however much they differed, the prayer was certain to fly up to God like the hymns of a choir of angels.

> The sum is this, If the man that makes the prayer be an unholy person, his prayer is not an instrument of a blessing, but a curse; but when the sinner begins to repent truly, then his desires begin to be holy. But if they be holy, and just, and good, yet they are without profit and effect, if the prayer be made in an evill communion, or if it be made without attention, or if the man soon gives over, or if the prayer be not zealous, or if the man be angry. A good man cannot prevail in his prayers, if his desires be cold, and his affections trifling, and his industry soon weary, and his society criminall.[19]

So, what made someone fit to be an intercessor, assuming that those prayed for were in a saveable condition (for no intercession, thought Taylor, could prevail upon an undisposed person)? Those who prayed for others *must be extraordinary!* It was like hospitality, when a generous person had enough to share what overflowed at his table. We all needed our prayer for ourselves, for the 'daily expences of our own infirmities'. We are usually absorbed in our own shipwrecks; 'and most good men are in this condition, that they have enough to doe to keep themselves above water.' Anyone with anything left over must be extraordinary.

Taylor's understanding of the work of intercessory prayer was that intercession was uncommon, not that anyone could do it at any time; but that it was exceptional, rare, and wonderful. He expected the ordained ministry to be able to do such work. He dreaded the intolerable shame of the clergy proving to be too frail for it. They were meant to be able to pray for others. No longer so taken up with themselves, they were free to give themselves continually to prayer for others. That is what it was to be a blessing for others. This ministerial care for others, which included love and concern, and pangs of conscience for others, this opportunity to be joined by the Eucharist to the work of Christ interceding, was not denied to anyone, nor to any group which recognized a duty of intercession. But it was ambitious to wish to join the saints who intercede. For the saints are always arresting the sun,[20] opening and shutting the store-houses of the rain, quenching the violence of fire, stopping the mouths of lions, and hastening the day of judgement.

THE MEASURE OF A PERFECT CLERGYMAN

In a letter to John Evelyn in the winter of 1661, Jeremy Taylor reported sending to his publisher 'a little collection of rules for my clergy'. *Rules and Advices to the Clergy of the Diocese of Down & Connor, For their Deportment in their Personal and Publick Capacities*, presented a short, stirring account of Anglican ideals for ministry.[21]

At the Restoration Jeremy Taylor was sent back to Ireland to apply the king's rules and religion, to re-establish episcopal order, to rebuild the Anglican Church, and a University in Dublin.[22] The new bishop was not thinking about advice for the conduct of his team of clergy for the first time in his life. His estimate of the work of a priest sprang directly out of the experience of having been a clergyman on the run, the elusive minister of a persecuted communion, in danger of imprisonment and exile, taking his life into his hands to do his pastoral duty, and dependent on his friends for financial support. His arrival in the diocese of Down and Connor did not cancel what had been learned in insecurity, though he could now probably afford to buy his clerical cloth.

The prospect of reconciling the Irish Churches was not good. It was not clear how he was to supply clergy, or secure the loyalty of Calvinist families. It was uncertain if anyone would be able to enforce the Episcopalian Establishment in Ireland at all, especially in those territories, like his own diocese, where the immigrant farming community was strong and Presbyterian. In *Holy Living* he had proposed a practical list of personal, political, and devotional aims for his friends in having to manage Christian faith without Church or clergy. Now he had to re-invent the idea of a diocese, with parishes and a new clergy. He would bring into the open some of the features of the heroic calling he learned in privation.

His clergy were going to have to be exceptional:

> Pray much and very fervently, for all your Parishioners,
> and all men that belong to you, and all that belong to God;
> but especially for the Conversion of Souls:
> and be very zealous for nothing but for Gods glory,
> and the salvation of the World, and particularly of your Charges:
> Ever remembring that you are by God appointed,
> as the Ministers of Prayer, and the Ministers of good things,
> to pray for all the World, and to heal all the World
> as far as you are able.[23]

It is clear that Taylor did not think that everybody was equipped to be an intercessor, but only the extraordinary, and those special, secret friends of God who might be suspected of being able to arrest the sun in its course. Jeremy Taylor did not require his clergy to be able to interfere so spectacularly. But his description of ministerial vocation shows him discriminating between a special vocational class and every other calling.

Religion should have 'proper' ministers, said *Clerus Domini* (1651). It was not to be 'bruised by the hard hand of mechanicks, and sullied by the ruder touch of undiscerning and undistinguished persons; for although the light of it shines to all, yet it were not handsome that every man should take the taper in his hand'. It was natural and reasonable that ministry should belong to 'certain persons, whose calling must be holy, and their persons taught to be holy' and 'that those persons being made higher than the people by their calling and religion, and yet our brethren in nature, may be intermediall between God and the people, and present to God the peoples needs, and be instrumentall to the reconveying Gods blessing'.[24]

Taylor was not exalting his profession. His brand of clericalism, the Anglican parson, had been distinctly unpopular; but his aim now was to show why it was necessary to inspire holiness of life by special examples. The measure of his ideal clergyman was this:

> He that is holy,
> let him be holy still, and still more holy,
> and never think he has done his work,
> till all be finished by perseverance,
> and the measures of perfection
> in a holy Life and a holy Death;
> but at no hand must he magnifie himself
> by vain separations from others,
> or despising them that are not so holy.[25]

Two Visitation sermons which comprise *The Whole Duty of the Clergy* (1663)[26] fasten upon the exemplary role of the spirituality peculiar to the clergy 'by whom God intends to plant holiness in the World'. All parishioners were called to live holy lives, and expected to grow in grace towards perfection. As for the clergy:

> you are the Choicest of his Choice
> the Elect of his Election
> a Church pick'd out of the Church

All Christians were meant to be lights in the world, and examples of good life to one another, but he insisted to the ministry:

> you are to be Examples even of the Examples themselves;
> that's your duty, that's the purpose of God[27]

About the clergy it had been complained nearly 300 years earlier 'that if gold ruste, what shal iren do?'[28] The scandalous example of a lazy or a drunken minister, or an ignorant and incompetent one, threatened Taylor's ideal of exemplary clergy. Even the Thirty-nine Articles of Religion offer the Church a refuge from human frailty in the paragraph entitled '*Of the Unworthiness of the Ministers, which hinders not the effect of the Sacrament*'. But Taylor did his best to demolish it. His argument was not just that a clerical life which should be edifying was made contemptible by insincerity, but that a bad conscience was certain to inhibit genuine preaching, and to vitiate prayer. Those whom he had described as Christ's under-labourers in the great work of intercession were not going to be allowed to rust: 'the Sermons of a wicked Minister may do some good, not so much as they ought: but the Prayer of a wicked Minister does no good at all; It provokes God to anger.'[29]

Taylor thought it an intolerable shame that the prayers of the parish might be frustrated by a mischievous parson. 'Can he minister the Spirit from whom the Spirit of God is departed? God will do his work alone; the *Amen* shall be more than all the Prayer, and the People shall prevail for themselves.' Such '*Hirelings*' and all for whom 'Theology is but a trade, to fill the belly and keep the body warm' cannot fulfil the vocation for which more than mere innocence is required:

> many things are lawful for the people
> which are scandalous in the Clergy; you are tied
> to more abstinences, to more severities
> to more renunciations and self-denials,
> you may not with that freedom receive
> secular contentments that others may;
> You must spend more time in Prayers,

> your Alms must be more bountiful,
> your hands more open
> your hearts enlarged;
> others must relieve the poor,
> you must take care of them;
> others must show themselves their brethren,
> but you must be their Fathers;
> they must pray frequently and fervently,
> but you must give your *selves up*
> *wholly to the Word of God and Prayer*,
> they must *watch and pray*
> *that they fall not into temptation,*
> but you must watch for your selves and others too;
> The people must mourn when they sin,
> but you must mourn for your own infirmities,
> and for the sins of others; and indeed,
> if the life of a Clergy-man does not exceed
> even the piety of the People,
> that life is in some measure scandalous:[30]

A summary of the 83 recommendations in *Rules and Advices* confirms the emphasis upon ministerial example. Thus priests were to be stricter with themselves than with others, having mastered their passions, never litigiously insistent upon their rights; neither covetous nor demanding; avoiding pride, and practising humility; spiritually wise, enabled by their self-understanding to understand others; detached not worldly, nor jealous of reputation; good tempered under reproach, cheerfully obedient, simple and honest, fervent in prayer, learning patience, bearing adversity meekly, doing all that needed to be done with unwearied industry, courage and constancy; persevering, prudent, unswayed by popular opinion, neither servile nor over-indulgent, nor deceived by the reputation of others, they were to be free from vainglory, and not given to gossip.

In preaching they were warned not to generalize, and not to be influenced by the views of the congregation; to preach to those who were present, not to those who were not; and to reprove sin without naming names. They were to preach holy life, peace, love – 'Press those Graces most that do most good, and make the least noise' – but should be severe against backbiting, and against all those faults which the law takes no cognizance of, like intemperance, extravagance, bragging, peevishness; dwelling upon the Last Things, but without mysteriousness. 'Speak but very little of the secret and high things of God, but as much as you can of the lowness and humility of Christ.' Without being judgemental they were to teach the humbler members of the congregation with special affection, using plain words, destroying popular errors, explaining faith so that it quickened love rather than excited dispute: 'let them be taught to believe, but not to argue' — not presenting heresies in order to refute them — 'they will much easier retain the Objection than understand the Answer'. They were not to be frivolous or profane; neither envious of better preachers, nor eager for praise.

Pastoral care for Taylor's clergy, who had been well trained in canon law, in casuistry, and in biblical criticism, would include catechizing both the young and old; teaching meditation; commending frequent confession and the observance of fasts and feasts, especially Sunday; preparing candidates for confirmation; visiting the sick and dying; and regularly visiting every home in the parish. The obligations to say the daily offices, to secure the baptism of infants, to exhort the parishioners to periodical Holy Communion, to see that the poor were provided for by the energetic collection of alms — 'Think it no shame to beg for Christs poor members' — and to supply everyone's need of comfort and advice, completed the list of duties.

Taylor wished his clergy to gain the love of their parishes by doing their duty not by seeking popularity; and he expected the parish to be submissive to firm leadership. Benevolent command was to be aimed at, reasonable not overbearing. The admirable clergy would always be seeking to reconcile quarrels, would be even and gentle with dissent, not partisan; discerning and merciful with the penitent, wary with the opinionated, nimble in directing the zealous into good works, and in finding work for the unemployed. They would discourage their parishioners from arguing about religion, and would not invite trouble by consulting them on doctrinal controversy. They were not to be pusillanimous. The responsibility of neighbouring rectors was not to be usurped. They should avoid meddling with the liturgy.

What was being described was a vocational style which was practical; not out of reach. Virtue and good sense were being continually applied. It was serious; but it was inspiring. It was a plain delight to Jeremy Taylor that someone could be called by God *to live for others* in that way, and could make a habit of it, and turn it into second nature, with the help of a direct and unmysterious set of rules to start off with. The ruled and methodical way in prayer and liturgy and clerical life was characteristic. He had no quarrel with the Benedictine strand in the English tradition of spirituality which reckoned discipline to be the secret of vocational freedom. *Licentia multos decipit*, said Anselm in introducing his favourite distinction in monastic life between the will that is free because it is obedient and the will that is enslaved because it is disobedient.[31]

The suspicion of élitism in Taylor's recipe should be answered. For it is evident among Church of England ordinands today that Taylor's expectation of a role for the clergy *as examples to the flock* is unwelcome. The results of a study[32] published in 1986 found them reluctant to distinguish the priest for good or ill from the rest of the household of faith. They were not disposed to imagine that the minister could have, or should have, higher moral standards than the congregation, or that the faults of the minister were more shameful than those of others. Holiness they judged is too powerful a concept to be attached to the responsibilities of the clergy. Enabling and caring they hoped to be, but not holier than anyone.

Differences between the seventeenth and the twentieth centuries might account for a shift in the use of language, as well as of the status of the clergy. Most important of these could be that Holy Orders are no longer required for ordinary members of the family to be active in Church ministry, education, pastoral practice, and in the senior management of the Church, with a confidence undreamed of in the Caroline Establishment. It was exactly that unordained life which Jeremy Taylor addressed in *The Rule and Exercises of Holy Living*, without failing to recognize there would be need for a sacramental priesthood as well. The awesomeness of the language of priestly vocation Taylor did not regret; but nor did it embarrass him to see the sovereignty of good in the light of Heaven. For him the heart of religion was to do well, and to go on doing it; there could not be anything holier than that. If the clergy were called to do better, that lay in the calling, not in a claim of superiority.

THE PHARISEE AND THE PUBLICAN

Jesus spake this parable unto certain which trusted in themselves and despised others: Two men went up into the temple to pray; the one a Pharisee, the other a publican. The Pharisee stood and prayed thus with himself, God I thank thee, that I am not as other men are, extortioners, unjust, adulterers, or even as this publican; I fast twice in the week, I give tithes of all that I possess. And the publican standing afar off, would not lift up so much as his eyes unto heaven, but smote upon his breast, saying, God be merciful to me a sinner. I tell you, this man went down to his house justified rather than the other:[33]

The parable presents the predicament of the religious professional. It takes care to convey the extraordinary piety of Pharisees. Precisely because he is a paragon, as saintly as anyone could imagine, the Pharisee prays without a trace of pride, scorn, or hypocrisy. The sacrificial life he has accepted, which is exacting, and more than the Law requires, is a life lived for others. He thanks God for it. Those listening must already be satisfied that this good person is going to be the hero.[34] Pharisees must smile to think how they are outclassed by a publican, a despairing swindler, in what follows. It might even be supposed that Pharisees, the only ones who ever study parables, have been reciting the publican's prayer ever since, uneasily suspecting that within they are still ravening Pharisees. Perhaps the Pharisee deserved to take comfort from the paradoxical taunt: *the first shall be last.* For those who long for Heaven and will not be deterred, who have always acknowledged that the love of God is full of expectation, that perfection needs effort as well as grace, these first friends of God will no doubt get there in the end.

To explain holiness to English people, Jeremy Taylor had begun with personal happiness. He argued that it sprang from old classical ideas about moderation and contentment, as well as from the Christian virtues of chastity in marriage, and humility. Good government came next, and fair dealing in a happy society. Holiness would be identified here chiefly as the responsibility of parents writ large. The third strand, the worship of the good society, would best be observed in charitable deeds. Taylor would congratulate a National Health Service as good prayer, and an encouraging sign of holiness. Meditative attention to the English Bible, and fasting, were also important, and a good imagination of more use than a taste for mysticism. The men and women fit to minister to such a godly realm would have to be perfect examples.

9

O the death of Phoebe!

THE PROSPECT of eternity puts in its place, among other things, church concern. *Holy Dying*, Jeremy Taylor's wonderfully sad, clear, primitive grasp of the end of everything exposes the unimportance of church rivalry, of theological controversy, or even of the good sense of tolerant Anglicanism and religious freedom. The Church has almost disappeared from these pages. There remains the modest task of being good at terminal care:

> For though the day be never so longe,
> At last the belles ringeth to evensonge.[1]

A commonplace of psychiatric opinion is that social adversity is the single most important factor in the onset of depressive illness. Jeremy Taylor was not a depressive. He had lost his job. He lost his home. He joined up on the losing side. He was a prisoner of war. He had been the king's chaplain; he lost his status. He lost his income. He tried the next thing that an unemployed scholar might do, which was to open a prep school out in the sticks with two other equally unqualified school-teachers. He was a part-time pastor to the aristocracy. He wanted to be a writer. His monarch did not applaud him making room in *The Liberty of Prophesying* for 'every dislik'd opinion'. It was too generous a plea for religious toleration. His working relationships as an employee of Charles I and William Laud were terminated, because they were executed. He lost his friend Frances Carbery who died in childbirth. He thought he could always remain *content* with whatever sadness life would bring, and that it must be possible to weep in moderation. He was a clergyman on the run, trying to explain the rules of happy family life. Then his wife Phoebe died.

Anti-depressants might have been tried on him today, with advice to escape after the funeral, particularly from winter's dull weather. Instead he put grief into writing.[2] We cannot even picture Phoebe. In the flying language of *Holy Dying* did he go on talking to her? Did he learn meanwhile to iron his own linen collars? From his mourning came a book which is eloquent about the end of everything which matters to us. Phoebe's cold nose and stiff hands were reckoned with, and despair on his own account. He was stripped of his old defence, contented, uncomplaining, English manners. He had to construct something not too chaotic, not too angry, out of tears. He did not show the book of Job's interest in the symptoms of agitated, reactive depression. He was not worried about that cardinal sign, early morning waking. He did not complain about itchy skin, or about disloyal friends. He did not suspect that everyone was shunning him, talking about him behind his back, or ganging up against him. Phoebe had left him nothing but a long walk by himself (they called it Taylor's Walk; see Chapter 10) to stare at Death; as if there might be, at the end of an avenue of trees, a familiar figure; and nothing to blame himself for. Crazy grief never had such a clear gaze. Imagine the instant fury which a bereaved Jeremy Taylor could have felt, at the same time as trying to compose a calm enquiry into mortality. He told his patron Richard Carbery that he intended the book for Frances Carbery, who 'knew how to live rarely well, and she desired to know how to die; and God taught her by an Experiment'.[3] But Taylor's words of dedication are a courteous excuse for the expression of his own near despair in losing Phoebe. 'In the coldness of his own hearthstone . . . he sat down and wrote one of the most beautiful prose compositions of the 17th century.'[4]

Just as *Holy Living* had been given to a scattered Church whose clergy had been driven out of office, *Holy Dying* was offered to the same Anglicans, to help them at their end, without the Church to depend on. '*It is a great Art to die well.*' Perhaps that was all that was left to them. He would even compile a service for them, a comfort for the dying, which a layman at the bed-side or 'any fit person' could conduct; it had never been done before. It would be '*the first entire Body of Directions for sick and dying People, that I remember to have been publish'd in the* Church of England'.[5]

The problem with the Catholic practice of extreme unction was that at the last moment it seemed *a priest* could be fetched, to overturn the whole exercise of holy living, and show that:

> *though* a holy Life *be not necessary,*
> *yet* a Priest is;
> *as if God did not appoint the Priest to minister to holy Living,*
> *but to excuse it;*
> *so making* the holy Calling

not only to live upon the Sins of the People,
but upon their Ruin[6]

Dying was to be faced in holy living; but since we all need help when health and strength are failing, Taylor would also set out

to preach to the Weary,
to comfort the Sick,
to assist the Penitent,
to reprove the Confident,
to strengthen weak Hands and feeble Knees,

and then he alluded to the hopeless state of the Anglican Church, so persecuted that its customary work of mercy to the dying was suspended:

having scarce any other Possibilities left me
of doing Alms, or exercising that Charity
by which we shall be judged at Doom's-day.

In five chapters Jeremy Taylor considered the shortness, vanity and misery of life, and therefore the importance of preparing for death by daily self-examination, and by practising a charitable life. With those who were seriously ill he discussed the chief temptations that were likely, impatience and fear, and their remedies. He commended patience, resignation, faith, penitence, amendment, confession, charity and justice. He wished to describe how the Church could have been a visitor at the death-bed. There was a discernible ministry here, whose task was to banish fear and despair, to seek reconciliation, and to administer Holy Communion. He knew that ministry, and could describe it:

they who received us in our Baptism,
are also to carry us to our Grave,
and to take care that our End be
as our Life was, or should have been.[7]

Visiting the sick should not be an ominous sign for the household:

It is a very great evil that they fear the Priest,
as they fear the Embalmer, or the Sexton's Spade:
and think his Office so much to relate to the other World,
that he is not to be treated with while we hope to live in this.

Time was needed to bring hard hearts to regret, to awaken the lethargic, to prick the conscience:

To dress a Soul for a Funeral,
is not a Work to be dispatch'd at one Meeting:

But all this time Jeremy Taylor was not really explaining how a clergyman should conduct a ministry to the dying; he was performing it himself. The book was written *instead of* an Office for the Visitation of the Sick. *Holy Dying* is not a handbook for the clergy. It is a self-help manual for those especially in the dismantled Church who have no priest. It is for those who need instructing about the danger they are in; who need to read that nothing can be hidden from God; who need to realize how few good works have been done; who need a practical and exemplary list to work through and what to be reminded of in order to make a good confession. Of course a convenient parson could help, because two heads are better than one; because some who have become deaf to their own calamity 'must be hallooed to'; because sins hide:

> Under the dark shadow
> of these unhappy and fruitless Yew-trees,
> The Enemy of Mankind makes very many to lie hid[8]

and because sins of omission, the bigger half of our failings, are difficult to discern. But the reader's own conscience can do all this, and is, therefore, 'invited to do the work of religion'. Even priestly absolution is not finally needed. To hear the words of absolution is 'of huge Comfort to them that cannot otherwise be comforted' but it is not strictly necessary. What *Holy Dying* aimed at was to convince the reader, in the absence of the Church of England and its ministry, of the reality of the divine mercy in pardoning sinners, and not to despair.

His lines upon the temptation finally to despair are written in the first person singular. At the lowest point in his own bereavement he preached this sermon to himself about what he was feeling:

> I can but mourn for my Sins,
> as I apprehend grief in other Instances:
> I hope this Cloud may pass:
> *Despair assents as firmly and strongly as Faith itself*;
> And I hope it is a Disease of Judgment,
> not an intolerable Condition that I am falling into;
> here we must live in a Cloud,
> in Darkness under a Veil, in Fears and Uncertainties,
> and our very living by Faith and Hope
> is a Life of Mystery and Secrecy[9]

Taylor was assailed; he did not finally despair, either of himself, or of his Royalist friends, or of the Anglican Church. But the death of his wife had sharpened his sad eye. He did not pronounce the Church of England defunct, even though it seemed that the fragile middle way of the Church of England had been completely eclipsed, and nothing appeared more likely to him than that these were the last of the Anglicans. *Holy Dying* insisted on a better perspective: that Heaven was more important, and more real, than the survival of the failing Church, or of any church:

> Let the sick Man mingle the recital of his Creed
> together with his Devotions,
> and in that let him account his Faith;
> not in Curiosity and Factions,
> in the Confessions of Parties and Interests:
> Let it be enough that we secure our Interest of Heaven,
> For every good Man hopes to be saved as he is a Christian,
> and not as he is a Lutheran, or of another Division.[10]

Thus he related to 'the other World' in the way those nervous parishioners suspected, and as they feared the sexton's spade. His realism about the life of the world to come is eloquent, though his anguish in writing it down in 1651 has been forgotten. Heaven is not a church matter. He was sure that we live our lives in the presence of Heaven, and that it was unrealistic and extraordinarily unpractical to avoid that. Heaven is the summary of a good life, its direction, its consequence, its real explanation.

The clarity of his language would arouse a different sort of nervousness today; for not every good Anglican who thinks about language could speak of a hope to be saved – except as a metaphor – or confess a final account with Heaven and hell – except as a mythological picture. Jeremy Taylor wrote as one who plainly believed in Heaven and hell. Salvation was not a metaphor for him. It was a matter of life and death.

TOWARDS A HOLY AND BLESSED DEATH

Where Taylor began was with this bubble, Man. As ephemeral as 'Morning-Mushrooms' his life is so brief and fragile that to create him is 'as much a miracle' as to preserve him 'from rushing into nothing'. It is not a diatribe, as in the first words of Isaiah:

> Cease ye from man whose breath is in his nostrels:
> for wherein is hee to be accounted of?[11]

nor is it a lament upon the evanescence of all things, as was sung in the Psalter, and in Job, and in the Prayer Book's choice of Psalms for the Burial of the Dead. It is more matter-of-fact. It fastens on the ageing body becoming 'useless and entangled like the Wheels of a broken

Clock'; so that 'there is not in the world any greater Instance of . . . laughter and tears'. It is natural; it is unavoidable:

> The Clock strikes, and reckons on our Portion of Eternity.
> Thus Nature calls us to meditate of Death.
> and you can go no whither, but you tread on a Dead Man's Bones.

He described death in his own experience: *infant mortality* – he knew exactly what it was like for parents to be made 'a little glad and very sorrowful', and he included a child's accidental death at the hands of 'a careless Nurse' (to add to his warning about wet-nurses in a previous chapter); *the death of women in childbirth* – he was publishing this work on the anniversary of the death of Frances Carbery; *casualties in the Civil War* –

> I have conversed with some Men
> who rejoiced in the Death or Calamity of others,
> and accounted it as a Judgment upon them
> *for being on the other side, and against them in the Contention*;
> but within the Revolution of a few Months
> the same Men met with a more uneasy and unhandsome Death[12]

The other, not unexpected, reference was to *death in classical literature*. For this section in *Holy Dying* he consulted Petronius' *Satyricon*. His version of the shipwrecked friends finding the body of the captain

> ballasted with Sand in the Folds of his Garment,
> and carried by his civil Enemy the Sea
> towards the Shore, to find a Grave

is such embroidery, that he might be supposed working from memory; but he referred to the Latin of Petronius at least a dozen times in *Holy Dying*. To be reminded of *The Satyricon* and of Trimalchio's feast is like bringing on the clowns for the Gravedigger's scene in *Hamlet*. Jeremy Taylor shared, what can still be found among clergy and sextons and undertakers' men, the unceremonious humour of the boneyard. Who could ever forget a foreman-gravedigger of Highgate Cemetery whispering to a curate: 'The corpse's brother says, would you like to stay for a cup of tea?'

In the same spirit he could describe the change of mortal beauty into decay, and recommend, as the best and most passionate sermon on common mortality, a visit to a royal tomb

> where their Ashes and their Glory
> shall sleep till Time shall be no more
>
> There the warlike and the peaceful,
> the fortunate and the miserable,

> the beloved and the despised Princes
> mingle their Dust
>
> and tell all the World, that, when we die,
> our Ashes shall be equal to Kings[13]

The policies which made sense to Jeremy Taylor when death was faced included:

(i) *Existential seriousness*: since death was sure, the future uncertain, and expectation could not reach out much further than planting an orchard for the next generation to enjoy, and since no one was 'Lord of to Morrow', the present moment was the time for living *in the presence of Heaven*.

> He that by a present and constant Holiness secures the present,
> and makes it useful to his noblest Purposes,
> he turns his Condition into his best Advantage,
> by making his unavoidable Fate become his necessary Religion.[14]

With Seneca he illustrated false expectation and anxiety stealing the present away from us.

(ii) *Heavenly aspiration*: the only reliable felicity, 'where Eternity is the Measure', is the house whose walls and foundation is God. Taylor had much to say about Christian hope in *Holy Living*, and about the increase of hope to cure despair. He had become no less sure of final hope for Heaven, but treated despair sensitively.

(iii) *Care of time*: one of the three motives of *Holy Living*, with its advice to the reader about being properly employed, and avoiding idleness and immorality (every hour so spent runs him backward[15]), now received some urgency:

> before a Man comes to be wise,
> he is half dead with Gouts and Consumptions,
> with Catarrhs and Aches, with Sore-Eyes and a worn-out Body
>
> Old-age seizes upon most Men
> while they still retain the Minds of Boys

Too busy to be virtuous, the reckless shortened life by wasting it. Taylor admitted that not everyone was able to use all his time writing good books, or even to be one who 'perpetually reads good books'. But the liveliness of the happy man, with his charitable deeds, was not tedious; rather was such a life so obviously fulfilling, that time was expanded. Virtue always had 'the seeds of immortality'.

The troublesome character of existence was reviewed, beginning with quaint nuisances, and working up to real misery:

> we have Gnats in our Chambers
> and Worms in our Gardens
> and Spiders and Flyes in the Palaces of the greatest Kings.[16]

> All the Inhabitants of *Arabia* the Desart are in continual danger
> of being buried in huge heaps of Sand

Then come more natural disasters, tempest, earthquake, fire and flood, but also *religious* disaster. For Taylor, who courted unpopularity by making room for quarrelsome versions of Christianity in *The Liberty of Prophesying*, had no experience of world religions, apart from Christian interpretation of the ancient, and now docile, religions of Greece and Rome, and of the Hebrew Bible. He would often refer to a writer like St John of Damascus, but without any recognition that his theology had been worked out within the hospitality of an Islamic country. In ignorance of anything else, Taylor shared seventeenth-century European anxiety about advancing Turks, and an exclusive view of salvation. Even the ferocity of Tertullian's demonizing of other faiths was echoed in Taylor:

> the greatest number of Men and Women born
> in so many Kingdoms and Provinces
> are infallibly made *Mahumetan*,
> Strangers and Enemies to Christ,
> by whom alone we can be saved.
> This Consideration is extremely sad,
> when we remember how universal and how great an Evil it is,
> that so many Millions of Sons and Daughters
> are born to enter into the Possession of Devils, to Eternal Ages.

He indicated a great variety of instances in which good and evil were inextricably mixed together, the prosperity of the world soured with evil, and joy measured merely by the absence of much sorrow. He did not solve the 'extremely sad' consideration of millions of strangers. Had they been less strange to him, these sons and daughters of other faiths, he may have judged how much of what he meant by a holy life and a holy and blessed death would have been readily understood by other religions. Conscious of the violence between Christians themselves, he surveyed the battlefields and the refugees from the muskets of the Civil War:

> But if we could from one of the Battlements of Heaven espy
> how many Men and Women at this time

lie fainting and dying for want of Bread,
how many young Men are hewn down by the Sword of War,
how many poor Orphans are now weeping
over the Graves of their Father,
by whose life they were enabled to eat;
if we could but hear
how many Mariners and Passengers
are at this present in a Storm,
and shriek out because their Keel dashes against a Rock,
or bulges under them,
how many People there are that weep with Want,
and are mad with Oppression,
or are desperate by too quick a Sense of a constant Infelicity,
in all reason we should be glad
to be out of the Noise and Participation of so many Evils.
This is a place of Sorrows and Tears,
of great Evils and a constant Calamity;
Let us remove from hence,
at least in Affections and Preparation of Mind.[17]

How many young men were being hewn down by the sword of war
was estimated at that moment by Oliver Cromwell, in his dispatch to
Parliament, 4 September 1650, giving news of his surprise, at dawn, in
a left-flanking attack out of Dunbar, where Leslie had thought to have
cornered him with no escape except by sea. The Scots were routed.

> The best of the Enemy's horse being broken through and through in less
> than an hour's dispute, their whole Army being put into confusion, it
> became a total rout: our men having the chase and execution of them
> near eight miles. We believe that upon the place and near about it were
> about Three-thousand slain. Prisoners taken . . . of private soldiers near
> Ten-thousand . . . What officers of theirs of quality are killed, we yet
> cannot learn . . . And, that which is no small addition, I do not believe
> we have lost twenty men.[18]

Between Dunbar and Cromwell's last battle at Worcester (exactly twelve
months later – as Cromwell pointed out to Parliament: 'remarkable for
a mercy vouchsafed to your Forces on this day twelvemonth in
Scotland'[19]) *Holy Dying* was being composed and published. Jeremy
Taylor did not need to be reminded of the noise of musketry and
the misery of war, or of the horrific wounds which could be hewn by
the sword. The description which Anne Halkett gave of caring for the
wounded after Dunbar is sobering.[20]

VERY HEAVEN OR HELL

Taylor turned to three words of advice in preparation for making a good end: to make death 'safe and friendly' by keeping it in view, and adopting the classical device of *memento mori*; not to wobble about at the prospect of death like those with 'both their feet in one shoe' but to stand on two feet, namely faith and patience; to take the beatitude seriously, 'Blessed are they that mourn'.

> He that would die holily and happily,
> must in this World love Tears,
> Humility, Solitude, and Repentance.[21]

So he commended *daily* self-examination; he immediately illustrated how much there was for a conscientious person to think about, and therefore how sensible it was that

> we should sum up our Accounts at the Foot of every Page.

Leaving everything to the last moment would not help. In order to be realistic, final judgement had to be acknowledged as something that begins in the present. Self-critical appraisal aimed at mending what was wrong at once, and at recovering the morale to persevere in a holy life. Because it prevented the habit of sin, and interrupted the piling up of faults, because it promoted conscientiousness, and fastened on immediate detail, the practice of daily self-examination was an easy cure. To refuse it was a sign of a guilty heart. It would take time to gain a quiet and disentangled life. But how much better that was, than to come to an end 'timorously and uncomfortably' (he was remembering the prayers that were needed of the army chaplain in the Civil War)

> like an amazed, wounded, affrighted Person
> from a lost Battel,
> without Honour, without a Veil,
> with nothing but Shame and sad Remembrances:[22]

Then, in one of the most important passages in the whole of *Holy Dying*, Jeremy Taylor composed his song of praise for charity; how at last, when all else fails, 'Charity shall bear you upon the Wings of Cherubims'.

> in the Day of Death and Judgment,
> the great Sentence upon Mankind shall be transacted
> according to our Alms, which is the other part of Charity.
> Certain it is, that God cannot, will not, never did reject
> a charitable Man in his greatest Needs,
> and in his most passionate Prayers;
> For *God* himself *is love,*

and every degree of Charity that dwells in us,
is the participation of the divine Nature;
And therefore, when upon our Death-bed
a Cloud covers our Head,
and we are enwrapped with Sorrow;
and when we feel the weight of a Sickness,
and do not feel the refreshing Visitations
of God's Loving-kindness;
when we have many things to trouble us,
and looking round about us we see no Comforter;
then call to mind what Injuries you have forgiven,
how apt you were to pardon all Affronts
and real Persecutions,
how you embraced Peace when it was offered you,
how you *followed after Peace* when it ran from you:
And when you are weary of one side, turn upon the other,
and remember the *Alms* that by the Grace of God,
and his Assistances, you have done;
and look up to God, and with the Eye of Faith
behold him coming in the Cloud,
and pronouncing the Sentence of Doom's-day,
according to his Mercies and thy Charity.[23]

To arrive in Heaven finally, he argued, was worth all our wit and industry. It was not salvation by works. Charity is God's work.

Then he warned the reader that his chapters towards death were reaching the end. He would describe what came next, '*The Circumstances of a dying Man's Sorrow and Danger*', by precise quotation from some of the Fathers. His authorities included St Nilus, St Basil, St John Chrysostom and St Ephraim Syrus. All of these represent a tradition of literal exegesis of biblical texts concerning the Last Judgement and eternal reward and punishment. Some of them, like Ephraim, were vehement about terror to come. But even Chrysostom, preaching on 'outer darkness' and 'weeping and gnashing of teeth'[24] and 'eternal fire, prepared for the devil and his angels',[25] set the hard question: Where now are they by whom hell-fire is disbelieved?[26]

Taylor had not only read Chrysostom. He knew Origen's refusal to treat parables literally, and his far-reaching attempt to reinterpret traditional imagery of the Last Judgement, to think of the pains of the wicked as remedial, and the fires of hell as purgative, and all talk of torment as a vivid expression of the conscience-stricken anguish of sinners *inside them*:

every sinner kindles for himself the flame of his own fire[27]

In *The Foolish Exchange*[28] Taylor examined Origen's desire to put a limit to damnation, but argued that *no amount of hell-fire* was worth enduring. Nor did it improve the prospects of the wicked to say that one day God's mercy would not be frustrated any more.

Between two world wars in this century, an Anglican commission of distinguished scholars (including Oliver Quick, Will Spens and William Temple) produced the Temple report on Doctrine. About hell-fire it was evasive, about divine judgement bashful, about the struggle between love's endeavour and perdition, it declared itself politely open: 'probably the majority feel strongly the force of the argument on both sides.'[29] That feelings were to be estimated thus, provides in itself a caricature of the uncertain proceedings of a commission, nervous about being thought literal, or even 'quasi-literal', about what is pompously called 'the drama of the Last Things'. The language of the report has no edge to it. The Anglican language of Jeremy Taylor is momentous:

hell could not be hell without the despair of accursed souls[30]

If the Doctrine Commission of the Church of England today could have produced its latest document on the subject (1995) without any mention of hell at all, it would have done so. Though still mealy-mouthed, it is braver than William Temple's commission. Its aim is to show that *The Mystery of Salvation* is so all-embracingly secular in its importance that there is simply no room left for Heaven's alternative, except a few words of moral protest against sadism and trying to frighten people.[31] It even issues an account of the Anglican heritage, as if the Litany and the Book of Common Prayer were innocent of all thoughts of everlasting damnation. Hooker, on the other hand, decided there was not a single petition in the Litany that we could ever say we did not need.[32] To resolve to be silent about the tradition is one thing; it might be said to display a seemly reticence about the life of the world to come. But to use the report's one paragraph on final judgement to refer to Dante's *Inferno*, which has no part in Anglican tradition, is a mistake (unless you were to believe that Miss Dorothy L. Sayers was the genius of Anglicanism). *Holy Dying*, by sticking so closely to mortality, has a realism which at once makes theology much more readable than any attempt to shift religious language in the supposed interests of science, feminism and religious pluralism.

First Jeremy Taylor watched the patient die. 'The manner of the Dissolution' is like a clinical description; it is simpler, yet without melancholy. It contributes to human understanding, to compassion. It is not intended to horrify, but to make us friendly to the facts. It does not linger; and not a word is out of place. Nothing is avoided. 'He speaks of one death, and we taste the death of all.'[33] When he reached the last breath of the dying –

> the Noise is like the faint Echo of a distant Valley

– he immediately distinguished the wicked from the good. They die; and hell and Heaven are instantly apparent. Everything happens so quickly for joy or ill, that the reader need have no doubt about the marvellous righteousness of God, or of his mercy, or of the vindication of the good, or of the pains of the damned being true and necessary. The last word is with the rejoicing souls

> being securely carried into the bosom of the Lord,
> where they shall rest till their Crowns are finished.[34]

There is such longing for Heaven, and such reason for repentance, such attention to glory, such knowledge of peril, that a classically heroic picture of holy living and dying in the imitation of Christ was being offered for the inspiration of beaten Anglicans. Taylor was not speculative about rights and wrongs after death. Heaven and hell have always to be left to God's decisiveness.

THE PATIENT'S HEALTH AND THE BEGINNINGS OF FELICITY

It is a striking feature of the funeral service of the Book of Common Prayer that it includes at the grave a petition:

> suffer us not at our last hour
> for any pains of death
> to fall from thee.

The modern rite has tidied away this complaint; for what distinguishes the end of the twentieth century from the seventeenth (or any other) century concerning human sensory experience is some skill in pain management. The world is not rid of painful diseases and accidents. But the expectation that sufferers can often be given pain relief, and helped in terminal care, makes us such different people from every previous generation, that Jeremy Taylor's order of priorities at a sick-bed now comes as a surprise. It puts the private wards of *Holy Dying* at a distance from us to recognize that the pains of death were expected there, irremediable, and sometimes atrocious. 'Friends that stand by the Bed-side' were told at the start not to be upset by the shrieks of pain which diseases can bring; and that it was a cruel mistake to think patients should be better behaved:

> That's the proper Voice of Sickness[35]

It asks for pity, not disapproval. Not everybody had the same temperament or capacity for bearing pain. Even-tempered self-control was admirable; it could not be asked of the delirious. Crying out in desperation could actually help. Taylor was reminded of the Roman accounts of gladiatorial combat.

Taylor had no anaesthetics, no analgesics, unless there was bark. Would chewing willow-bark do, where there was no aspirin? He showed no interest in poppy, apart from classical references in Homer and Pliny.[36] He knew neither laudanum nor paregoric Elixir. The East India Company was founded in 1600. It imported calico and important spices. Was not opium already an habitual narcotic as well as a medicine in Bengal? Could there have been in Taylor's day an alcoholic solution of opium and aniseed, a sort of seventeenth-century Brompton Cocktail? Is that what he had in mind when he trusted that the patient 'would use no indirect Means for his Recovery'? Taylor's world was too young for chloroform and laughing gas. He was equipped only with the news of the crucifixion:

> when our blessed Saviour
> suffered his last and sharpest pang of Sorrow,
> *he cried out with a loud voice,*
> and resolved to die, and did so.[37]

Jeremy Taylor set out to show it possible to be reconciled to sickness and pain. Loud crying imitated Christ; but the complaint must be without despair. Hope was needed. It must be without murmur, that is without reproach of God. Resignation was needed, and the ability to sing God's praises. The complaint must be without peevishness, for that was directed against those who stood around to ease the sufferer. Obedience should be shown to the doctor, and civility to the nurse.

There were remedies against impatience. They included: noticing the way children put up with illness, without any of our sophistication, and how they showed that

> Nature hath in them Teeth and Nails enough
> to scratch and fight against their Sickness;[38]

When pain was instant, it was tolerable. All pain did not have to be added together. To ask how much could be endured, found some of its answer in the examples of courage in men and women who suffered. Sickness dismissed life's other problems:

> Here all Losses and Disgraces,
> domestick Cares and publick Evils,
> the apprehensions of Pity and a sociable Calamity,

> the fears of Want and the troubles of Ambition,
> lie down and rest on the sick Man's Pillow.[39]

Desire for life and recovery battled with the progress of illness at every step. Nothing was intolerable if it was necessary. Nobody escaped illness; the classical, pagan world showed the noble and good contemptuous of pain. Impatience only made matters worse:

> Nothing is more unreasonable
> than to entangle our Spirits in wildness and amazement,
> like a Partridge fluttering in a Net,
> which she breaks not, though she breaks her Wings.[40]

Patience took pain as God-given, and humbling; patience was able to give thanks that pain was not eternal; and that what was sent could not be more than a Christian could bear. Sufferings were to be united to the Cross, understood as chastening, even as part of the work of love:

> the truth of Love is hardly known,
> but by somewhat that puts us to Pain.[41]

Accepted as punishment for sins, as a last opportunity to be virtuous (looked back on gratefully in convalescence) sickness did not extinguish hope and joy in recovery. There was even

> Recovery by Death,
> as it is easier and better than the Recovery by a sickly Health,
> so it is not so long in doing;
> It suffers not the tediousness of a creeping Restitution,
> nor the Inconveniences of Surgeons and Physicians,[42]

Thinking about reasons for patience was itself remedial. Taylor asked what made groans of pain 'apt to be joined to the Musick of Angels' but the fact that illness prepared the patient for eternity. It untied the strings of vanity, knocked off the fetters of pride, especially the self-importance of being wise; it stripped off anger like a garment, and made a sinner so weak to continue badly that he was obliged to take a step of innocency. Then was summed up all that had brought Taylor to write *Holy Living* and *Holy Dying*:

> all is well as long as the Sun shines,
> and the fair Breath of Heaven gently wafts us
> to our own Purposes.
> But if you will try the Excellency, and feel the work of Faith,
> place the Man in a Persecution,
> let him ride in a Storm,
> let his Bones be broken with Sorrow,
> and his Eye-lids loosened with Sickness,

let his Bread be dipped in Tears,
and all the Daughters of Musick be brought low;
let God commence a Quarrel against him,
and be bitter in the Accents of his Anger or his Discipline:
Then God tries your Faith.
Can you then trust his Goodness,
and believe him to be a Father, when you groan under his Rod?
Can you rely upon all the strange Propositions of Scripture,
and be content to perish if they be not true?
Can you receive Comfort in the Discourses of Death and Heaven,
of Immortality and the Resurrection,
of the Death of Christ and conforming to his Sufferings?
Truth is, there are but two great Periods
in which Faith demonstrates itself
to be a powerful and mighty Grace:
And they are *Persecution* and *the Approaches of Death*[43]

Why should the persecuted Church of England and the last of the Anglicans be afraid of dying? Was Heaven just a dream? Were faith and hope without content, and the strange propositions of Scripture just a story? Anyone who loves the operatic scenery of *Paradise Lost* will see in an instant how different *Holy Dying* is from a work of art. Taylor was not in the least interested in spinning a magnificent mythology, but in helping the patient to write his will and to make a good confession without fear. Heaven and hell are not make-believe. Nor are they a mediaeval drama; nor a Baroque masque; nor magic. It is important to ask why Milton's work is essentially irreligious. The decline in the belief in Heaven and hell is not just a threat to the last of the Anglicans. It threatens the last of Christianity. How could a poem begin to destroy a religion?

HOLY DYING AND *PARADISE LOST*

Milton's use of the Bible includes reproducing it, as Christopher Hill judges, 'not . . . as earlier verse paraphrases had done', but 'half-way between Biblical verse paraphrases and the novel'.[44] Copious pages of *Paradise Lost* are indeed a metrical version of the Bible, and suffer the limitations of that. I do not mean the thump of the poetry which F. R. Leavis found awful and compelling: 'the foreseen thud that comes so inevitably, and, at last, irresistibly.'[45] The Bible is not only a final text, but, as the long haul of historical-critical method has shown, it is composite. The varieties of authorship, editing, and historical setting, even in the strands of the same chapter (as in the Creation accounts in Genesis which Milton was very interested in), cannot be preserved by turning out the Bible as a song on one string, however melodious. The effect of rewriting it in one poetic idiom, an effect which Milton could not possibly have intended, since the unparaphrased original is astonishingly fresh and knotty, is to iron out biblical material more monumentally flat and tedious than even F. R. Leavis bargained for. If Milton had been pleased to show how long and dull the Bible is, and how rebellious 'under Browes / Of dauntless courage' (I.602f.) one ought to sit fuming at it, he could have hardly done better than *Paradise Lost*. The irreligious do still think that the Bible is boring.

Christopher Hill quotes Milton's private theory of interpretation, as going to the logical extreme of Protestant reading of the Bible: 'No one else can usefully intepret for him unless that person's interpretation coincides with the one he makes for himself and his own conscience.' 'Each man is his own arbiter.'[46] It is a noticeable feature of *Paradise Lost* that Milton insisted on his way of hearing the Bible. He had to close his ears. To suppose that the fundamental teaching of the Bible is about an epic battle, even a magnificent one, or that the Bible is essentially about a proud rebellion, is to use one verse in the Book of Revelation to unlock the rest of Scripture. But if the one with such a fabulous key was stirred by the very human heroism and defiance of falling Lucifer, and also oppressed by the everlasting almightiness of the power of God, and resentful 'Against the high Supremacie of Heav'n' (III.205), it is understandable that he might hear *that* being read out as every creaking page of the Bible was turned. Tillyard's famous joke,[47] retailed by Empson, that if Milton had been in the Garden he would have eaten the apple at once and written a pamphlet to prove that it was his duty, captures the aggression nicely.

The suggestion that Milton was half-way to a novel points to his most remarkable achievement. For a novel, the story of the Garden of Eden has obviously to be a love story. Plot is critical. Character, including in this case plausible psychological characterization of (formally unimaginable) human temperament before the Fall, as well as relationships after the apple, must be credible. If the mutual love of Adam and Eve is to be the paradigm of true love, of conjugal love, 'Leaning half-rais'd, with looks of cordial Love / Hung over her enamour'd' (V.12f.), nothing must stand in its way, certainly not, as A. J. A. Waldock excellently puts it, 'the mere doctrine that God must be obeyed'.[48] Of course, there is no coherent plot in the Genesis creation narrative. If it was the Tree of the Knowledge of Good and Evil, how could Adam know that it was wrong to eat of it, or wrong not to do as he was told, or wrong to listen to anyone else but God? Genesis is also dumb about the characters of the lovers, and as unhelpful as the Bible can be, and usually is, about the development of character. Genesis is *not intricate and is wholly sublime*; but the moment Milton takes the glances of the lovers seriously, or is determined to describe the fragrance of Eve half hidden by roses, or her marvellously intelligent curtain speech

> On me exercise not
> Thy hatred for this miserie befall'n,
> On me already lost, mee, then thy self
> More miserable; both have sin'd, but thou
> Against God onely, I against God and thee (X.927–31)

at that moment he knows that Adam and Eve are right, that God's justice is indefensible, that reality has broken the story to pieces, messed up the whole tradition of Original Sin, buried Calvinism, parted company with St Augustine, and left him with no one to turn to except that Caroline divine Jeremy Taylor. Milton did abandon Presbyterianism, but did not find his way into the English Church of the Restoration.

The seventeenth century, says Christopher Hill, re-imagined biblical myths in the light of the problems of their own society. 'The background for *Paradise Lost* . . . is the defeat of the cause in which Milton believed so profoundly and to which he had sacrificed so much.'[49] The rebel angels, guilty of pride, ambition, self-interest, greed, portray the vices which had led to the fall of the Commonwealth. But it is when Christopher Hill refers us to the fact that Gideon in the Old Testament, for example, was taken to mean Cromwell (Gideon also refused a crown) that the coarseness of such a use of the Bible is exposed. The Bible ransacked for a contemporary political cartoon, or as a dressing-up box of barely disguised characters and events, in order to take comfort in allegory, is miserable theology; it is irreligious. That this has been endlessly tried, and is almost impossible to resist, though it is a tribute to the persistence of biblical types and images, is no recommendation.

To notice Milton's historical context in his work is instructive. Tyranny and superstition were the evils in England to be resisted, loss of political liberty was to be deplored; every reason, therefore, for the archangel Michael (hinting at what had happened so disastrously since the Restoration) to tell Adam that

> upstart Passions catch the Government
> From Reason, and to servitude reduce
> Man till then free. Therefore since hee permits
> Within himself unworthie Powers to reign
> Over free Reason, God in Judgement just
> Subjects him from without to violent Lords;

> Who oft as undeservedly enthrall
> His outward freedom: Tyrannie must be,
> Though to the Tyrant thereby no excuse.[50]

Imagine a violent lord like Charles II attacking freedom with his Act of Uniformity (1662), Proclamation requiring Church attendance (1663), First Conventicle Act (1664), Five Mile Act (1665). According to Milton, none of that had deserved to succeed, and would not have, if Milton's fellow citizens had not been so passionately unreasonable.

Milton's 'magnificent invention' removes the authority of the Bible, dethrones it, and brings on the Enlightenment, by treating it as mythology. C. S. Lewis was right. Milton was 'trying to make Heaven too like Olympus',[51] the home of the Greek gods. This is the moment at which a classical education (described in Chapter 2) destroys Christian belief. The classical tradition is no longer a source to plunder, but an infection, atheism beautifully arrayed. That is not a poetic disaster. It is irreligious. Heaven and hell become fictions, as arty as Venus rising from the waves.

Lewis wondered for a moment if Milton could have got away with it by making God more *vague*, about whom 'all the Sanctities of Heaven / Stood thick as Starrs' (III.60f.). But Milton was inviting his readers to look at the whole cosmic plot from outside. 'In the religious life man faces God and God faces man. But in the epic it is feigned, for the moment, that we, as readers, can step aside and see the faces both of God and man in profile.'[52] C. S. Lewis concludes that the epic cannot be religious.

The attempt to replace the text of the Bible as it stands with a literary form, with a work of art, with *Paradise Lost*, or to use it for a political allegory, is mistaken. But a preference for the plain text, as Jeremy Taylor would put it, is often labelled fundamentalism. Whenever a literary approach to biblical interpretation today offers to sort out which texts are secondary, or late, or mythological, great care to pick up the pieces from the literary editor's floor seems appropriate, in order that another generation may consider the language of the kingdom of Heaven in as complete and uncorrupt a state as possible. A refusal to replace the text, and a wariness about proposals to translate the text 'to make it modern', need not obstruct the wish to make Heaven and hell as intelligible as the teaching of the parables of Jesus about reality.

Holy Dying does seek intelligibility: it does this, partly by remedying the fear of death and hell by recounting how Jesus was pleased to legitimate fear by his agony and prayer in Gethsemane; but chiefly by a constant rejoicing in the names of the saints and martyrs, the triumphant Church in Heaven. The martyrs are the Church to belong to. The dying Anglican patient and the stricken Church of England have to transfer their allegiance to that Church.

> Now thou art to enter into the Action of a new Religion.[53]

Even sophisticated television audiences at nightfall are ready to mistake make-believe for the real thing. It is not to be supposed that everyone switching off recites Shakespeare:

> Our revels now are ended. These our actors,
> As I foretold you, were all spirits, and
> Are melted into air, into thin air;
> And like the baseless fabric of this vision,
> The cloud-capped towers, the gorgeous palaces,
> The solemn temples, the great globe itself,
> Yea, all which it inherit, shall dissolve;[54]

It is difficult to put down *Paradise Lost* without recognizing that the loveliness of Milton's Adam and his Eve and his

> Heav'n by many a Towred structure high,
> Where Scepter'd Angels held thir residence,[55]

is insubstantial, compared either to Heaven which is the aim and consequence of holy living, or to the family love of Phoebe Taylor and to Jeremy Taylor's real sorrow and real joy.

It could be said that Jeremy Taylor did recover from *Holy Living* and *Holy Dying*, and that his generation was not quite the last of the Anglicans, but that his message in those books remained when the peril of the Church for which they were written had passed. The questions raised in the first chapter of this book may now be given brief answers:

There was no need for him to revise *Holy Living* and *Holy Dying* at the Restoration. His publisher would say they remained popular just as they were. They became English classics because what they proposed was too sharply practical to be relegated to what is called spirituality. Like so much of the revolutionary theology of the day, Taylor's work found itself shaken free from the Church establishment just long enough to become quite unsanctimonious. The two books are about political life, unemployment, market prices, parental anxiety, and terminal illness. Piety gets turned into generosity. The highest moral expectations are set out so invigoratingly, because shops, schools, and law-courts, sex, violence, and family holidays, are all secular concerns, and not hidden from the endless and immediate certainty of Heaven and hell.

About church and doctrine Taylor was blessedly ecumenical; he would adore with the High Church, and always earnestly reform himself with puritans and Evangelicals. He would challenge the disunity of the churches now. If it was a matter of doctrinal argument, he would argue in favour of bishops, and against infallibility. But argument should not separate. He would wonder, for example, why nothing but the vanity and self-importance of the bishops and clergy of the Church of England should get so spitefully in the way of reconciliation with the Methodists, and how many scandals should continue to appal the Catholic Church before the marriage of the clergy and the ordination of women became accepted in universal Church order.

That it was all rules and exercises that the reader was invited to take on could never conceal the spirit, so affectionate, courteous and forgiving, of such a pile of Heavenly legislation.

IO

The search for Jeremy Taylor

THERE is such a meagre hatful of details about the life of Jeremy Taylor, despite the fame of his writing, that it is disappointing not to find a society which exists to prove that his work had actually been written by another. Robert Aris Willmott, a Victorian clergyman, solved the problem with the title *Bishop Jeremy Taylor, His Predecessors, Contemporaries and Successors* (1846), so that he was able not only to fill a book, but also to disguise the embarrassment of short paragraphs on his chief subject.

Lecturing in King's College, London in 1877, F. W. Farrar[1] allowed himself plausible conjecture to eke out scant history. His invention is like dealing with the infancy of Christ by expanding with apocryphal stories the amazing brevity of the gospel narratives. Was not Jeremy Taylor baptized at Trinity Church Cambridge on 15 August 1613, and was not his father Nathanael a barber by trade? Yes; they were. But these facts encouraged the wistful Farrar: 'As the little boy stood at the shop door he may often have noticed the stern and gloomy lineaments of an undergraduate of Sidney Sussex College, whose name was Oliver Cromwell, and may have admired (on the other hand) the calmer and more untroubled face of the Public Orator of the University, George Herbert.' It is not reported if anyone interrupted the lecturer to ask if the demon barber of Petty Cury had ever *shaved* the stern and gloomy lineaments, and if so why he had not struck an anticipatory blow for the divine right of kings by cutting the throat of young Cromwell. As for romancing with history, would not even the most superficial acquaintance with the poetry of (on the other hand) George Herbert have saved the lecturer from describing him as untroubled?

Jeremy Taylor died at Lisburn, Co. Antrim, 13 August 1667, and was buried at Dromore. His first biography is in the funeral sermon preached by George Rust. C. Barksdale's short description of Taylor in

A Remembrancer of Excellent Men (London, 1670), even his commendation 'none of God's ordinary', is copied from Rust, who said:

> He was born at *Cambridge*, and brought up in the Free-School there, and was ripe for the University, afore custome would allow of his Admittance; but by that time he was Thirteen years old, he was entred in *Caius* Colledge; and as soon as he was Graduate, he was chosen fellow ... From the University, by that time that he was Master of Arts, he removed to *London*, and became publick Lecturer in the Church of Saint *Paul's*; where he preached to the admiration and astonishment of his Auditory; and by his florid and youthful beauty, and sweet and pleasant air, and sublime and rais'd discourses, he made his hearers take him for some young Angel, newly descended from the Visions of Glory; the fame of this new Star, that out-shone all the rest of the Firmament, quickly came to the notice of the great Arch-Bishop of *Canterbury* ... he placed him in his own Colledge of *All-Souls* in *Oxford*, where Love and Admiration still waited upon him ... He had not been long here, afore my Lord of *Canterbury* bestowed upon him the Rectory of *Uphingham* in *Rutland-shire*, and soon after preferred him to be Chaplain to King *Charles* the Martyr of blessed and immortal Memory.
>
> This Great man had no sooner launch'd into the World, but a fearful Tempest arose, and a barbarous and unnatural War disturb'd a long and uninterrupted Peace and Tranquillity; but his Religion taught him to be Loyal, and ingag'd him on his *Prince's* side, whose Cause and Quarrel he always own'd and maintain'd with a great courage and constancy; till at last, he and his little Fortune were shipwrackt in that great *Hurricane*, that overturn'd both Church and State: This fatal Storm cast him ashore in a private corner of the World, and a tender Providence shrowded him under her Wings, and the Prophet was fed in the Wilderness; and his great worthiness procur'd him friends, that supplied him with bread and necessaries. In this Solitude he began to write those excellent Discourses ...
>
> When he had spent some Years in this Retirement, it pleas'd God to visit his Family with Sickness, and to take to Himself the dear Pledges of his Favour, three Sons of great hopes and expectations, within the space of two or three Months: And though he had learned a quiet Submission unto the Divine Will; yet the Affliction touch'd him so sensibly, that it made him desirous to leave the Countrey; And going to *London*, he there met my Lord *Conway*, a Person of great Honour and Generosity; who making him a kind Proffer, the good man embraced it, and that brought him over into *Ireland*, and settled him at *Portmore*, a place made for Study and Contemplation, which he therefore dearly lov'd; and here he wrote his *Cases of Conscience* ...
>
> By this time the Wheel of Providence brought about the Kings happy Restauration ... It was not long ere his Sacred Majesty began the settlement of the Church, and the great Doctor *Jeremy Taylor* was resolv'd

upon for the Bishoprick of *Down* and *Connor*; and not long after, *Dromore* was added to it ... he was made a Privy-Councellor; and the University of *Dublin* gave him their Testimony, by recommending him for their Vice-chancellor: which honourable Office he kept to his dying day.[2]

In 1668 David Lloyd's long, gripping title *Memoires of the lives, actions, sufferings and deaths of those noble, reverend and excellent personages that suffered by Death, Sequestration, Decimation or otherwise for the Protestant Religion, and the great Principle thereof, Allegiance to the Soveraigne, in our late Intertestine Wars, from the year 1637 to the year 1660. and from thence continued to 1666. with the life and martyrdom of King Charles I* was published. Of Taylor he wrote:

So exquisitely quick and exact were his Reasonings, so fluent his Language, and so prodigiously ready and various his Learning, as being a very strict and pious man, he writ several taking books of Devotion, as *Holy Living* and *Dying*, his *Life of Christ*, his *Eniautos* or Course of Sermons throughout the year, the *Doctrine and practice of Repentance*, his *Golden Grove*, or a *Manual of daily Prayers*, the *Worthy Communicant*, *A Collection of Offices or Forms of Prayer, fitted to the needs of all Christians*, the *Nature, Offices, and Measures of Friendship*, and his *Cases of Conscience*, by which doing the Church in the time of her sufferings great services, the latter adorning and assisting the former, and his indeavor to make men holy and serious, preparing to his pains, to make or keep them good Subjects and Church-men.[3]

The books named are most of Taylor's work between 1649 and the Restoration. Taylor's 'unwary sentiments', as Lloyd called them, about freedom of conscience, prompted him to omit *The Liberty of Prophesying* from mention. The Establishment had still not forgiven Jeremy Taylor for writing so humanely about such intolerable sectarians as those who opposed infant baptism. Then Lloyd composed a description of Jeremy Taylor as a bishop in Ireland, by making a collage of extracts out of Taylor's own pamphlet *Rules and Advices to the Clergy of the Diocese of Down & Connor*, without telling us of this source.

This demonstrates Jeremy Taylor already being remembered not for his 'actions, sufferings, and Sequestration', but for his *writing*, and already having to be reconstructed out of his own writings. Lloyd did see the books and the persecution going hand in hand. Thus, in the year after the publication of his defence of episcopacy, a bill for the abolition of episcopacy was passed in both houses of Parliament; the issuing of the *Directory for Publique Worship* which outlawed the Book of Common Prayer is met by Taylor's *Discourse concerning Prayer Extempore*, revised as *Apology for Authorised and Set Forms of Liturgy* (1647); when compulsory attendance at the parish church was abolished in 1650,

Taylor was providing *The Rule and Exercises of Holy Living* for those parishioners of the Church of England whose parish priest had been ejected. The books are interlocked with the times. They also survived them.

His *Sermon preached in Saint Mary's Church in Oxford upon the Anniversary of the Gunpowder-Treason* he dedicated to the Archbishop of Canterbury, William Laud, signing it: 'Your Graces *most observant and obliged* Chaplaine, Ier. Taylor.'[4] The title page of *Great Exemplar*, and several of his other books, also describe him as Chaplain in Ordinary to Charles I. Both of these grand employers and patrons of his had their heads chopped off. The plain evidence that Jeremy Taylor was willing to go on and on writing in opposition to such a government reflects upon his character. He must have been irrepressibly and recklessly talkative, or very brave, or both.

In Lloyd's list of Taylor's titles prominence is given to a letter written to 'the most ingenious and excellent' Mrs Katherine Philips, published as the discourse *Of Friendship*. Taylor wrote a good, witty letter to Katherine, the Matchless Orinda, whose love poems, especially to Anne Owen, whom she named Lucasia, were a gentle expression of homosexual relationship.[5] Jeremy Taylor was a kind, wise friend to her. 'A person of a most sweet and obliging Humour, of great Candour', his conversation was described as having 'all the pleasantness of a Comedy, and all the usefulness of a Sermon . . . he never spake but he charm'd his Hearer'.[6]

Katherine was married to a Roundhead colonel. Taylor was openly Royalist. This friendly man dedicated his books to Cavaliers: to Christopher Hatton and Mary Compton, to Richard and Fanny Vaughan, to Alice Egerton (who took a part in Milton's *Comus* when it was performed at Ludlow Castle, and later married Richard Vaughan, Lord Carbery), to James Butler and his wife Elizabeth Preston, and to Christian Cavendish, all of whom belonged to the peerage and to the court. To Charles I he dedicated *Apology for Authorised and Set Forms of Liturgy*; to Charles II *Ductor Dubitantium*; to Princess Mary of Orange *Worthy Communicant*; to Lord Hatton of Kirby Hall *Episcopacy Asserted, The Liberty of Prophesying*, and the first instalment of *Great Exemplar*. To Lord Carbery of Golden Grove he dedicated *Holy Living, Holy Dying, The Sermons*, and *Unum Necessarium*; to Lady Carbery and Lady Northampton parts of *Great Exemplar*; to the dowager Countess of Devonshire *Deus Justificatus*; to the Duke of Ormond *A Discourse of Confirmation*; and to the Duchess of Ormond *The Supplement to The Sermons*. They admired him. They patronized him. But like John Evelyn, they needed his spiritual help and friendship, and were loyal friends in return.

The lively references to Jeremy Taylor in John Evelyn's *Diary* begin in 1654: '15th April. I went to London to heare the famous Doctor Jeremy Taylor (since Bishop of Downe and Connor) at St. Gregg: on 6 Matt. 48 (*sic*) concerning evangelical perfection.' Evelyn was actually referring to chapter 5: 'Be ye perfect as your heavenly Father is perfect'. Taylor's sermon that morning at St Gregory, near St Paul's Cathedral, is not preserved; but the section of *Unum Necessarium* (1655) where he argues that repentance and the command to be perfect can stand together, is quite likely to be exactly what he said in the pulpit. When it came out, Evelyn got a copy of this book.

The next relevant entry comes in 1655.

> 18 March: Went to London on purpose to heare that excellent preacher, Dr. Jeremy Taylor on 14 Matt. 17 shewing what were the conditions of obtaining eternal life: also concerning abatements for unavoidable infirmities, how cast on the accompts of the Crosse. On the 31st I made a visit to Dr. Jer. Taylor to conferr with him about some spiritual matters, using him thenceforward as my ghostly father.

The entry for 28 August conveys not only the intellectual temperature at Wotton, Evelyn's country mansion, in the middle of the seventeenth century, before he had helped to found the Royal Society, but also the context from which Taylor's work escaped into the modern world. The passage shows how chemistry and astronomy are not as yet sharply distinguished from alchemy and millenary anxiety.

> Came that renown'd mathematician Mr. Oughtred to see me, I sending my coach to bring him to Wotton, being now very aged. Amongst other discourse he told me he thought water to be the philosopher's first matter, and that he was well perswaded of the possibility of their elixir; he believ'd the sunn to be a material fire, the moone a continent, as appears by the late Selenographers; he had strong apprehensions of some extraordinary event to happen the following yeare, from the calculation of coincidence with the diluvian period;[7] and added that it might possibly be to convert the Jewes by our Saviour's visible appearance, or to judge the world; and therefore his word was *Prepare to meet trouble!* He said original sin was not met with in the Greeke Fathers, yet he believ'd the thing; this was from some discourse on Dr. Taylor's late booke which I had lent him.

To the ancient clergyman Evelyn had lent *Unum Necessarium*, the latest book, in which Taylor had included the words on a repentant sinner trying to be perfect, from the sermon which had first drawn Evelyn to seek him out. What this book chiefly shows is Taylor's courage and common sense in repudiating as bad theology the fashionable

Presbyterian gloom about human depravity. But Evelyn was now anxious for his spiritual director to meet agreeable and philosophical company, like the deposed Royalist governor of Virginia, and the Warden of Wadham College, whose lodgings full of 'artificial, mathematical and magical curiosities' are described in Evelyn's tour of Oxford colleges, 13 July 1654, and Boyle, the Sceptical Chymist, himself:

> 1656, 12 April. Mr. Berkeley, and Mr. Robert Boyle (that excellent person and great virtuoso), Dr. Taylor and Dr. Wilkins, din'd with me at Sayes Court, when I presented Dr. Wilkins with my rare burning-glasse. In the afternoon we all went to Colonel Blount's to see his new-invented plows . . . 6 May. I brought Monsieur le Franc, a young French Sorbonnist, a proselyte, to converse with Dr. Taylor; they fell to dispute on original sinn, in Latine, upon a booke newly publish'd by the Doctor, who was much satisfied with the young man . . . 7th. I visited Dr. Taylor and prevail'd on him to propose Mons. le Franc to the Bishop that he might have orders, I having some time before brought him to a full consent to the Church of England her doctrine and discipline, in which he had till of late made some difficulty; so that he was this day ordain'd both Deacon and Priest, by the Bishop of Meath. I paid the fees to his Lordship, who was very poore and in greate want, to that necessity were our Clergy reduc'd!

Letters exchanged between them show that Jeremy Taylor was not just poor but imprisoned in the Tower of London. Evelyn's letter to the Lieutenant of the Tower pleads his friend's innocence.

> 1657, 7th June. My fourth sonn was born, christen'd George (after my Grandfather): Dr. Jer. Taylor officiating in the drawing-room.
> 1658. 15 Feb. The afflicting hand of God being still upon us, it pleased Him also to take away from us this morning my youngest sonn, George, now 7 weeks languishing at nurse, breeding teeth, and ending in a dropsie. God's holy will be done! He was buried in Deptford church the 17th following. 25th. Came Dr. Jeremy Taylor & my Brothers with other friends to visite and condole with us. March 7. To London to hear Dr. Taylor in a private house on 13 Luke 23, 24. After the sermon followed the blessed Communion of which I participated. In the afternoone Dr. Gunning at Excester House expounding part of the Creede. This had ben the severest winter that any man alive had known in England. The crowes feete were frozen to their prey. Islands of ice inclos'd both fish and fowl frozen, and some persons in their boates.

Taylor's sermon on that text is called *The Gate to Heaven a Strait Gate*.[8] There is even topical reference to the weather. Early ardour may cool 'from very hot to be tepid, from tepid to be cold, from cold to be quite frozen and incrustated'. If he was writing this sermon for his penitent, he did not spare him. To read the harmless flattery in which Taylor couched his book dedications to royalty and the nobility is a reminder of the desperate obsequiousness of court protocol. But in office, in the pulpit and in his work as a priest, he was not afraid of anyone:

> You may see in a little,
> that a Man may go a great way in Piety,
> and yet not enter into Heaven.
> What then shall we think of such persons,
> whose Piety hath no more age than a Fly;
> no more labour in it
> than walking in a shadow;
> no more expence
> than in the farthing-alms
> of the street or highway;
> no more Devotion
> than going to Church on Sundays;
> no more Justice
> than in preserving the rules of Civil Society,
> and obeying the compulsion of Laws;
> no more Mortification
> than fasting upon a Friday,
> without denying one Lust,
> and the importunity of sinful Desires?
> These certainly are far
> from entring into the Gate,
> because they are far
> from striving to enter.
> And yet there want not some Men,
> will not do a quarter of this,
> and yet would spit in your face
> if you should put them in doubt
> or question their Salvation.

Of the correspondence between these two friends 21 letters survive.[9] Evelyn wrote from Sayes Court, his beautiful manor house of West Greenwich, Deptford. Taylor was sometimes in London, sometimes in Wales. His letter which began: 'Not long after my coming from prison' probably refers to a sentence served in Chepstow Castle. Of his last five letters, four came from Portmore and Lisburn, Co. Antrim where Edward Conway, a friend of Evelyn's, had helped Jeremy Taylor to safety before the Restoration. The last letter came from Dublin. What do the addresses in this small packet of correspondence suggest? Evelyn sat still. His poor friend hopped about like a bird in the frost.

In Evelyn's *Diary* there is this entry, 26 February 1680: 'To the Royal Society, where I met an Irish Bishop with his Lady, who was the daughter to my worthy and pious friend, Dr. Jeremy Taylor, late Bp. of Downe and Connor; they came to see the Repository. She seemed to be a knowing woman, beyond the ordinary talent of her sex.' The Irish prelate was Francis Marsh, Bishop of Limerick and Kilmore, later Archbishop of Dublin. His wife, the highly intelligent Mary Taylor, was one of the three daughters of Jeremy Taylor and Joanna Bridges of Mandinam in Wales, his second wife.

Taylor had come through the Civil War unscathed. It is recorded by Anthony à Wood that he 'attended in his majesty's army in the condition of a chaplain; where tho' he had not a command of his time and books, yet he laid the foundation of several treatises . . . Upon the declining of the King's cause he retired into Wales . . . in a private corner, as t'were, of the world.'[10]

Thus Willmott was prompted to sniff Taylor's treatises for musketry and the whiff of grape-shot. He found some. The sermon *Apples of Sodom* and *Holy Dying* have examples of 'martial imagery'.[11]

> no man buy's death and damnation at so dear a rate,
> as he that fights for it, and endures cold and hunger,
> *Patiens liminis atq; solis*[12]
> the heat of the sun, and the cold of the threshold;
> the dangers of war, and the snares of a crafty enemy;
> he lies upon the ground
> with a severity greater
> then the penances of a Hermit,
> and fasts beyond the austerity
> of a rare penitent;[13]

> so have I known a bold trooper
> in the confusion of a battell,
> and being warm with heat and rage
> received from the swords of his enemy,
> wounds open like a grave;
> but he felt them not,
> and when by the streams of bloud
> he found himself mark'd for pain,
> he refused to consider then,
> what he was to feel to morrow.
> But when his rage had cool'd
> into the temper of a man,
> and a clammy moisture had checked
> the fiery emission of spirits,
> he wonders at his own boldnesse,

and blames his fate,
and needs a mighty patience
to bear his great calamity.[14]

as a man under the Chirugeons hands,
smarting and fretting all the while[15]

what can we complain
of the weakness of our Strengths,
or the pressures of Diseases,
when we see a poor Soldier stand in a Breach
almost starved with Cold and Hunger,
and his Cold apt to be relieved only
by the Heats of Anger, a Fever, or a fired Musket
and his Hunger slacked by a greater Pain and a huge Fear?
This Man shall stand in his Arms and Wounds,
patiens luminis atque solis,
pale and faint, weary and watchful;
and at Night shall have a Bullet
pulled out of his Flesh
and shivers from his Bones
and endure his Mouth to be sewed up
from a violent rent, to its own Dimension;
and all this for a Man he never saw[16]

J. Wheeldon's *Life of Bishop Taylor*[17] (first published 1789) hardly deserves the name. He is enthusiastic about

the purest writings of a *Man clothed with a multitude of Mind* . . . It were extravagant and almost impossible, in a general encomium to give the common reader an adequate idea of Taylor's amazing capacity. They who would fathom his mighty mind must read all his works, which many cannot, which many will not, and which most are unable either to purchase or understand.

Wheeldon's remedy, therefore, was to select 'these little pearls, which I have drawn from his ample store' and to excuse himself from fathoming any further. Some sermons and extracts follow. Thus Wheeldon brought into the open what Lloyd had hinted. The only way to find Jeremy Taylor is to read him.

There is one last ruse. Although Henry Kaye Bonney's *Life of the Right Reverend Father in God Jeremy Taylor DD* (1815) also took refuge in offering a book of selected passages, in tapping the 'flow of divine truth proceeding from Taylor', and in paying tribute rather than examining the argument, there are some forays into Taylor's countryside. It was too much to hope that Taylor might be met round the next corner; but

Bonney did his best with the mansion of Lord Carbery which Taylor knew so well:

> Golden Grove is seated in one of the finest parts of the celebrated vale 'of winding Towy, Merlin's fabled haunt' and near the banks of that beautiful river, which runs through the grounds. The surrounding country is highly picturesque. It is well wooded: but was much more so in the days of Taylor. Dynevor Castle, the seat of the ancient Prince of South Wales, with its fine hanging groves of venerable oaks, stands about a mile and a half to the north of Golden Grove; Dryslwyn Castle on a rocky hill in the middle of the vale is about three miles to the west, in full view of the principal front of the house; and Grongar Hill forms a striking feature in the prospect, about a mile and a half to the north west. The natural beauties of Golden Grove are scarcely exceeded in any country. In the edition of 1657 of the collection of Polemical Discourses is a vignette, containing a view of Golden Grove, embosomed in woods, with the romantic hills in the back ground to the north-east, not ill delineated. The present house is by no means suitable to the princely property attached to it. It stands on part of the ruins of the ancient mansion; and some of the old walls remain, but not enough to convey any idea of the former place, which has been represented as approaching to magnificence. In the year 1729, the old manor house was burnt down, together with all the furniture, library (excepting two or three hundred volumes that the Duchess of Bolton, then proprietor, had in the house in London) grants, deeds, valuable writings, and family memorials. The name of Taylor is still held in great veneration in that neighbourhood; and there is a walk or avenue near the house, which to this day is called Taylor's walk.[18]

With Bonney showing the way, a search for Jeremy Taylor would have to start chronologically, not with Golden Grove, but in Cambridge, probably in Petty Cury. Barber-shops there are in the town; but no longer Nathanael Tailor's establishment. The font of Trinity Church is missing. Mr Lovering was schoolmaster of Dr Perse's foundation. That school has moved to the edge of the town; but Gonville and Caius College remains sufficiently recognizable, especially the chapel roof, for a seventeenth-century shade to be sought loitering in doorways and at the turnings of stairs. At Uppingham church, the Caroline pulpit, what is left of it, is said to be Jeremy Taylor's furniture: small, the carved oak dark, each of the six sides coffered, with decent, formal designs of round arches and trees of paradise. Here it would be fitting to open *Great Exemplar* at the 'duty that women should nurse their own children',[19] or at the use of the short, mysterious Lord's Prayer,[20] parish sermons, to be found in the book he dedicated to Lord Hatton of Kirby Hall, six miles away. Unlike Golden Grove, and Evelyn's Sayes Court, now lost in

London SE8, and Lord Conway's mansion at Portmore by Lough Neagh, the skeleton of Kirby Hall is conspicuous still.

Of all the homes of Jeremy Taylor's friends, John Evelyn's house and garden by the Thames at Deptford is the greatest loss. A most beautiful place, Pepys called it, in 1665:[21] 'we walked in his garden and a lovely noble ground he hath endeed. And among other rarities, a hive of Bees; so, as being hived in glass, you may see the Bees making their honey and Combs mighty pleasantly.'[22] This was a gift (from the magical Dr Wilkins) which Evelyn had brought home from Oxford.[23] 'And here he showed me his gardens, which are for variety of Evergreens and hedge of Holly, the finest things I ever saw in my life. Thence in his coach to Greenwich and there to my office, all the way having fine discourse of Trees and the nature of vegetables.'[24] 'He read to me very much also of his discourse he hath been many years and now is about, about Guardenage, which will be a most noble and pleasant piece.'[25]

Dr Taylor cannot be found in the vanished oval garden at Sayes Court.[26] But in the silence of the shell of Kirby Hall's great inner court-yard, its Renaissance loggia holding up nothing but the blue sky, its derelict ranges and gables, giant porches and empty parlours, its door-way going nowhere, but ornamented with bands of rusticated ashlar (ordered by the third Christopher Hatton when Jeremy was ordering the organ for his church), in those theatrical façades of stone, untroubled by subsequent history, is the exact scenery of a seventeenth-century encounter between the nobility and the young saint. White and golden upon green lawns, with chimneys tall and hollow, and with deep shadows, Kirby is almost a miracle, an illusion in two dimensions, a piece of architectural space from an elaborate past.[27]

Neither prisoners' quarters in Cardigan Castle nor dungeons in the Tower of London echo with the secrets of Jeremy Taylor. Nor does Hampton Court, where he visited the imprisoned Charles I to receive the last of the king's swag of jewellery. Chepstow Castle with its Marten's Tower is described in Chapter 1; its little chapel is a hollow place. But plain Ballinderry Church, on the once great Lisnagarvey (Lisburn) estates of his friend Edward, Lord Conway, in Co. Antrim, is more eloquent. It is a single, atmospheric, oblong room of villagers' Laudian, built by the new Bishop Jeremy Taylor. A wooden table for worthy communicants, enclosed in Wm Laud's prescribed rails; three-decker pulpit half-way down the nave with its back to the wall; box pews and balcony, all country joinery, elegantly modest; plain bull's-eye glass in square windows; it is the place for learning the *Rules and Advices to the Clergy of the Diocese of Down & Connor, For their Deportment in their Personal and Publick Capacities given by Ier. Taylor Bishop of that Diocese at the*

Visitation at Lisnagarvey. Admirably restored, maintained in its bare severity, Ballinderry's little church is now more severely Protestant than the bishop himself might have chosen. The altar needs a splendid table carpet[28] of Turkeywork, or other prize Oriental throw-over tapis. Best linen, candlesticks, and plump cushions with 'great tassells of crimson silke' would match the ones he put in at Uppingham.[29]

Edmund Gosse, literary critic and author of *Jeremy Taylor* (1904), was closer to the ground than most investigators. He found the letter which Taylor, on his appointment as bishop, wrote 19 December 1660 to James Butler, about to be created Duke of Ormond and reinstated as Lord Lieutenant of Ireland.[30]

> I perceive myself thrown into a place of torment. The country would quickly be very well, if the Scotch ministers were away, at least some of the prime incendiaries. All the nobility and gentry, one only excepted, are very right, but the ministers are implacable . . . They talk of resisting unto blood, and stir up the people to sedition . . . and intend to petition to his Majesty that I may not be their bishop . . . I have invited them to a friendly conference, desired earnestly to speak with them, went to them, sent some of their own to invite them, offered to satisfy them in anything that was reasonable; I preach every Sunday amongst them, somewhere or other; I have courted them with most friendly offers, did all things in pursuance of his Majesty's most gracious declaration; but they refused to speak with me; they have newly covenanted to speak with no bishop, and to endure neither their government nor their persons . . . They threaten to murder me.[31]

Butler, a great survivor, but accustomed to being trapped between competing claims over Irish property and allegiance, wondered how an English Act of Uniformity could work in Ireland.

> Do you know what Gilbert Sheldon the great Bishop of London has written to me about the Act of Uniformity which some minds would like to moderate? 'Tis only a resolute execution of the law that might cure this disease – all other remedies have and will increase it – and tis necessary that they who will not be governed as men by reason and persuasion, should be governed as beasts by power of force: all other courses will be ineffectual, ever have been so, ever will be.'[32]

The resolute Sheldon could not be accused of sending Jeremy Taylor deliberately on an impossible mission which would break his heart; nor could John Drysdale, the most formidable of the intractable Presbyterian ministers, be said to be the death of him.

His London publisher Richard Royston, at the sign of the Angel, *Ivie-lane*, did not work him to death either. The publisher was 'most wary about securing his rights in Taylor's works'.[33] Taylor's own industry was unsparing. 'In all the changes of his life whether in his Welsh retirement or in the midst of the distractions of his Irish see, his pen seems to have been scarcely ever out of his hand.'[34]

If Taylor was not murdered by Presbyterians (he died of a fever) a fully orchestrated murder did take place in Dublin in 1663 at the brilliant opening of 'Pompey. A Tragedy', Mrs Katherine Philips' translation of Pierre Corneille's *Mort de Pompée*, at the brand new theatre in Smock Alley. 'Had not the Duke himself [Ormond] and all the considerable persons here hasten'd its being acted', wrote Matchless Orinda, the blushing playwright, 'I might have had hopes of preventing it, or at least have delay'd it till I was gone hence; but there was no resisting the stream.'[35] Was her wise friend the new Irish bishop part of that irresistible stream? It is clear that Dublin, with its first Restoration theatre, had stolen a march on London.[36] On Tuesday afternoon, 10 February 1663, Pompey was murdered to loud applause.

Between Act III, when Caesar was looking forward to meeting Cleopatra:

> Caes: Antonius, have you this bright Princess seen?
> Ant: Yes, sir, I have, and she's a matchless queen.

and Act IV, in which Ptolemy was discovered plotting with the Gypsies (Egyptians):

> Two miles from hence, six thousand Souldiers wait
> Which I forseeing some new discontents
> Have kept in readiness for all Events.

the Ghost of Pompey enters, *and sings a song* to Cornelia asleep:

> From lasting and unclouded Day
> From joys refined above allay
> And from a spring without decay
> I come by Cynthia's borrowed beams
> To visit my Cornelia's dreams
> And give them yet sublimer Theams.[37]

The music for this entr'acte survives. It has been happily discussed by Curtis Price, who judged the dream sequence to be the only moment 'of this stilted tragedy that could be safely called dramatic'.[38] Nobody knows if the bishop and Mrs Jeremy Taylor were among the considerable persons with the Butlers attending the opening of Katherine's play. As well as in the diocese of Down and Connor, he had important business in Dublin. Smock Alley was just down the hill from Ormond's castle. The fabric of the theatre, with its pit, and three storeys of galleries, its apron, and music loft above the proscenium,[39] lasted for sixty years, and like the insubstantial dramas on stage, has left not a rack behind.

Anthony à Wood, the seventeenth-century biographer, gives this note about Katherine:

> the wife of Jam. Phillips of the Priory of Cardigan esq; daughter of John Fowler of Bucklersbury in Lond. merchant, by Catherine his wife daughter of Dan. Oxenbridge doctor of physic. Which Kath. Fowler alias Philipps (by the way it must be observed) was born in the parish of St Mary Wool-church in Lond. and baptised there on the eleventh of January 1631, bred up in a school at Hackney under Mrs Salmon, where she then much delighted in poetry, notwithstanding brought up in the presbyterian way. After her marriage with Ja. Philipps she went into Ireland with the Viscountess of Dungannon and at Dublin she translated from French into English the tragedy called Pompey, which was several times acted in the new theatre there, with great applause, an 1663 and 64 in which last year it was made public. While she was young she was very forward in English learning, by the blessedness of a quick and happy memory; at riper years she was esteemed the most applauded poetess of our nation, and not without reason, since her name is of a fresh and lively date from a published vol in fol. of her poetical works, bearing the title, *Poems by the most deservedly admired Mrs Katherine Phillips, the matchless Orinda. To which is added Monsieur Corneille's Pompey and Horace tragedies with several other Translations out of French.* Lond 1667. fol. with her picture, a shoulder piece before them standing on a pedestal and underneath written Orinda. These poems which were first printed in Oct an 1664 without the translations are commended to the world by the poems of Abr Cowley, Tho. Flaxman, Jam Tyrrel esq &c. At length she being overtaken with the small pox, died of it in Fleet Street and was buried 22 June 1664, in the church of S. Bennet Sherehog (at the end of Syth's-lane) in London, under a great grave stone where her father, grandfather, and grandmother were before buried.[40]

The bishop and his wife might have attended the first night of *Pompey* out of friendship to Katherine. Taylor's chief business in Dublin, however, was putting his practical solution to Irish sectarianism into practice. There was no way out of torment for any Englishman in trying to reconcile irreconcilable Christians in Down and Connor. But Taylor was too good at intercessory prayer to be defeated by that. He proposed *The Way of Understanding* to deal with religious prejudice and the murderous anger that is born of ignorance and fear; and that meant recovering proper university education in Ireland. Elizabeth I had put an English University in Dublin. Ussher learned there, taught there, crossed the Irish sea; and Trinity College collapsed as an unsuccessful experiment in planting the seeds of learning in uncultivated soil. Jeremy Taylor raised it up, restored it, ordered it, and endowed it 'like a gardener in winter'.[41] That invaluable work is no longer visible in the eighteenth-century architecture of Trinity College, not even in the great Library which came with the Restoration. But the civilized aspiration, both English and Irish, which brought Jeremy Taylor and Robert Boyle to sit down excitedly together at John Evelyn's table, pointed forward not only to the 'peculiar achievements of eighteenth-century Anglo-Irish culture',[42] but to every sign of agreement between Dublin, Westminster and Belfast that is worth pursuing today.

It is curious that so little remains of Jeremy Taylor's places. But there is a marvellous house, which is just the same today as it was when he recovered his happiness. It was his second wife Joanna's home in Wales. Gosse described it: 'a small country house, romantically situated on a hill above the south side of the Bran River, just where that stream narrows its gorge before spreading into the Vale of Towey; it commands a fine view south to the Rhiwiau Hills and the Black Mountain.'[43] Hidden Mandinam! It is exactly right; hospitable, much loved today, and undisturbed by 350 years. The spirit of contentment found Jeremy Taylor perched on a steep Welsh hill under Heaven. His skill in writing was the object of this study. As Gosse observed,[44] theologians who write brilliantly are an object of the deepest suspicion. To have chosen another excellent wife (was she indeed a princess in disguise?) and a home as beautiful as this, can only make him an object of the highest admiration as well.

Admiration inspired the following portrait of Jeremy Taylor. It is an elegy composed in 1667 after the funeral by the enthusiastic and dotty Lemuel Mathew:

> Open great volumn of Fame, open wide,
> Written fair and full on every side;
> To all the world his story show,
> Though all the learned world already know,
> But Fame, be elegant like him;
> Be quaint, be copious; and not obscure;
> And Book unsullied be and trim;
> Have a large character; but specially be sure
> without; within
> No blot, no stain be seen,
> For this to latest ages must endure.
>
> He was the man; so pure, so innocent,
> So careless of forbidden fruit,
> Richly supplied with Natures own recruit;

So masculine his soul, and so content
To be but man; so little bent
To vice, that you might call
Him one not bruis'd by *Adams* fall.
Iv'e never but with admiration seen
His generous looks, his glorious meen,
They made me think of heaven, and of the Saints above.
So Angels live, and smile, and love!

So vast his knowledge, he
Had tasted oft of each allowed tree,
On all their sweets had daily fed
The Bird of Paradise, he kindly bred
A gaulless Dove within the Serpents head:
The Cherubs bow'd, and sheath'd their swords;
For's tongue had all the charm of words,
And all that language and wit affords,
And new and fitter names did wear;
And's lucky pen (as if a pencil 'twere)
Made gold, by guilding it, more golden to appear.

His soul from golden Fetters free,
Rapt to its own dear liberty,
To highest Heaven knew all the wayes,
For there't had been ten thousand times in pray'r and praise
Wrapt in a commendatory prayer,
A mouthful of artic'late Air,
Air rarifyed with hearty zeal
was its first vehicle;
A nimble Cherub quickly flyes
From the best wardrope in the skies;
For soon the news had fill'd those starry rooms,
The Prelat comes;
The welcom guest is quickly cloath'd upon
With Albes of pure etherial lawne;
Subtile as Angels joy, and fine
As is the breath divine:
Clad in that Robe of white,
Of soft and never with'ring light,
He gently passes through
A long admiring row
Of sainted Ghosts to martyr Charle's wain
Come, *Taylor*, come!
Here's *Hammond*, there is *Sanderson*;
The lesser Angels all make room,
And they embrace – ill-natured men! in vain

Ye kept these three from the entreating Soveraign;
Enter bright Soul this general Convention,
This Quire of Priests; hither's thy translation,
Bishop elect! there shortly will be given
To thee a Diocess in the large Hierarchy of Heaven.[45]

Postscript: Orinda's love letter

THERE is no room in these pages to set Jeremy Taylor among his own fellow Anglican scholars, and compare him with the other Caroline divines. This postscript offers instead a test case. It fastens upon seventeenth-century thinking about homosexual relationships. It shows how wittily and gently Taylor could deal with a difficult topic; how original and imaginative he was; and, in contrast to almost all his contemporaries, how his words did not get stuck in the past.

These Caroline divines knew what sins were, and said so; and were in no doubt that the physical expression of homosexual love was sinful as well as criminal. Statute law (25 Henry VIII, c. 6) remained in force from the previous century. It defined homosexuality in terms of buggery. From the pulpit Robert Sanderson (1587–1663) denounced it as 'abominable filthiness'.[1] That is typical of seventeenth-century moral theology. Discussing the choice of the lesser evil, but advising his listeners to choose neither, he cited Lot's predicament (Genesis 19.8):

> And so *Lot* should have done: he should rather have adventured his own life, and theirs too, in protecting *the chastity* of his Daughters, and the safety of his Guests; than have offered the exposal of his *Daughters* to the lusts of the beastly *Sodomites*; though it were to redeem his *guests* from the abuse of fouler and more abominable filthiness.

Also typical was homophobic anxiety, which treated homosexual relationships as serious evidence of national decadence. Sanderson compared the destruction of Sodom and Gomorrah to the calamities of the Civil War:

> Here is a warning for us ... When God sendeth his *Angel* to pluck out his righteous *Lots*, what may *Sodom* expect but *fire* and *brimstone* to be rained down upon them? When he plucketh out the fairest and choicest *flowers* in his garden, and croppeth off the tops of the goodliest *Poppies*:

who can think other, than that he meaneth to lay his *Garden* wast, and to turn it into a wild *Wilderness?* when he undermineth the main *Pillars* of the house, taketh away the very *Props* and *Butteresses* of Church and Common-weal; sweepeth away Religious *Princes*, wise *Senators*, zealous *Magistrates*, painful *Ministers*, men of eminent *ranks*, *gifts*, or *example* . . . Think not, ye *filthy Sodomites*, it is for your own sakes, that ye have been spared so long . . . O the goodness of our God! that would have spared the five Cities of the Salt Sea, if among so many thousands of beastly and filthy persons there had been found but *Ten Righteous ones.*[2]

It was assumed both in Church and State that homosexuality was unnatural. Commenting upon Genesis 19.5–7:

And they called unto Lot, and said unto him, Where are the men which came in to thee this night? Bring them out unto us that we may know them. And Lot went out at the doore unto them, & shut the doore after him, And said, I pray you, brethren, doe not so wickedly.[3]

Simon Patrick (1626–1707) wrote:

'that we may know them' A modest word for a lewd Fact. Some indeed will have it understood simply, of their examining what they were, whence they came, and what their business was. Which might perhaps be their pretence; but *Lot's* answer to them, *ver.* 7, 8. interprets their meaning to be filthy. 'doe not so wickedly' As to break the Rights of Hospitality; and violate the Laws of Nature.[4]

An example of animus against homosexuality was included in the explanation that every sort of vice was weak and womanish, of which a manly Christian should surely be ashamed. Henry Hammond (1605–60) contrasted the 'civil, manlike exercise' of Christian virtue with 'those womanish, sluggish abusers' and noted:

an unmanlike, impotent, effeminate heart; all its actions are mixed with so much passion and weakness, they are so raw and womanish, that it would grieve one to behold a fair, comely manlike Christian . . . one who had undertaken to be a champion for Christ, led away and abused and baffled by every pelting paltry lust.[5]

These writers, with the exception of Patrick, grew up in the reign of James I, whose homosexual orientation must have been obvious to them. Historians no longer find it necessary to hold their tongues.[6] It must have been specially obvious to Lancelot Andrewes (1555–1626) who preached before the king and the Court at Whitehall for eighteen years. Not once did that prelate say anything in public on this subject. If he had an opinion about the promiscuous nature of the king's homosexual friendships, or of what was unseemly about favouritism, he kept it private; but he plainly redoubled his own penitential exercises in *Preces Privatae* on behalf of a gay court.[7] This combination of silence with the willingness to suffer in one's conscience *for others* (described by Jeremy Taylor, but also by Dietrich Bonhoeffer, as 'bearing guilt for the sake of our neighbour', the mark of a mature conscience which has been set free by Christ[8]) is instructive. It suggests that the Caroline divines might be found agreeing that the place for this topic was private confession rather than public debate.

They had been relieved of centuries of having to judge the case in Church Courts (with a finely graded tariff of penances, all the way from snogging choirboys to nuns with appliances). Buggery was on the statute book now, as a felony punishable by death. It was, consequently, simply unmentionable; and no doubt it was an accusation as frightening as sorcery and witchcraft, with which it might be linked. Trevor-Roper accused the seventeenth-century Church of England of being lukewarm about witchcraft, a reluctant compliment.[9] Was it also to be blamed for becoming discreet about homosexual relationships?

Calling a spade a spade, a phrase used by Jeremy Taylor in *Ductor Dubitantium* when he was dealing with outspoken sermons before kings, was not laudable, he argued, because public reproof of royalty 'can very hardly be done without diminution of their dignity'; because such utterances amount to 'publick *seditions*, not *sermons*'; because if the 'reproof of Kings be in Pulpits', the king cannot answer back. It was imprudent, because the king, far from being helped in private, 'may be provok'd by your ungentle Sermon, or may be hardened by your fire'.

> And if the Bishop calls a spade a spade, it is very possible the People may do so too, for they are soon taught to despise their rulers. If once they come to despise their Prince, they will soon unclasp his royal Mantle.[10]

There is to be found in Taylor only one reference to 1 Corinthians 6.9f. (He is silent on Leviticus 18.22 and 20.13; and on Romans 1.27.) In *Unum Necessarium* he clears the decks for the repentance of sins by setting out a catalogue of them, which includes, under Wantonness:

> Every thing by which a Man or Woman is abominable in their lusts; to which the lusts not to be named are reducible: amongst which *St Paul* reckons the effeminate and abusers of themselves with Mankind; that is, they that do, and they that suffer such things . . . *Mollities* or softness is the name by which this vice is known, and the Persons guilty of it, are also called the abominable.[11]

He goes on to explain that his catalogue comprises the works of the flesh which are less notorious than the obvious ones like adultery. But for all that they are 'sometimes esteem'd innocent, often excused, commonly neglected, always undervalued' their scriptural reward is undoubtedly the lake of fire and brimstone. He does not deviate from that official line. He has, however, one chance to speak off the record, as it were, in the role of a private spiritual director rather than public casuist. There he reveals another world, a world in which official faith has been informed by love.

Before leaving the Pauline text to look at Taylor's more important contribution, it is useful to observe how John Hales (1584–1656) in the course of a sermon which argued for the 'gracious interpreting of each others imperfections' commented on 1 Corinthians 6.9f.:

> Know yee not that the unrighteous shall not inherite the kingdome of God? Bee not decceived: neither fornicators, nor idolators, nor adulterers, nor effeminate, nor abusers of themselves with mankinde, nor theeves, nor covetous, nor drunkards, nor revilers, nor extortioners, shall inherit the kingdom of God.[12]

Hales had been discussing how important it was that those who were intellectually weak, 'who out of *weakness* of understanding fall into many errors', deserved 'to be received & cherisht by us'. Next he turned to the morally weak, 'a man of *prophane* and wicked life, one more dangerously ill then the former, have we any *recipe* for this man?'

> The condition of conversing with heathen men, be they never so wicked is permitted unto Christians by our Apostle himself, whereas with this man all commerce seems by the same Apostle to be quite cut off. For in the 1 *Cor.*6. St. *Paul* distinguishes between the *fornicators* of this world, and the *fornicators* which were Brethren. But saith he, *if a brother be a fornicator or a thief, or a railer with such a one partake not, no not so much as to eat.* Wherefore the case of this person seems to be desperate. Is Christ contrary to *Paul*? It is the main drift of Christ's message and unavoidably he is to converse, yea, eat and drink with allsorts of sinners. We must therefore entertain even near friendship with such a one to discover him.[13]

> Christian curtesie spreads it self to all sorts of men, to the *Infidel*, to the gross *notorious sinner*, then will it without any streining at all come home to all the *infirmities* of our weaker brethren.[14]

The sermon breathes that tender and sociable spirit of goodness which Hales loved to describe. Nor would he 'pass by that *singular moderation of this Church of ours*'. What is contained here is a sense of the style of the pastoral care that would be recommended for cases of homosexual relationship. It was certainly being regarded as an error, but one which deserved very courteous and patient treatment, because we are to look for the good in everyone. How different Richard Baxter (1615–91)! In *Directions for Weak distempered Christians* there is never any escape for the weak Christian, or (even worse) for the seeming Christian, in page after merciless page of unflattering comparison with the strong Christian. No wonder in the end that Baxter was complaining about the way the strong Christian's holiness 'maketh him an eyesore to the *ungodly world*'.[15] Baxter's heroes were not just uninviting; they were simply impossible for the carnally frail world to join.

The single most rewarding document from the Caroline divines is the letter written by Jeremy Taylor to 'the most ingenious and excellent M. K. P.', Mrs Katherine Philips. It was subsequently published under the title *A Discourse of the Nature and Offices of Friendship* (1657). Reginald Heber described it as a 'splendid and powerful little essay' valuable for its 'good sense and practical wisdom'. But nowadays it is admitted that Katherine was a lesbian, and that as a married woman she was consulting the clergyman she loved and trusted about the nature of her special friendships, and how far she could go. He understood what she was asking and why. So he composed a letter which anyone could read without suspecting that the context was homosexual love. He wrote without scolding. He encouraged her to fasten upon everything that is noble and worthy in friendship.

Katherine was eighteen years younger than him. 'Brought up in the presbyterian way',[16] she was married ('but they were all deceiv'd') to James Philips of Cardigan, one of Cromwell's staff officers. Known as 'the matchless Orinda', in her literary circle she was celebrated for her passionate love poetry. To her special friend 'my excellent *Lucasia*' (Anne Owen) she wrote:

> I did not live until this time
>   Crown'd my felicity,
> When I could say without a crime,
>   I am not thine, but Thee.
>
> This Carcass breath'd, and walkt, and slept,
>   So that the World believ'd
> There was a Soul the Motions kept;
>   But they were all deceiv'd.
>
> For as a Watch by art is wound
>   To motion, such was mine:
> But never had *Orinda* found
>   A Soul till she found thine;
>
> Which now inspires, cures and supplies,
>   And guides my darkned Breast:

> For thou art all that I can prize,
> My Joy, my Life, my Rest.
>
> No Bridegrooms nor Crown-conquerors mirth
> To mine compar'd can be:
> They have but pieces of this Earth,
> I've all the World in thee.
>
> Then let our Flames still light and shine,
> And no false fear controul,
> As innocent as our Design,
> Immortal as our Soul.[17]

The giggles of the bridegroom in verse five (James Philips, rejoicing with the crown-conqueror Oliver himself) refers to Katherine's marriage, celebrated in the summer of 1648 during Cromwell's successful Welsh campaign, when she was not yet seventeen, and the bridegroom 54. Taylor, an army chaplain aged 35, had been a Royalist prisoner in Cardigan Castle, and was now living at Golden Grove, forty miles away in the vale of Towy. In case the love being protested in this poem is thought to be exclusive, as well as immortal, similar poems of loving intensity were also composed by Katherine. Thus for Rosania (Mary Aubrey) she begins:

> Soul of my Soul, my Joy, my Crown, my *Friend*

So when she asks Jeremy Taylor 'how far a dear and perfect friendship is authorized by the principles of Christianity', he begins by teasing her: 'it is not so much as named in the New Testament; and our Religion takes no notice of it.' (He knows exactly what she means by a dear and perfect friendship.) 'You think it strange; but read on.'[18]

What the New Testament is about, of course, is Charity, that is, 'friendship to all the World'. 'When men contract friendships, they enclose the Commons; and what Nature intended should be Everymans we make proper to two or three.' Christianity restores universal friendship. 'He who was to treat his enemies with forgiveness was to have all Friends.' Nevertheless, friendship is bound to be limited 'because we are so'. We cannot include everyone, like the sun which is 'indifferent to the Negro or the cold Russian, to them that dwell under the Line, and them that stand near the Tropicks, the scalded Indian, or the poor boy that shakes at the foot of the *Riphean* hills'. But:

> There must be in friendship something to distinguish it from a
> Companion, and a countryman, from a School-fellow or a gossip, from
> a sweet-heart or a fellow-traveller: friendship may look in at any one of
> these Doors, but it stays not anywhere till it come to be the best thing

in the World: And when we consider that one Man is not better then another, neither towards God nor towards Man, but by doing better and braver things, we shall also see that which is most beneficent is also most excellent . . . a fool cannot be relied upon for Counsel, nor a vicious person for the advantage of Vertue, nor a beggar for relief, nor a stranger for conduct, nor a tattler to keep a Secret, nor a pitiless person trusted with my complaint, nor a covetous man with my Child's Fortune, nor a false person without a Witness, nor a suspicious person with a private Design; nor him that I fear with the Treasures of my Love: But he that is wise and vertuous, rich and at hand, close and merciful, free of his Money and tenacious of a Secret, open and ingenuous, true and honest, is of himself an excellent Man; and therefore fit to be lov'd.

Taylor was not being mercenary, but just his usual practical self, in noticing that my best friend is the one who can do me the most good when I need it. Physical attractions and wealth are the least important considerations for choosing such a friend.

A pretty face or a smooth chin? I confess it is possible to be a friend to one that is ignorant and pitiable, handsome and good for nothing, that eats well and drinks deep; and I love him with a fondness or a pity, but it cannot be a noble friendship.

Katherine, however, wanted to know, besides all the worthy stuff, if she could fancy her friend. He agreed that there were 'little partialities' and 'innocent passion' to take account of.

Even our blessed Saviour himself loved St *John* and *Lazarus* by a special love . . . and of the young man that spake well and wisely to Christ, it is affirm'd Jesus loved him: that is he fancied the Man, and his Soul had a certain cognation and similitude of temper and inclination . . . and a witty answer may first strike the flint and kindle a spark, which if it falls upon tender and compliant natures may grow into a Flame; but this will never be maintained at the rate of friendship, unless it be fed by pure materials, by worthinesses which are the food of friendship.

He warned Katherine of the sort of 'tinsel dressing' relationships 'which will shew bravely by Candle-light, and do excellently in a Mask' and of fantasies 'that build castles in the air, and look upon friendship as upon a fine romance'.

How far can friendship go? He was immediately reminded of David and Jonathan, 'both good men . . . they stood like two feet supporting one Body', and asked how far Jonathan's willingness 'to lay down his Life for his friend' expected heroism of every friendship. He indicated some of the boundaries. We should 'love our friends as we love ourselves' and go as far 'as our friend fairly needs in all things where we

are not tied up by a former Duty, to God, to ourselves, or some pre-
obliging relative . . . No friendship can excuse a sin . . . a Man may not
be perjured for his friend . . . he that does a base thing in Zeal for his
friend, burns the golden Thread that ties their Hearts together.'

The natural affinity of parents and children, the society of brothers
and sisters, are relationships distinct from friendship; Taylor concluded
that 'friend is more than Brother, and I suppose no one doubts that
David loved *Jonathan* far more than he loved his Brother *Eliab*'. But, and
here was the question Katherine needed answering, can a friend be
more than husband or wife?

> to which I answer, that it can never be reasonable, or just, prudent or
> lawful: but the reason is, because Marriage is the Queen of friendships,
> in which there is a communication of all that can be communicated by
> friendship: and it being made sacred by Vowes and Love, by Bodies and
> Souls, by Interest and Custome, by Religion and by Laws, by common
> Counsels, and common Fortunes; it is the Principal in the kind of
> friendship, and the measure of all the rest.

Taylor here touched upon how friends might have to cope with marital
incapacity (the spiritual director was writing to his dear young friend
with an ancient husband): 'so must these best friends, when one is
useless . . . they must love ever and pray ever.' Then, in what is,
perhaps, his tenderest message to her:

> Add to this, that other friendships are parts of this, they are Marriages
> too, less indeed than the other, because they cannot, must not be all that
> endearment which the other is; yet that being the Principal, is the
> measure of the rest, and are all to be honoured by like Dignities, and
> measured by the same Rules, and conducted by their portion of the same
> Laws: but as friendships are Marriages of the Soul, and of Fortunes, and
> interests, and Counsels; so are they Brotherhoods too; and I often think
> of the excellencies of friendship in the Words of *David*, who certainly was
> the best friend in the world: 'it is good and it is pleasant that brethren
> should live like friends.' Such friendships are the beauties of Society, and
> the pleasure of Life, and the festivity of minds: and whatsoever can be
> spoken of Love, which is God's eldest Daughter, can be said of virtuous
> Friendships.

He turned to friendships between the sexes, which, if they are
prudent and honourable, are not to be frightened by gossip. Then he
praised women for their special capacity for friendship:

> A female friend in some cases is not as good a counsellor as a wise man
> . . . but a woman can love as passionately . . . and retain a secret as
> faithfully . . . and she can die for her friend as well as the bravest Roman

knight . . . we cannot grudge to virtuous and brave women that they be
partners in a noble friendship . . . we may as well allow women as men
to be friends.

He concluded with ten guiding instructions, beginning: 'The first law
of friendship is, they must neither ask of their friend what is undecent;
nor grant it if themselves be asked' – but ending – 'so must the love
of friends sometimes be *refreshed with material and low caresses*; lest by
striving to become too divine it become less humane: it must be allowed
its share of both.'

The published letter, in Jeremy Taylor's customary style, contains
numerous quotations in Greek and Latin. But they are translated into
English couplets, something not to be found elsewhere in Taylor's work.
Katherine was the poetess and translator most likely thus to have
adorned her greatly loved friend's advice.

> They loved each other with a love
> That did in all things equal prove.

She would have wept over it too. She knew he would tell her to behave
herself, would tell her to be good, that the loveliest and noblest things
are costly, and that real friendship contains all that she can desire. Poor
Orinda! She invented The Society of Friendship.

If the Caroline divines were chiefly silent about homosexual
relationships, it was not just for reasons of patriotic prudence at the
court of King James. They would discuss unlawful love, as Sanderson
did in his *Cases of Conscience*[19] (a far-fetched case, whether a married
woman can promise a married man to wed if both their spouses were
to die before them). A preference for the privacy of counselling, where
the persuasive appeal of John Hales and Jeremy Taylor might be effective, rather than a public hearing, in which the Church would inevitably
be found lining herself up with the law and the popular hostility,
counted with them; so that a national campaign for gay liberation they
would think intrusive and counter-productive, and for Christians to join
in it discourteous, a threat to the weaker brethren. As for Christians
betraying the sexual orientation of fellow-Christians, they would
describe it as destructive of friendship, and therefore infamous and
despicable.

Notes and references

REGINALD HEBER was the nineteenth-century editor of Jeremy Taylor. His work was revised and corrected by Charles Page Eden with the help of Alexander Taylor. *The Whole Works of the Right Reverend Jeremy Taylor, DD, with a Life of the Author*, edited by Reginald Heber, revised and corrected by Charles Page Eden (10 volumes; London, 1847–52), is the edition used here; and referred to as Works, followed by volume and page number.

The present study began not with Heber–Eden but with a single-folio third edition of *Ductor Dubitantium* (printed by R. Norton for R. Royston 1676) belonging to the remarkable library of Wells Theological College, and with a quarto first edition (1649) of *Great Exemplar*, in Wells Cathedral Library. The unrevised and uncorrected spelling of the seventeenth century keeps quietly insisting that Jeremy Taylor, who is much more modern than Victorian, has his own *Sitz im Leben*. So although the page references of Heber–Eden have been stuck to in these notes, old spelling has been preferred in the text. The question is: which old spelling? A work like *Great Exemplar* ran to four editions during Taylor's lifetime (1649, 1653, 1657, 1667). It seems to me doubtful that Taylor saw the fourth edition through the press. He was dying in Ireland. *Great Exemplar* of 1657 might be considered Taylor's own best shot at a satisfactory text; it is used here. The stability of sense, and of vocabulary, is obvious throughout all the editions; the spelling and punctuation has an antinomian air. Like Taylor's drunken man in Chapter 1, their tongues are sometimes 'full as spunges', sometimes 'full of sponges'. My policy with each of Taylor's works was to start with his first edition and to stop with the last edition he might have corrected. The Library of Gonville and Caius College, Cambridge, has all of this, and more, treasure.

Coleridge loved and defended every semi-colon in Jeremy Taylor's long sentences. Gosse swore it would be an act of real editorial kindness to mend the punctuation to make the stuff intelligible. Taylor piles phrases to make them balance, to make them roll, to make them climb, accumulate and fall. It is possible to expose his rhetoric by setting his prose as if it were verse; or as if it were liturgical prayer. It is usually both. At Cambridge he was Rhetoric Praelector. Sometimes the *shape* of what he was saying out loud in his sermons is so revealed by the printed profile of short lines, that it is to be wondered if that is exactly how he wrote them down on paper. Where it seemed appropriate, I have centred the text, to expose the theological architecture.

1. TO BEGIN HOLY LIVING

1 Works, Vol. III, *Holy Living*, p. 24.
2 R. Gough, *The History of Myddle* (London: Penguin Books, 1981), pp. 42f.
3 Works, Vol. III, p. 1.
4 Titus 2.11–13, Revised English Bible.
5 Works, Vol. VIII, *Collection of Offices*, p. 588.
6 Works, Vol. III, p. 44.
7 Henry Vaughan, Silurist, *Silex Scintillans or Sacred Poems and Private Ejaculations* (London, 1650), p. 68.
8 Works, Vol. III, pp. 1–3.
9 L. Wittgenstein, *Tractatus Logico-Philosophicus* (London: Routledge & Kegan Paul, 1922), 6.54.
10 Works, Vol. III, p. 47.
11 Ibid., p. 55.
12 Works, Vol. IV, p. 184, echoing Tertullian, *De Jejunio*, cap. IX, on the diet of Daniel, *leguminum pabulum et aquae potum* (Daniel 1.12).
13 Ibid., p. 191; cf. Clement, *Paedagogus*, Book II, ch. 1, 'On eating'.
14 Ibid., p. 199.
15 Works, Vol. X, *Ductor Dubitantium*, pp. 631–6.
16 François de Sales, *Introduction à la Vie dévote* (1619), Part I, ch. 3.
17 Tertullian, *Ad Uxorem*, Book I, ch. 1.7–14.
18 Works, Vol. III, p. 68.
19 Works, Vol. IV, *The Marriage Ring*, pp. 207–33, esp. pp. 224 and 226.
20 Works, Vol. III, p. 57.
21 Ibid., pp. 65f.
22 Ibid., p. 113.
23 Works, Vol. X, pp. 415–40.
24 Iris Murdoch, *The Sovereignty of Good* (London: Routledge & Kegan Paul, 1970), p. 95.
25 Works, Vol. III, pp. 69f.; where he refers to Apuleius (author of *The Golden Ass*), *De Demon. Socratis*, p. 670.
26 See Murdoch, pp. 78f.
27 Works, Vol. III, p. 72.
28 Ibid., p. 77.
29 Ibid., p. 74.
30 Cf. Matthew 11.25.
31 Ecclesiasticus 35.17 (the primary text for *The Cloud of Unknowing* in its treatment of humility, chs XIII–XV, as the threshold of contemplative prayer, chs XXXVII–XXXVIII. Taylor had probably not read the fourteenth-century English mystics).
32 James 4.6.
33 Cf. Matthew 7.3; Luke 6.41.
34 Cf. John 8.7.
35 Cf. John 13.15.
36 Works, Vol. VII, *Unum Necessarium*, Preface, pp. 15f.

37 Works, Vol. III, p. 77.

38 Hebrews 12.28f.; and *Sermon VII, VIII* and *IX*, Works, Vol. IV, pp. 85–117.

39 Works, Vol. III, p. 81.

40 Ibid., p. 79.

41 Ibid., p. 23.

42 Ibid., p. 88.

43 Edmund Gosse, *Jeremy Taylor* (London: Macmillan, 1904), p. 219 and footnote, attributing the epithet to Wm Mason.

44 Shakespeare, *King Lear*, III.2, lines 10–13.

45 P. Reps, *Zen Flesh, Zen Bones* (London: Penguin Books, 1971), p. 19.

46 George Eliot, *Silas Marner* (1861), ch. XIX.

47 Works, Vol. III, p. 86.

48 Ibid., p. 100; cf. Psalm 129 *Saepe expugnaverunt* v. 3; cf. Plutarch, *Consol. ad Apollon.*, tom. vi.398.

49 Works, Vol. III, p. 98.

50 Works, Vol. I, p. cccxxiii.

51 Works, Vol. III, p. 87; in *Collection of Offices*, the form of prayer for prisoners includes 'give us patience and a way for us to escape': Works, Vol. VIII, p. 666.

52 Ibid., p. 91.

53 Ibid., p. 93.

54 Ibid., p. 87; Philippians 4.11.

55 Horace, *Odes*, Book I.11 (*Tu ne quaesieris*).

56 Works, Vol. III, p. 87.

57 Romans 8.28.

58 Works, Vol. III, p. 103.

59 See, for example, Origen, *Contra Celsus*, Book VII, ch. 24; John Chrysostom, *Homilies, On Matthew*, XXI and XXII; S. Kierkegaard, *The Lilies of the Field and the Birds of the Air* (1849) in *Christian Discourses*, trans. W. Lowrie (Princeton University Press, 1961); P. Tillich, *The Shaking of the Foundations* (New York: C. Scribner's Sons, 1948).

60 Works, Vol. III, p. 104.

61 Ibid., p. 100.

62 Ibid., pp. 98f.

63 Ibid., p. 90.

64 Ibid., p. 88.

65 Ibid., p. 101.

66 Ibid., p. 85.

67 Ibid., p. 96.

68 Ibid., p. 110.

2. THE TEARS OF ACHILLES

1 Works, Vol. IV, *The Marriage Ring*, p. 232; cf. Homer, *Odyssey*, Book X.237.

2 C. Marlowe, *The Tragicall History of D. Faustus* (1604), Act V.i.107f.

3 Works, Vol. IV, *The Foolish Exchange*, p. 570, quoting in Greek, Homer, *Iliad*, Book III.156f.

4 Ibid., Vol. VIII, *Via Intelligentiae*, p. 368.

5 But see also Works, Vol. II, p. 124; Vol. III, pp. 198, 318; Vol. IV, pp. 223, 327, 387; Vol. VII, p. 508; Vol. VIII, p. 435; Vol. X, pp. 116, 143, 463.

6 In the sermon *The Foolish Exchange*, for example (Works, Vol. IV, pp. 547–72), half of the 30 quotations in Greek or Latin are not translated.

7 An instance of a mistaken translation by Taylor (Works, Vol. IX, *Ductor Dubitantium*, p. 16) comes in the slanging match between Achilles and Hector, in which, according to Taylor, Achilles says: 'I would my *conscience* would give me leave to eat thy very flesh.' A better translation would be: 'I wish I *had the guts* to chop you up and eat you raw!' (*Iliad*, Book XXII.346). There is also a mistaken following of Lancelot Andrewes, averring that Simoisius '*refus'd* to nourish his loving parents, and therefore liv'd but a short life' (Works, Vol. X, p. 463). But Book IV.477 merely recorded that life was simply too short for the young man to repay his parents for their loving care: he fell to the spear of Ajax in an early engagement in the *Iliad*.

8 Works, Vol. II, *Great Exemplar*, p. 124.

9 *Odyssey*, Book XI.488f.

10 *Iliad*, Book III.156f.

11 *Odyssey*, Book XIV.330; Book XIX.299; cf. Works, Vol. IV, p. 620; Vol. X, pp. 109ff.

12 *Iliad*, Book III.308; cf. Works, Vol. VIII, p. 437.

13 Ibid., Book II.24; cf. Works, Vol. III, p. 121. For other examples of familiar classical quotation, see also: Works, Vol. III, pp. 52, 121; Vol. IV, pp. 119, 213, 220, 283, 418; Vol. VII, p. 508; Vol. VIII, p. 254; Vol. X, p. 584.

14 D. Coleridge (ed.), *Notes on English Divines by Samuel Taylor Coleridge* (London: Edward Moxon, 1853), Vol. I, p. 198.

15 R. Pfeiffer, *History of Classical Scholarship* (Oxford: Clarendon Press, 1968), p. 144.

16 L. D. Reynolds and N. G. Wilson, *Scribes and Scholars* (Oxford: Clarendon Press, 2nd edn, 1974), p. 35.

17 Works, Vol. IV, *Of Growth in Sin*, p. 536.

18 Homer, *Iliad*, Book II.384; Book X.294.

19 Works, Vol. IV, *Death-Bed Repentance*, p. 394.

20 Homer, *Odyssey*, Book XVIII.339; Book IX.291; cf. Works, Vol. VIII, p. 326.

21 *Iliad*, Book XXIII.222.

22 Works, Vol. III, *Holy Dying*, p. 447.

23 Ibid., p. 315; Vol. VII, pp. 151, 428.

24 Homer, *Iliad*, Book I.15, 40; cf. Works, Vol. I, pp. 9, 16. Gosse, *Jeremy Taylor*, p. 223: 'he forces [the classics] to illustrate him, generally very much against their will.'

25 Works, Vol. IV, p. 223.

26 Homer, *Iliad*, Book XV.16.

27 Ibid., Book XIV.205; 209 *et passim*.

28 *Odyssey*, Book VIII.240–366. For other examples of Taylor quoting out of context, see: Works, Vol. II, pp. 428, 445; Vol. III, p. 125; Vol. V, p. 55; Vol. VIII, p. 437.

29 R. Watkins, *Moonlight at The Globe* (London: Michael Joseph, 1946), pp. 49f.

30 Shakespeare, *Julius Caesar*, Act II.i.73f.

31 Works, Vol. VIII, *Frances Carbery's Funeral*, p. 435. (Pepys reported in his *Diary*, 31 December 1663: 'The Turks very fur entered into Germany and all that part of the world.')

32 Works, Vol. II, p. 393.

33 Homer, *Iliad*, Book XIII.6.

34 Ibid., Book XXIV.10.

35 Works, Vol. IV, *The House of Feasting*, p. 185.

36 Ibid., p. 189.

37 Works, Vol. II, p. 646.

38 Homer, *Odyssey*, Book X.291–306; H. Baumann, *The Greek Plant World in Myth, Art and Literature*, trans. Stearn (1993), p. 110.

39 D. Page, *Folktales in Homer's Odyssey* (Cambridge, MA: Harvard University Press, 1973), pp. 51–66.

40 Homer, *Odyssey*, Book IV.221.

41 H. Wine, *Claude: The Poetic Landscape* (London: National Gallery Publications, 1994), pp. 12, 43.

42 Works, Vol. VII, *Deus Justificatus*, p. 508; also Vol. IV, p. 418.

43 Homer, *Iliad*, Book XIX.86f.

44 Cf. C. Westermann, *Genesis I–XI* (London: SPCK, 1984), p. 211.

45 Works, Vol. IV, *Miracles of Divine Mercy*, p. 635.

46 Ibid., p. 209.

47 Works, Vol. VII, pp. 497f.

48 Ibid., p. 521.

49 Ibid., *Unum Necessarium*, p. 282.

50 Works, Vol. II, p. 36 commends the *Florilegium* of John Stobaeus, an anthology of stock classical quotations.

51 Works, Vol. I, p. ccxlvi. In *Notes on English Divines by Samuel Taylor Coleridge*, Vol. I, p. 194 the exuberance of Taylor's classical quotations is complained of as: 'a procession of all the nobles, and magnates of the land in their grandest, richest, and most splendid *paraphernalia*: but the total impression is weakened by the multitude of lacqueys and ragged intruders running in and out between the ranks.'

52 Works, Vol. II, p. 469.

53 Horace, *Odes*, Book I.4.15; Book II.16.25, 11.11f.

54 Works, Vol. I, pp. 71–98. Taylor's *Letter to the most ingenious and excellent M. K. P.* (Mrs Katherine Philips) contains many classical quotations, fourteen of which have been translated into English couplets without attribution. Taylor nowhere else translated his sources into verse; but the ingenious Katherine was well known for her verse translations. These adornments in his letter about friendship are plainly in her style, and could be her work. Classical love poetry was fashionable in the literary circle of 'the matchless Orinda'. (See Postscript, pp. 186–90 above.)

55 Horace, *Odes*, Book III.29.57.

56 Horace, *Epistles*, Book I.16.60.

57 Works, Vol. II, p. 465.

58 Ibid., pp. 131f.

59 Tertullian, *De Spectaculis*, ch. 8; the authorship of *The Passion of S. Perpetua* is usually attributed to Tertullian.

3. POLITICAL HOLY LIVING

1 See J. Morrill, *The Nature of the English Revolution* (London and New York: Longman, 1993), ch. 7, pp. 148–75.

2 H. B. Porter, *Jeremy Taylor, Liturgist* (London: Alcuin Club/SPCK, 1979), pp. 158–60.

3 Works, Vol. III, *Holy Living*, p. 114.

4 Romans 13.1, and referring also to Titus 3.1; 1 Peter 2.13; Hebrews 13.17; 2 Corinthians 2.9.

5 Works, Vol. III, p. 119.

6 *S Benedicti Regula*, cap. v, 'De Obedientia'.

7 Works, Vol. III, p. 120.

8 Ibid., p. 122.

9 C. Russell, *The Causes of the English Civil War* (Oxford: Clarendon Press, 1990), p. 148.

10 Morrill, p. 24.

11 The Tanner MSS, 58, shows Charles I consulting his clergy in August 1647 on religious toleration, with Jeremy Taylor a signatory. See C. J. Stranks, *The Life and Writings of Jeremy Taylor* (London: SPCK, 1952), pp. 72f.

12 Works, Vol. IX, *Ductor Dubitantium*, p. 36.

13 C. Carlton, *Charles I, the Personal Monarch* (London: Routledge, 2nd edn, 1995), ch. 11.

14 J. R. Tanner, *English Constitutional Conflicts of the Seventeenth Century, 1603–1689* (Cambridge University Press, 1928), ch. 5; Morrill, ch. 15, pp. 285–306.

15 Works, Vol. III, p. 123.

16 Russell, pp. 131f.

17 Works, Vol. III, p. 125.

18 Carlton, p. 157.

19 C. Hill, *Society and Puritanism in Pre-Revolutionary England* (Peregrine edition; Penguin Books, 1984), ch. VIII.

20 Ibid., ch. XI.

21 W. S. Holdsworth, *History of English Law* (London: Methuen, 3rd edn, 1922), Vol. IV, p. 353.

22 C. Wilson, *England's Apprenticeship, 1603–1763* (London: Longman, 2nd edn, 1984), ch. 5, pp. 89–107.

23 Russell, ch. 7, pp. 161–84.

24 Wilson, p. 95.

25 J. Bunyan, *The Pilgrim's Progress*, 'The Town of Vanity'.

26 Russell, p. 176.

27 C. Hill, *The World Turned Upside Down* (Penguin Books, 1984), pp. 272f.

28 G. Davies, *The Oxford History of England: The Early Stuarts, 1603–1660* (Oxford: Clarendon Press, 1936), p. 80.

29 Works, Vol. III, p. 125.

30 Ibid., p. 141.

31 J. Locke, *Two Treatises of Civil Government* (1690), Book II, cap. 6.55.

32 J. L. Houlden, *Paul's Letters from Prison* (London: SCM Press, 1977), pp. 335f.

33 Works, Vol. III, pp. 126–28.

34 Stranks, p. 109.

35 Works, Vol. VIII, *Frances Carbery's Funeral*, pp. 425–50.

36 Gosse, p. 227.

37 Works, Vol. III, *Holy Dying*, p. 329.

38 Works, Vol. II, *Great Exemplar*, pp. 72–81.

39 Ibid., p. 67.

40 Wilson, ch. 3, 'The trade of England: the seventeenth-century crisis', pp. 36–65; and ch. 6.

41 Samuel Pepys, *Diary*, 15 January 1665.

42 George Herbert, *The Countrey Parson* (first published 1652), ch. XXXII, 'The Parson's Surveys'. Professor Wilson noted a Somerset clergyman's answer to unemployment, Richard Eburne's *A Plaine pathway to the Plantations* (1624): see Wilson, p. 118.

43   Works, Vol. III, pp. 189, 191.
44   Works, Vol. X, pp. 478–90.
45   Ibid., p. 482.
46   Helen Oppenheimer, *The Marriage Bond* (London: Faith Press, 1976) and *Marriage* (London: Mowbray, 1990).
47   Homer, *Odyssey*, Book VI.180–185, translated by T. E. Lawrence (1932).
48   Works, Vol. III, p. 128.
49   Ibid., p. 132.
50   C. F. Evans, *Saint Luke* (London: SCM Press, 1990), p. 661.
51   Works, Vol. VII, *Unum Necessarium*, p. 471.
52   Works, Vol. III, p. 138.

4. MERELY SPIRITUAL POWER

1   Works, Vol. I, p. cccxxv.
2   *Diary of John Evelyn FRS*, 25 December 1655.
3   Ibid., 25 March 1657.
4   Ibid., 23 May 1658.
5   Kenneth Fincham (ed.), *The Early Stuart Church 1603–1642* (London: Macmillan, 1993), p. 45.
6   Works, Vol. IX, Preface to *Ductor Dubitantium*, p. xi.
7   Works, Vol. X, *Ductor Dubitantium*, p. 282.
8   Ibid., pp. 393f.
9   1 Timothy 3.3.
10   Works, Vol. X, p. 267.
11   Works, Vol. I, *Rules and Advices*, p. 107.
12   Works, Vol. X, p. 272.
13   Ibid., p. 274.
14   *Odyssey*, Book XIX.109ff.: 'as the glory of some god-fearing king of a populous powerful race, by virtue of whose equity and good governance the masses prosper and the dark earth abounds with wheat or barley and the trees bow down with fruit' (trans. T. E. Lawrence).
15   Works, Vol. X, p. 261.
16   Ibid., p. 250.
17   Ibid., p. 295.
18   Hill, *Society and Puritanism in Pre-Revolutionary England*, p. 348.
19   Works, Vol. IX, p. xi.
20   Works, Vol. X, p. 319.
21   Works, Vol. IX, pp. xiif.
22   Works, Vol. X, p. 338.
23   Ibid., p. 392.
24   Ibid., p. 390.
25   Works, Vol. II, *Great Exemplar*, pp. 346f.
26   Works, Vol. IV, *Of Growth in Grace*, pp. 496–519.
27   Works, Vol. II, p. 475; Vol. IV, p. 83; Cassian, *Collations*, ix.32.
28   Works, Vol. IV, p. 496.
29   Ibid., p. 498; cf. 2 Peter 3.18.
30   Ibid., p. 512.
31   Ibid., p. 514.

5. DEVOUT HOLY LIVING

1 D. Cressy, *Literacy and the Social Order: Reading and Writing in Tudor and Stuart England* (1980), p. 74.

2 Works, Vol. III, *Holy Living*, pp. 164–7.

3 Works, Vol. IV, *Miracles of the Divine Mercy*, p. 635.

4 Works, Vol. I, *Rules and Advices*, p. 109, Rule LIII, and LIV.

5 Stranks, pp. 67f.

6 Works, Vol. VIII, *Via Intelligentiae*, pp. 359–91.

7 J. D. Rayner and B. Hooker, *Judaism for Today* (London: Union of Liberal and Progressive Synagogues, 1978), p. 108. The introduction of universal education in Palestine in the first century BC came about 2,000 years earlier than in most Gentile societies. Rabbi Joshua ben Gamla ordered that teachers should be appointed in every district and in every city and that boys should be sent to them at the age of six or seven years (Baba Batra 21a).

8 G. Vermes, *The Religion of Jesus the Jew* (London: SCM Press, 1993), p. 15. The claim of Geza Vermes that Jesus is shown in the Gospels to be chiefly interested in *private* prayer, and that the *public* liturgy described in Luke 4.16–30 must be exceptional, brings into relief the problem of the intimacy of prayer with biblical literacy.

9 What is striking about critical literacy today is that 'one of the most telling stories in the gospels', as Christopher Evans puts it, the Lukan composition of Jesus in the opening scene of his ministry reading aloud verses from Isaiah and *appropriating* them (and effectively, for Luke and the Church almost up to the present, turning the Hebrew Bible into a Christian book), comes under suspicion of promoting an abuse of the Hebrew Bible: Evans, *Saint Luke*, pp. 58f., 269.

10 Works, Vol. IX, *Ductor Dubitantium*, pp. 463f.

11 T. G. A. Baker, *Questioning Worship* (London: SCM Press, 1977), p. 28.

12 G. J. Brooke, *Exegesis at Qumran* (Sheffield: JSOT, 1985); see also 'Pesher' in R. J. Coggins and J. L. Houlden (eds), *A Dictionary of Biblical Interpretation* (London: SCM Press, 1990), pp. 531f.

13 Tertullian, *De Jejunio*, cap. III: Ante-Nicene Christian Library (1870), Vol. XVIII, pp. 127f.

14 L. L. Martz, *The Paradise Within: Studies in Vaughan, Traherne and Milton* (New Haven, CT: Yale University Press, 1964), ch. IV.

15 John Chrysostom, *Homilies*, XIII.2.

16 1 Kings 17.2–6; the suggestion to read *arabim*, Arabs, for *orebim*, ravens, as J. Gray, *I & II Kings* (London: SCM Press, 1964), pp. 338f., is a temptation open to scholarship only.

17 B. K. Lewalski, *Milton's Epic* (Providence, RI: Brown University Press, 1966); or see 'Theme and action in *Paradise Regained*' in C. A. Patrides (ed.), *Milton's Epic Poetry* (Penguin Books, 1967), pp. 325, 331.

18 N. Frye, 'The typology of *Paradise Regained*' in Patrides, p. 313.

19 Ibid., p. 303.

20 Works, Vol. X, p. 344.

21 Ibid., p. 350.

22 Ibid., p. 385; Taylor's eloquence may owe a word or two to the Homily on Fasting in *The Second Tome of Homilies* (Oxford edn, 1832, pp. 255–71) provided by John Jewel: 'Some do fast and abstain both from fish and flesh. Others there are, which, when they fast, eat all of water-fowls, as well as of fish, grounding themselves upon

Moses, that such fowls have their substance of the water, as the fishes have. Some others, when they fast will neither eat herbs nor eggs.'

23 Works, Vol. X, p. 387.
24 Ibid., p. 381.
25 Works, Vol. II, *Great Exemplar*, pp. 191–3.
26 Ibid., p. 198.
27 Ibid., p. 200.
28 Ibid., pp. 202f.; not in the 1st edition (1649), these words first appear in 1653 and in all subsequent editions of *Great Exemplar*.
29 Tertullian, *De Jejunio*, cap. VI; cf. Works, Vol. VIII, pp. 221f.; Vol. IX, p. 269; Vol. X, p. 338.
30 John Cosin, a member and junior fellow before the arrival of Jeremy Taylor, was thought to have undermined his constitution 'by excessive fasting as an under-graduate and junior fellow of Caius': C. Brooke, *A History of Gonville and Caius College* (The Boydell Press, 1985).
31 Works, Vol. II, p. 490.
32 *Liturgical Services of the Reign of Queen Elizabeth* (The Parker Society, 1847), pp. 478–90; 'The Order for the general Fast', p. 490, paras 4 and 5.
33 Works, Vol. III, p. 168.
34 Ibid., p. 171.
35 Ibid., p. 176.
36 Ibid., p. 192.
37 Ibid., p. 191.
38 Ibid., p. 192.
39 Porter, *Jeremy Taylor, Liturgist*, pp. 75f.

6. THE GREAT EMPLOYMENT

1 Works, Vol. I, *Rules and Advices*, p. 111, rule 67; cf. Works, Vol. VII, *Agenda*, pp. 611–17, with instructions for a scheme of meditation.
2 Jeremy Taylor was an undergraduate at Gonville and Caius College when Cambridge was afflicted by the plague in 1630, with 347 recorded deaths. It was severe enough for a Royal Brief to be issued 'towards the releife and succor of the poore distressed inhabitants of our Towne of Cambridge'. See M. McCrum, 'Doctor Henry Butts', *Letter of The Corpus Association*, no. 73 (1994), pp. 42–53.
3 Works, Vol. IV, *Christ's Advent to Judgment*, p. 10.
4 Works, Vol. III, *Holy Dying*, p. 297.
5 Works, Vol. II, *Great Exemplar*, p. 144.
6 Ibid., p. 142.
7 Ibid., p. 1.
8 Ibid., p. 48.
9 Ibid., p. 37.
10 Ibid., pp. 334f.; Mark 2.13–17 (with parallels in Matthew 9.9–13; Luke 5.27–32); and Mark 2.18–20 (Matthew 9.14f.; Luke 5.33–35).
11 E. Cousins, trans., *Bonaventure* (London: SPCK, 1978), p. 125.
12 Works, Vol. II, *Discourse, On Meditation*, pp. 133f.; 'Lanthorn' in the first three editions of *Great Exemplar* does not become 'lantern' until 1667.
13 Ibid., p. 83.
14 Ovid, *Metamorphoses*, Book X.560–680.

15 Works, Vol. II, p. 139.

16 Ibid., p. 141.

17 E. Colledge and J. Walsh (trans.), *Julian of Norwich, Showings* (New York: Paulist Press, 1978), p. 22.

18 H. A. Allen, *English Writings of Richard Rolle, Hermit of Hampole* (Oxford: Clarendon Press, 1931), p. 43.

19 G. Worley, *Jeremy Taylor* (London: Longmans, Green & Co., 1904), pp. 67–9.

20 Helen C. White, *English Devotional Literature (Prose) 1600–1640* (Madison: University of Wisconsin Press, 1931), chs 5 and 6, esp. pp. 125, 134.

21 Gosse, *Jeremy Taylor*, pp. 59f. If Gosse is right to think that the discourses embedded in *Great Exemplar* were first sermons preached from the pulpit at Uppingham, then *Of Meditation* was delivered between April 1638 and August 1642. From its position among the infancy narratives near the beginning of the work, it would not be surprising to think that it was preached on or about Christmas 1639 when Taylor was 26. Cf. H. McAdoo, *First of Its Kind: Jeremy Taylor's Life of Christ* (Norwich: Canterbury Press, 1994), pp. 75f.; T. K. Carroll, *Jeremy Taylor, Selected Works* (New York: Paulist Press, 1990), p. 18.

22 Works, Vol. II, p. 143.

23 Ibid., p. 87.

24 Ruusbroec had reached the same conclusion in *Vanden Blinckenden Steen (The Sparkling Stone)* in describing 'the common life' as a life equally ready for contemplation and for action: R. C. Petry (ed.), *Late Medieval Mysticism* (Philadelphia: Westminster Press, 1957), p. 319; J. A. Wiseman, *John Ruusbroec* (New York: Paulist Press, 1985), p. 18.

25 Works, Vol. II, pp. 164–69.

26 *The Temple*, 'The Son'; see *The Works of George Herbert*, ed. F. E. Hutchinson (Oxford: Clarendon Press, 1941; 2nd edn, 1945); or *George Herbert: The Country Parson, The Temple*, ed. J. N. Wall (London: SPCK, 1981), p. 293.

27 Izaak Walton, *Life of George Herbert* (1670). But see F. L. Huntley, *Essays in Persuasion* (University of Chicago Press, 1981), ch. 7 for discussion of Nicholas Ferrar's editing of Herbert.

28 R. Tuve, *A Reading of George Herbert* (London: Faber, 1952), p. 108, complains of 'a grasshopper plague of explainers of poems'. A useful survey of literary criticism of Herbert can be found in B. L. Harman, *Costly Monuments* (Cambridge, MA: Harvard University Press, 1982), pp. 1–32, with notes on Palmer, Empson, Tuve, Summers, Fish, Vendler and Lewalski. More recently, J. B. White, *This Book of Starres* (Ann Arbor: University of Michigan Press, 1994), pp. 276–81, on Martz, Stein, Bloch, Strier, Shuger and Shoenfeldt.

29 *The Temple*, Antiphon I.

30 *Keble's Lectures on Poetry 1832–1841*, trans. E. K. Francis (1912), p. 99.

31 *The Temple*, 'The Agony'.

32 Ibid., 'The Sacrifice'.

33 J. A. W. Bennett, *Poetry of The Passion* (Oxford: Clarendon Press, 1982), p. 29.

34 T. S. Eliot, *George Herbert* (Writers and Their Work; London: Faber, 1962), pp. 15–25.

35 W. H. Auden, *George Herbert: Selected* (London, 1973), p. 10.

36 *The Temple*, 'Perirrhanterium', lines 73–84.

37 Proverbs 6.6, 9; 10.26; 13.4; 15.19; 19.15, 24; 20.4; 21.25; 22.13; 24.30; 26.10, 13–15.

38 Proverbs 22.13.

39 J. H. Summers, *George Herbert, His Religion and Art* (London: Chatto and Windus,

1954), pp. 187–9, points to Herbert's simplicity of the spirit, which was the reverse of naivety.

40 S. Sykes, *Unashamed Anglicanism* (London: Darton, Longman and Todd, 1995), p. 62.

41 *The Temple*, 'Matins'.

42 R. Baxter, *Poetical Fragments* (1681), preface.

43 *The Temple*, 'Denial'.

44 Ibid., 'Prayer I'.

45 Vaughan, *Silex Scintillans*, 'The World', p. 91.

46 *The Temple*, 'Affliction IV'.

47 Ibid., 'The Holdfast'.

48 William Cowper: 'I was advised by a very near and dear relation to lay him aside, for he thought that such an author was more likely to nourish my melancholy than to remove it': *Memoir of the Early Life* (1816).

49 *The Temple*, 'The Collar'.

50 Ibid., 'Easter II'.

51 H. White, *The Metaphysical Poets* (New York: Macmillan, *c.* 1936), pp. 228–30.

52 *The Temple*, 'A Parody'.

53 R. Crashaw (1613?–49), 'On Mr. G. Herbert's booke intituled the Temple of Sacred Poems, sent to a Gentlewoman' in *English Poems*, ed. J. R. Tutin (Great Fencote, Yorks: Tutin, 1900).

54 S. T. Coleridge, *Miscellaneous Criticism*, ed. T. M. Raysor (London: Constable, 1936), p. 244.

55 L. C. Knights, *Explorations 3* (London: Chatto and Windus, 1976), p. 68.

56 *The Temple*, 'The Forerunners'.

57 E. P. Sanders, *The Historical Figure of Jesus* (London: Allen Lane, The Penguin Press, 1993), p. 233.

58 *The Temple*, 'Bitter-sweet'.

59 Ibid., 'Discipline'.

60 E. Clarke, 'George Herbert's *The Temple*' in G. Rowell (ed.), *The English Religious Tradition and the Genius of Anglicanism* (Wantage: IKON, 1992), pp. 131f.

61 H. Gardner, *The Poems of George Herbert* (Oxford University Press, 1961), p. xx.

7. A TERRIBLE IMAGINING

1 Plutarch, *Vitae, Julius Caesar*, to which Taylor *directly* and not infrequently refers, and not indirectly via Sir Thomas North's translation, *Lives of the Noble Grecians and Romans* (1579), or Shakespeare's *The Tragedy of Julius Caesar* (1623) (Act III.ii), which version of North every schoolboy knows.

2 Aristotle, *The Art of Rhetoric*, 2.2. Cf. Works, Vol. II, p. 437.

3 Works, Vol. II, *Discourse On Meditation*, pp. 133f.

4 E. V. C. Plumptre in H. Mallalieu (ed.), *The Harrow Achievement* (The Old Harrovian Players, 1982), p. 19.

5 McAdoo, *First of Its Kind*, p. viii.

6 Works, Vol. VIII, *The Minister's Duty*, pp. 522f.

7 Ibid., pp. 526f.

8 Rembrandt, *Abraham's Sacrifice*, St Petersburg, Hermitage Museum, Cat. No. 92.

9 Authorised Version, 1611.

10 C. Tumpel, *Rembrandt* (Amsterdam, 1986), p. 164.

11 John 3.16–19.

12 M. Buber, *Tales of the Hasidim: The Later Masters* (New York: Schocken Books, 1948), p. 96.

13 M. Kitson, *Rembrandt* (Oxford: Phaidon Press, 1982), p. 19.

14 *Abraham's Sacrifice*, Munich, Alte Pinakothek. Cf. K. Voll, 'Das Opfer Abrahams von Rembrandt in Petersburg und in München' in *Vergleichende Gemälde Studien* (Munich and Leipzig, 1907), Vol. I, pp. 174–9.

15 C. Brown, *Rembrandt: The Master and His Workshop: Paintings* (New Haven, CT and London: Yale University Press/National Gallery Publications, 1991), p. 182.

16 R. Askew, *The Tree of Noah* (London: Geoffrey Bles, 1971), p. 67.

17 Works, Vol. VIII, *Fides Formata*, p. 298.

18 Works, Vol. II, p. 614.

19 S. Kierkegaard, *Fear and Trembling*, trans. W. Lowrie (Princeton University Press, 1954), p. 26.

20 Ibid., pp. 35–7.

21 S. Kierkegaard, *Concluding Unscientific Postscript*, trans. W. Lowrie (Princeton University Press, 1954), p. 327.

22 R. A. Willmott, *Bishop Jeremy Taylor, His Predecessors, Contemporaries and Successors* (London, 1846), p. 234.

23 Helen Waddell, *Lyrics from the Chinese* (London: Constable and Co., 1949), XII, p. 13.

24 Iris Murdoch, *Metaphysics as a Guide to Morals* (London: Chatto and Windus, 1992), p. 122.

25 Ibid., p. 146.

26 See R. M. Sainsbury, *Paradoxes* (Cambridge University Press, 1988).

27 Book of Common Prayer, 1662, Kalendar, 7 March.

28 Tertullian, *De Spectaculis*, Ante-Nicene Christian Library, Vol. XI.I, p. 32. See also *The Passion of Saint Perpetua*, trans. R. Waterville Muncey (London: J. M. Dent & Sons, 1927); Augustine, *Confessions*, Book VI, ch. 8; Cyprian, *Epistle to Donatus*, Ante-Nicene Christian Library, Vol. XIII.I, pp. 6f.; *On the Public Shows*, Vol. XIII.II, pp. 221–30; *The Passion of the Holy Martyrs Perpetua and Felicitas*, Vol. XIII.II, pp. 276–92.

29 J. Bunyan, *The Pilgrim's Progress* (1678), 'The Town of Vanity'.

30 Murdoch, p. 131.

31 Ibid., pp. 82f.

32 Ibid., p. 86.

33 Works, Vol. X, pp. 623f.

34 Murdoch, p. 132.

35 Works, Vol. II, *Great Exemplar*, pp. 703f.

36 Works, Vol. IV, *The Righteous Cause Oppressed*, pp. 435–7.

8. ARRESTING THE SUN

1 Works, Vol. III, *Holy Living*, p. 212.

2 Cf. Symeon the New Theologian, *The Discourses*, IV.12.

3 B. F. Westcott, *The Epistle to the Hebrews* (London: Macmillan, 1906), pp. 231f.

4 Works, Vol. III, p. 32.

5 Ibid., p. 245.

6 Ibid., p. 247.

7 Works, Vol. VII, *Golden Grove*, pp. 636–8.

8 Romans 8.26.

9 Works, Vol. V, pp. 240f.

10 Works, Vol. VII, *Credenda*, p. 596.

11 Ibid., p. 605.

12 Works, Vol. VIII, *The Worthy Communicant*, p. 226.

13 George Herbert, *The Temple*, 'Prayer I'.

14 Works, Vol. IV, *The Return of Prayers*, pp. 76f.

15 Works, Vol. VIII, *Collection of Offices*, pp. 628f.

16 Porter, *Jeremy Taylor, Liturgist*, pp. 65–7.

17 Works, Vol. IV, pp. 47f.

18 Ibid., p. 56.

19 Ibid., pp. 69f.

20 Joshua 10.12f.; Habakkuk 3.11.

21 Works, Vol. I, *Rules and Advices*, pp. 101–14.

22 Stranks, *The Life and Writings of Jeremy Taylor*, pp. 226–9.

23 Works, Vol. I, p. 103.

24 Ibid., *Clerus Domini*, pp. 6f.

25 Ibid., p. 103.

26 Works, Vol. VIII, *The Whole Duty of the Clergy*, pp. 499–539.

27 Ibid., pp. 504f.

28 Chaucer, *The Canterbury Tales*, line 500.

29 Works, Vol. VIII, p. 512.

30 Ibid., p. 517.

31 R. W. Southern (ed.), *The Life of St Anselm, Archbishop of Canterbury, by Eadmer* (London: Thomas Nelson and Sons, 1962), p. 77.

32 R. Askew, 'Taylor's *Abbreviature Projected*' in J. Butterworth (ed.), *The Reality of God* (London: Severn House Publishers, 1986), pp. 123–37.

33 Luke 18.9–14.

34 E. Linnemann, *Parables of Jesus* (London: SPCK, 1966), p. 60. Cf. J. Jeremias, *The Parables of Jesus* (London: SCM Press, 1954), pp. 111–15; E. P. Sanders, *Jesus and Judaism* (London: SCM Press, 1985), pp. 278f.

9. O THE DEATH OF PHOEBE!

1 Stephen Hawes, *Passetyme of Pleasure or History of Graunde Amoure*, printed by Wynken de Worde (1509), cap. 42.

2 W. Hamper, *Life, Diary and Correspondence of Sir W. Dugdale* (1827), p. 250: a torn letter from Jeremy Taylor to Sir William Dugdale, 1 April 1651, with news of Phoebe's recent death, and work on *Holy Dying*. See also Gosse, *Jeremy Taylor*, pp. 87f.

3 Works, Vol. III, *Holy Dying*, p. 257.

4 Gosse, p. 89.

5 Works, Vol. III, p. 264.

6 Ibid., p. 261.

7 Ibid., p. 403.

8 Ibid., p. 413.

9 Ibid., pp. 432f.

10 Ibid., pp. 366f.; cf. *The Gate to Heaven a Strait Gate*: 'Some Men are so fond as to think Heaven is intail'd upon a Sect or an Opinion': Works, Vol. I, p. 126.

11 Isaiah 2.22 (Authorised Version); O. Kaiser, *Isaiah 1–12* (London: SCM Press, 1983), p. 63; see also Isaiah 40.7, and U. Simon, *A Theology of Salvation* (London:

SPCK, 1953), pp. 43–7; C. Westermann, *Isaiah 40–66* (London: SCM Press, 1969), pp. 40–3.

12 Works, Vol. III, p. 270.

13 Ibid., p. 272.

14 Ibid., p. 276.

15 Ibid., p. 12.

16 Ibid., pp. 284f. The worms referred to were, presumably, wireworms, eelworms, cutworms, slugworms, maggots, leatherjackets; the common earthworm assists gardening.

17 Ibid., p. 291.

18 T. Carlyle, *Oliver Cromwell's Letters and Speeches* (London: Ward, Lock, Bowden & Co., 2nd edn, 1892), p. 387.

19 Ibid., p. 457.

20 Anne, Lady Halkett, *Memoirs* (Camden Society, 1875), quoted in R. Hudson (ed.), *The Grand Quarrel* (London: The Folio Society, 1993), pp. 206–8.

21 Works, Vol. III, p. 295.

22 Ibid., p. 301.

23 Ibid., pp. 302f.

24 Matthew 22.1–14; John Chrysostom, *Homilies in the Gospel of St Matthew*, Library of Fathers trans. (Oxford: John Henry Parker, 1852), Part III, Homily LXIX, pp. 932f., 937.

25 Matthew 25.31–41; Chrysostom, Homily LXXIX, p. 1050.

26 Chrysostom, Homily XI.7, p. 155.

27 Origen, *De Principiis*, Book II, cap. 10.4; J. W. Trigg, *Origen, The Bible and Philosophy in the Third-century Church* (London: SCM Press, 1983), pp. 114f., 186.

28 Works, Vol. IV, *The Foolish Exchange*, pp. 567–9.

29 *Doctrine in the Church of England* (London: SPCK, 1938), p. 219.

30 Works, Vol. IV, p. 568.

31 The Doctrine Commission of The Church of England, *The Mystery of Salvation* (London: Church House Publishing, 1995), p. 199.

32 Richard Hooker, *Ecclesiastical Polity*, Book V, cap. xli.4.

33 K. Rahner, 'Poetry and the Christian', *Theological Investigations*, Vol. IV (London: Darton, Longman and Todd, 1966), pp. 357–67.

34 Works, Vol. III, p. 307.

35 Ibid., p. 311.

36 Works, Vol. II, p. 646; Vol. IV, p. 240.

37 Ibid., Vol. III, p. 312.

38 Ibid., p. 314.

39 Ibid., p. 316.

40 Ibid., p. 320.

41 Ibid., p. 322.

42 Ibid., p. 323.

43 Ibid., p. 327.

44 C. Hill, *The English Bible and the Seventeenth-century Revolution* (London: Allen Lane, The Penguin Press, 1993), p. 372. William Empson indicates E. M. W. Tillyard as 'the first I think to point out that Milton scrutinizes the approach to the Fall like a novelist': *Milton's God* (London: Chatto and Windus, 1961), ch. IV, p. 150.

45 F. R. Leavis, *Scrutiny*, II (Cambridge, 1933), p. 124.

46 Hill, p. 374.

47 E. M. W. Tillyard, *Milton* (London: Peregrine Books, 1968), p. 239.

48 A. J. A. Waldock, '"Paradise Lost" and its critics' (1947) in C. A. Patrides (ed.), *Milton's Epic Poetry*, p. 86.
49 Hill, p. 373.
50 John Milton, *Paradise Lost* (1667), Book XII.88–96.
51 C. S. Lewis, *A Preface to Paradise Lost* (Oxford University Press, 1942), p. 127.
52 Ibid., p. 128.
53 Works, Vol. III, p. 354.
54 Shakespeare, *The Tempest*, Act IV.i.148–154.
55 *Paradise Lost*, Book I.733f.

10. THE SEARCH FOR JEREMY TAYLOR

1 F. W. Farrar DD, FRS, Canon of Westminster, Rector of St Margaret's, and Chaplain in Ordinary to the Queen, contributed to A. Barry (ed.), *Masters in English Theology* (being the King's College Lectures for 1877; London: John Murray, 1877), pp. 176f.
2 G. Rust, *A Funeral Sermon Preached at the Obsequies of the Right Reverend Father in God Jeremy Lord Bishop of Down* (1667), in Works, Vol. I, pp. cccxxi–ccxxiii.
3 D. Lloyd, *Memoires* (London, 1668), pp. 702ff.
4 Works, Vol. VIII, *Anniversary of the Gunpowder-Treason*, p. 455.
5 See Postscript. Katherine Philips (1631–64) is represented by two poems in *The Oxford Book of Seventeenth Century Verse* (Oxford: Clarendon Press, 1934); but by seven in *The Penguin Book of Renaissance Verse* (London: Allen Lane, Penguin Press, 1992).
6 Rust, in Works, Vol. I, p. cccxxiv.
7 Cf. Walter Ralegh, *Historie of the World*: 'by the gravest Astrologian it was observed that in the year 1524 there should happen the like conjunction as at Noah's Floud; than which . . . there was never a more faire, dry and seasonable year.'
8 Works, Vol. I, *The Gate to Heaven a Strait Gate*, pp. 115–27.
9 W. Bray, *Diary and Correspondence of John Evelyn FRS* (revised edn 1854), Vol. III, pp. 65–135.
10 A. Wood, *Athenae Oxonienses*, ed. Philip Bliss (London: 1813–20), Vol. XIII, p. 783.
11 R. A. Willmott, *Bishop Jeremy Taylor, His Predecessors, Contemporaries and Successors*, p. 110.
12 Horace, *Odes*, Book I.8; Book III.10.
13 Works, Vol. IV, *Apples of Sodom*, p. 238.
14 Ibid., p. 245; cf. C. Carlton, *Going to the Wars* (London: Routledge, paperback edn 1994), p. 191.
15 Works, Vol. IV, *Apples of Sodom*, p. 236.
16 Works, Vol. III, *Holy Dying*, pp. 315f.
17 J. Wheeldon, *The Life of Bishop Taylor and the Pure Spirit of his Writings, Extracted and Exhibited for General Benefit* (London, 1793), Preface (to the Hon Frederic Cavendish).
18 H. K. Bonney, *Life of the Right Reverend Father in God Jeremy Taylor DD* (London, 1815), pp. 52f.
19 Works, Vol. II, *The Duty of Nursing Children*, pp. 72–81.
20 Ibid., pp. 464–83.
21 *The Diary of Samuel Pepys*, 1 May 1665.
22 Ibid., 5 May 1665.
23 John Evelyn, *Diary*, 13 July 1654.
24 Pepys, 2 October 1665.
25 Ibid., 4 November 1665.

26 John Evelyn, *Diary*: '17 Jan 1653. I began to set out the ovall garden at Sayes Court which was before a rude orchard, and all the rest one intire field of 100 acres, without any hedge, except the hither holly hedge joyning to the bank of the mount walk. This was the beginning of all the succeeding gardens, walks, groves, enclosures and plantations there.'

27 Ibid., 25 August 1654: 'To see Kirby, a very noble house of my Lord Hatton's, in Northamptonshire, built *a la moderne*; the gardens and stables agreeable, but the avenue ungraceful, and the seat naked.' (The ruins of Kirby Hall are now marvellously cared for by English Heritage.) Cf. Gosse, *Jeremy Taylor*, p. 25.

28 P. Thornton, *Seventeenth-Century Interior Decoration in England, France and Holland* (New Haven, CT and London: Yale University Press, 1978), pp. 109–11, 239–43.

29 H. B. Porter, *Jeremy Taylor, Liturgist*, p. 140, quoted from Uppingham Vestry Book.

30 R. F. Foster, *Modern Ireland 1600–1972* (London: Allen Lane, Penguin Press, 1988), p. 88n.

31 Gosse, pp. 173f.

32 R. B. Bosher, *The Making of the Restoration Settlement* (London: A. & C. Black, 1951), p. 265.

33 R. Gathorne-Hardy and W. P. Williams, *A Bibliography of the Writings of Jeremy Taylor to 1700* (Illinois: de Kalb, 1971), p. 82.

34 *Quarterly Review*, Vol. 131 (July–October 1871), p. 126.

35 *Letters from Orinda to Poliarchus*, 2nd edn, with additions (London, 1729), pp. 114ff.

36 W. S. Clark, *The Early Irish Stage* (Westport, CT: Greenwood Press, 1955), pp. 50–65. His description of Mrs Philips as 'a dynamic untitled visitor from Cardigan, Wales' is spoken like an American. Cf. P. W. Souers, *The Matchless Orinda (i.e. K. Philips)* (Harvard Studies in English 5; Cambridge, MA: Harvard University Press, 1931), esp. pp. 180–7.

37 *Pompey a Tragedy*, printed for H. Herringman (London, 1667).

38 C. A. Price, 'The songs for Katherine Philips' "Pompey" (1663)', *Theatre Notebook*, Vol. XXXIII, no. 2 (1979), pp. 61–6.

39 Clark, pp. 54f.

40 *Athenae Oxonienses*, Vol. III, p. 787.

41 Works, Vol. I, p. cvii, in a letter to Ormond, 20 November 1661.

42 Foster, p. 126.

43 Gosse, pp. 126f.

44 Ibid., pp. 212f.

45 Lemuel Mathew, *Pandarique Elegie upon the death of the R R Father in God JEREMY Late Lord Bishop of Doune, Connor and Dromore* (Dublin, 1667).

POSTSCRIPT: ORINDA'S LOVE LETTER

A member of the Working Party which produced the Report *Homosexual Relationships* (London: CIO Publishing, 1979) for the General Synod of the Church of England, the author was invited in September 1996 by the House of Bishops to write an opinion on seventeenth-century attitudes to homosexuality. 'Orinda's love letter' is an abbreviated version of that paper.

1 R. Sanderson, *XXXV Sermons* (London: Tho. Hodgkin, 7th edn, 1681), Sermon II, *Ad Clerum*, at a Visitation at Boston, Lincoln, 24 April 1621.

2 Ibid., Sermon II, *Ad Populum*, 'at Grantham, Linc Feb 27, 1620' (but reference to

the sweeping away of religious princes, wise senators, painful ministers, viz. Charles I, Strafford, Laud, suggests a date of 1649 at the earliest).

3 Authorised Version (1611).

4 S. Patrick, *A Commentary upon Genesis* (London: printed for D. Midwinter, etc., 1694; 5th edn, 1738).

5 H. Hammond, *The work of an imperious whorish woman*, from *XIX Sermons preached on Several Occasions* (c. 1648) (LACT edn, 1849), pp. 273–96, esp. pp. 274f.

6 See, for example, Carlton, *Charles I, the Personal Monarch*, pp. 18f.

7 It is interesting to notice that P. A. Welsby, *Lancelot Andrewes 1555–1626* (London: SPCK, 1958), pp. 267f., who has correctly noted the great emphasis on penitence in the *Preces*, does not understand the nature of a *ministerial vocation* to share that Christ-like intercession of weeping not for his own sins but for the sins of others, described by Jeremy Taylor in *The Return of Prayers, ENIAUTOS*, Sermon VI (Works, Vol. IV, pp. 47–85).

8 D. Bonhoeffer, *Ethics*, trans. N. Horton-Smith, ed. E. Bethge (London: SCM Press, 1955), p. 213.

9 H. R. Trevor-Roper, *Religion, the Reformation, and Social Change* (London: Macmillan, 1967), p. 142, n. 1.

10 Works, Vol. X, *Ductor Dubitantium*, Part III, ch. IV, Rule 7.14, pp. 306–8.

11 Works, Vol. VII, *Unum Necessarium, Or The doctrine and practice of repentance*, ch. IV, section 1.9; 21 (pp. 127, 132).

12 Authorised Version.

13 J. Hales, *Golden Remains of the ever Memorable Mr John Hales of Eton College &c* (London: Tim Garthwait, 1659), 'Of dealing with Erring Christians', p. 42.

14 Ibid., p. 50.

15 R. Baxter, *Directions for Weak distempered Christians, to Grow up to a confirmed State of Grace, With Motives opening the lamentable Effects of their Weaknesses and Distempers* (London: Nevil Simmons, 1669), Part II, p. 157.

16 A. Wood, *Athenae Oxonienses*, Vol. III, p. 787.

17 K. Philips, *Poems by Mrs Katherine Philips the Matchless Orinda, To which is added M Corneilles' Pompey and Horace, tragedies* (London, 1667); ed. P. Thomas, *The Collected Works*, Vol. I: *The Poems* (Stump Cross, Essex, 1990).

18 Works, Vol. I, *A Discourse of the Nature and Offices of Friendship. In a Letter to The Most Ingenious and Excellent M. K. P.*, pp. 71–98.

19 R. Sanderson, *The Case of Unlawful Love* in *Five Cases of Conscience determined by a late learned hand* (London, 1666): *The Works of Robert Sanderson DD. sometime Bishop of Lincoln*, ed. W. Jacobson (Oxford University Press, 1854), Vol. V, case viii, pp. 88–103.

Index

Abraham's Sacrifice xi, 117–19, 201, 202
Adam 40–1, 79, 81, 83, 104–5, 160–1, 163
addiction ix, 10–11, 78
Aeschylus 42
affective prayer *see* prayer
à Kempis, Thomas 102
Allen, H. A. 200
almsgiving 60, 90–2, 141, 153–4
Ambrose 16
anaesthetics 157
Ancyra, Council of 16
Andrewes, Lancelot 106, 183–4, 207
Anselm 16, 141, 203
Apostolic Constitutions 17
Apuleius 192
Ariston of Chios 22
Aristotle 42, 113, 201
Arles, Council of 16
Arminius 75–6
Askew, Anne 116
Askew, R. J. A. 142, 202, 203, 206
Athens 49
Aubrey, Mary 187
Auden, W. H. 105, 111, 200
Augustine 10, 30, 33, 39–40, 43, 59, 75–6, 119, 121, 161, 202
awe 20–1, 66, 121, 142
Ayscue, Sir George 59

Baker, Augustine 102
Baker, T. G. A. x, 80, 198
Ballinderry 175–6
Barksdale, C. 165–6
Barry, A. 205
Basil the Great 154
Baumann, H. 195
Baxter, Richard 106, 110, 186, 201, 207
Benedict, Benedictines 9, 41, 48, 102, 141, 196
Bennett, J. A. W. 200

Bernard 15, 87
Blow, John 104
Board of Trade 59
Bonaventure 99, 199
Bonhoeffer, D. 184, 207
Bonney, H. K. 173–4, 205
Book of Common Prayer vii, viii, ix, xii, 1, 2, 4, 8, 27, 36, 40, 45, 46, 61, 92, 108, 112, 127, 133–4, 147, 148, 155, 156, 167, 202
Bosher, R. B. 206
Boyle, Robert 170, 179
Bray, W. 205
breast-feeding 55, 57–9, 174
Brooke, C. 199
Brooke, G. J. 198
Brown, C. 202
Buber, M. 202
bubonic plague 35, 94, 199
Buckingham, Duke of 53
Bunyan, John ix, 52, 105, 123, 196, 202
business ethics *see* ethics
Butler, James *see* Ormond

Caesar, Sir Charles 52
Caius College *see* Gonville and Caius College
Cambridge xi, 75, 81, 94, 103–4, 117, 165, 174, 191, 199
canon law 67–74, 85–6
Carbery, Richard Vaughan, Earl of xi, 5, 56, 64, 92, 145, 168, 174; Frances Altham xii, 36, 56–7, 59, 144–5, 149, 168, 194; Alice Egerton 168
Cardigan Castle xi, 175, 187
Carlton, C. 196, 205, 207
Carlyle, T. 204
Carroll, T. K. 200
Cassian 22–3, 76, 85, 197
Catesby 36
Cavendish, Christian *see* Devonshire
charity 153–4, 187

Charles I xi, xii, 1, 24, 46, 49–55, 60, 69, 71, 75, 81, 113, 117, 144, 168, 175, 196, 207
Charles II xii, 68, 128, 162, 168
chastity 3, 11–17, 46; and celibacy 15–17; and virginity 13–14, 16, 81; in marriage 11–13, 15–16, 81
Chaucer 139, 203
Chepstow Castle xii, 25, 171, 175
children and parents 54–61
see also breast-feeding
Chrysippus 22
Chrysostom, John 27, 83, 154, 193, 198, 204
Church and State 66, 68–75, 183
Cicero 30, 42, 45, 99, 113
civil obedience 47–9
Clark, W. S. 206
Clarke, E. 201
Claude Lorrain 39, 195
Cleanthes 22
Clement of Alexandria 10, 22–3, 26, 192
Climacus, John 22–3, 72
Cloud of Unknowing, The 102, 109, 192
Coggins, R. J. 198
Coke, Sir John 51
Coleridge, Samuel T. xii, 32, 111, 191, 194, 195, 201
Colet 32
Colledge, E. 200
common sense 66, 73, 169
Compton, Mary *see* Northampton
confession, private 19–20, 112, 147
conscience 2, 46–7, 50, 72, 81, 85, 139, 147, 153–4, 194
contemplation *see* prayer
contentedness 3, 17, 22–9, 30, 37, 44, 46, 71, 145, 179; and fate 26–7, 40–1; and providence 27–8; and environment 28
Conway, Edward, Viscount 68, 171, 175
corruption 51–3
Cosin, John 199
Cousins, E. 199
Coverdale, Miles 112
Cowper, William 111, 201
Cranmer, Thomas 112
Crashaw, Richard 110, 201
Cressy, D. 78, 198
Cromwell, Oliver 25, 71, 81, 152, 161, 165, 186–7, 204
Cyprian 15, 202
Cyril of Jerusalem 131

Dante Alighieri 155
Davies, G. 196
death 90, 149–50, 154–6; fear of 159, 162; impatience 157–8; pains of 156–9; trial of faith 158–9
debt *see* restitution
despair 145, 147, 150
Devonshire, Countess of 168
divorce and remarriage 61, 74

Dublin xii, 34, 39, 79, 123, 137, 171, 177–9
Dugdale, Sir William 203
Dunbar 152

East India Company 157
Eburne, R. 196
Eden, Charles Page 42, 191
Egerton, Alice *see* Carbery
Eliot, George 23, 193
Eliot, T. S. 105, 109, 111, 200
Empson, W. 160, 200, 204
Ephraim Syrus 154
Epictetus 22, 26
Erasmus 32
Erastian theory 69–71
ethics, in business 62–4; in professional life 64
Euripides 42
Evagrius 23
Evans, C. F. 65, 197, 198
Evelyn, John xii, 1, 4, 33, 63, 68, 93, 137, 168, 169–72, 174–5, 179, 197, 206
excommunication 72

Farrar, F. W. 165, 202
fasting *see* prayer
Ferrar, Nicholas 104, 200
Fincham, K. 197
Foster, R. F. 206
Francis, E. K. 200
François de Sales 11, 192
Freud 18
friendship 187–90
Frye, N. 83, 198

Gardner, Helen 201
Gathorne-Hardy, R. 176–7, 206
Globe, The xi, 36, 61, 114
Golden Grove 5, 56, 62, 174, 187
Gonville and Caius College x, xi, 94, 174, 191, 199
Gosse, Sir Edmund xii, 57, 62, 176, 179, 191, 193, 194, 196, 200, 203, 206
Gough, R. 3, 192
grace 75–7, 78
Gray, J. 198
Gregory VII 16
Gregory the Great 42
Guy Fawkes 36

Hadley, George 21
Hakuin 23
Hales, John 185–6, 190, 207
Halkett, Anne, Lady 152, 204
Hammond, Henry 183, 207
Hamper, W. 203
Harman, B. L. 200
Hatton, Christopher, Lord 26, 96, 168, 174, 175, 206; Lady 59; Christopher (son) 42
Hawes, Stephen 144, 203

Heaven ix, 2, 9, 41, 80, 81, 88, 97, 126, 142, 143, 148, 150, 154–6, 159, 162–4, 179
Heber, Reginald xii, 42, 186, 191
hell ix, 27, 41, 81, 84, 100, 148, 154–6, 159, 162–3
Herbert, George x, xi, 5, 59–60, 95, 103–6, 165, 196, 200, 201, 203; prayer of 106–12, 132
Herodotus 42
Herrick, Robert 110
Highgate Cemetery 149
Hill, C. 51–2, 116, 159–61, 196, 197, 204, 205
Hilton, Walter 102, 109
Hobbes, Thomas xii, 63
Holdsworth, W. S. 52, 196
holy dying 144–64
holy living, as politics 46–73; as virtue 9–29; as worship 78–143; summarized 28–9, 66–7, 143, 163
Homer 30–42, 44, 62, 71, 157, 193, 194, 195, 197
homosexual relationships 168, 182–90, 206
Hooker, Richard 69, 155, 204
Hopkins, G. Manley 111
Horace 27, 31, 37, 42–5, 193, 195, 205
Houlden, J. L. 196, 198
Hudson, R. 204
Hugh of St Victor 102
humility 3, 17–20, 46, 82, 192
Huntley, F. L. 200
Hutchinson, F. E. 200
Huxley, A. 107

Ignatius 99, 120
imagination 80, 86, 99–100, 112, 113–25; and extreme violence 114, 121–5; in Kierkegaard 116, 119–23; in Rembrandt 117–19, 122–3; of the Passion 114–15
infant baptism 75, 86, 167
intercession x, 11, 116, 126–38, 178; Christ's work of 126–7, 131–2, 137; language of 127–31; post-communion 126, 131–4, 137; qualifications for 134–7; special vocation of 126, 128, 136–8, 207
Islam 151

James I 79, 183, 190
Jeremias, J. 203
Jerome 16, 33
Jewell, John 78, 198–9
John of Damascus 151
John of the Cross 101, 109
Jones, Inigo 68
Julian, emperor 30
Julian of Norwich 102, 200
Julius Caesar 113–14, 123
justice 46–67, 77; see also canon law; Church and State; ethics; monarchy
Juvenal 37, 42–3

Kaiser, O. 203
Keble, John 104, 200
Kierkegaard, Søren 27, 116, 119–23, 193, 202
Kirby Hall 174, 175, 206
Kitson, M. 202
Knights, L. C. 111, 201

last judgement 94–5, 153–4
Laud, William xi, 51, 69, 144, 168, 175, 207
law and order see civil obedience; ethics; justice; monarchy
Lawrence, T. E. 197
Lea, Sir James 52
Lear, Edward 20
Leavis, F. R. 159–60, 204
Lewalski, B. K. 198, 200
Lewis, C. S. 162, 205
Linnemann, E. 203
Llanfihangel Aberbythych 42, 79
Lloyd, David 167–8, 173, 205
Locke, John 54–5, 196
Louis XIV 63
love see marriage
Lucian 37
Ludolf of Saxony 99
Luther, Martin 112
Lysimachus 63

McAdoo, H. 115, 200, 201
McCrum, M. 199
Mandinam 172, 179
Mark Antony 113–14
Marlowe, Christopher 31, 193
marriage, consent 54, 60–1; love 11–15, 62, 189
Marsh, Francis 172
Martial 42
Martz, L. L. 198, 200
Mary, Princess of Orange 168
Mathew, L. 179–81, 206
Maximus Confessor 23
meditation 80, 95–100, 112, 114–15, 116, 121, 123; Ignatian 99; and contemplation 100
Mendel, Menahem, of Kosov 118
Milton, John xi, xii, 36, 40, 81–4, 86, 159–63, 168, 198, 204, 205; *Lycidas* 81; *Paradise Lost* xii, 40, 159–63; *Paradise Regained* xii, 81–4; mythology 161–3
ministry see priest
modesty 3, 17, 20–2, 46
moly 38–9
monarchy, defects of 49–54
Morrill, J. 195, 196
Muncy, R. W. 202
Murdoch, Iris 18, 122–4, 192, 202
Myddle 3
Mystery of Salvation 155, 204
mysticism 100–2
mythology see Homer; Milton

National Health Service 143
national lottery 91
nepenthe 39
Nero, emperor 71
Newton Hall 79
Nicholson, William 42
Nilus 154
North, Sir Thomas 201
Northampton, Countess of 168

Oppenheimer, Helen 61, 197
ordination of women *see* priest
Origen 27, 154–5, 193, 204
original sin 39–40, 161
Orinda *see* Philips, Katherine
Ormond, James Butler, Duke of 168, 176, 177, 206
Ovid 42, 100, 199
Owen, Anne 186–7

Page, D. 195
parental responsibility 54–61
Patrick, Simon 183, 207
Patrides, C. A. 198, 205
Pepys, Samuel 59, 175, 194, 196, 205
Perpetua and her companions 45, 112, 123, 195, 202
Perse School xi, 35, 174
Petronius 149
Petry, R. C. 200
Pfeiffer, R. 194
Philips, James 178, 186–7
Philips, Katherine 123, 168, 177–8, 186–90, 195, 205, 206, 207
Pius II 15
Plato 18, 42
Plautus 42
Pliny 157
Plumptre, E. V. C. x, 114, 201
Plutarch 24, 37, 42–3, 113, 193, 201
politics *see* holy living
Porter, H. B. 92, 134, 195, 199, 203, 206
Portmore xii, 68, 171, 175
Posidonius 22
prayer 2, 53–4, 78–92; affective 110; contemplative 95, 100–3, 192, 200; and alms 90–2; and fasting 81–8, 89, 198–9; and illiteracy 78–80; *see also* imagination; intercession; meditation; mysticism; priest
Preston, Elizabeth *see* Ormond
Price, C. A. 177, 206
priest, vocation of 2, 5, 137–43; as example 138–40, 142–3; as intercessor 136–8; as pastor 141, 145–7; in preaching 70, 79, 140–1; ordination of women 74, 143, 164; *see also* chastity and celibacy
professional ethics *see* ethics
Prudentius 85
Purcell, Henry 104

Rahner, K. 155–6, 204
Ralegh, Sir Walter 205
Rayner, J. D. 80, 198
Raysor, T. M. 201
Rembrandt van Rijn xi, 117–19, 122–3, 201, 202
Reps, P. 23, 193
restitution of debt 65–6
Reynolds, L. D. 194
Richardson, Sir Thomas 52
Rolle, Richard 102, 200
Rome 31, 49, 71, 113
Royal Society, The 21, 169, 172
Royston, R. 137, 163, 176–7, 205
Russell, C. 49, 52, 196
Rust, George 24, 68, 165–7, 205
Ruusbroec, Jan van 200

Sainsbury, R. M. 202
Sanders, E. P. 201, 203
Sanderson, Robert 182–3, 190, 206, 207
Sartre, J.-P. 18
Sayes Court 171, 174, 175, 205–6
Seldon, John 53
self-examination 153
Seneca 22, 26, 37, 42, 55, 57, 150
Shakespeare xi, 23, 36, 61, 105, 113–14, 123, 149, 163, 193, 194, 201, 205
Sheldon, Gilbert 176
Simon, U. 203
sobriety 3, 9–29, 96
social justice *see* justice
Sophocles 42, 45
Souers, P. W. 206
Southern, R. W. 203
Spenser, Edmund 36, 83
Stobaeus, John 195
Stoicism 22, 26, 28, 30, 57
Strafford, Earl of 53, 207
Strangeways, Sir John 50
Stranks, C. J. 196, 198, 203
Suidas 99
Summers, J. H. 200
Sunday viii, 2, 4–5
Sykes, S. 106, 201
Symeon, New Theologian 72, 202

Tacitus 42
Tanner, J. R. 52, 196
Taylor, Jeremy, life of 165–81; dates xi–xii; classical education 29–45, 104, 174; royal chaplain 49, 117, 144, 168; army life ix, xi, 6, 24, 26, 47, 86–7, 151–2, 153, 172–3, 187; sequestration xi, 91, 144, 167; imprisonment ix, xi, xii, 25, 170, 171; adversity 6–8, 24–6, 91–2, 94, 137, 144; as bishop xii, 34, 137, 167, 175; in Ireland 68, 117, 137, 176–9, 191; his haunts 173–9; his obituary 166–7; elegy 179–81; discovered in his writing 167, 173

Taylor's family: Joanna Bridges xii, 172, 177, 179; Mary Marsh 172; Nathanael Taylor xi, 165, 174; Phoebe Landisdale xi, xii, 15, 24–6, 59, 144–5, 163
temperance 3, 9–11, 87–8
Temple, William 155
Teresa of Avila 101
Tertullian 12, 45, 81–2, 85, 123, 151, 192, 195, 198, 199, 202
Thornton, P. 206
Tillich, Paul 27, 193
Tillyard, E. M. W. 160, 204
Torricelli 21
tort 65–6
Tower of London xi, 51, 170, 175
Trevor-Roper, H. R. 184, 207
Trigg, J. W. 204
Trinity College see Dublin
Tumpel, C. 201
Tuve, R. 200
Tyndale, William 79, 84, 112

unction, extreme 145–6
unemployment 59–60, 77, 105–6, 141, 163, 196
Uppingham xi, 26, 57, 174, 176, 200

Vanity Fair 52, 123, 202
Vaughan, Henry 4–5, 104, 108, 110, 192, 198, 201
Vaughan, Richard and Frances see Carbery
Venice 49
Vermes, G. 198
Virgil 42, 82
virtue see holy living
Vision of a Rood, A 104–5

Voll, K. 202

Waddell, Helen 121, 202
Waldock, A. J. A. 160, 205
Walton, Izaak 111, 200
Warr, John 52
Watkins, Ronald x, 36, 194
Welsby, P. A. 207
Wesley, John xii, 9
Westcott, B. F. 127, 202
Westermann, C. 195, 204
Wheeldon, J. 173, 205
White, Helen 102, 110, 200, 201
White, J. B. 200
Willmott, R. A. 121, 165, 172–3, 202, 205
Wilson, C. 52, 59, 196
Windebank, Sir Francis 53
Wine, H. 195
Wingfield Digby, Venetia 58
Wiseman, J. A. 200
Wittgenstein, L. 9, 192
Wood, Anthony à 172, 178, 207
Worcester 152
Worley, George 200
worship see holy living
Wren, Sir Christopher 29
Wyatt, William 42
Wyclif, John 72

Xeno 99

Yelverton, Sir Henry 52

Zen 23
Zeno of Citium 22